IMAGES
of America

DELPHI

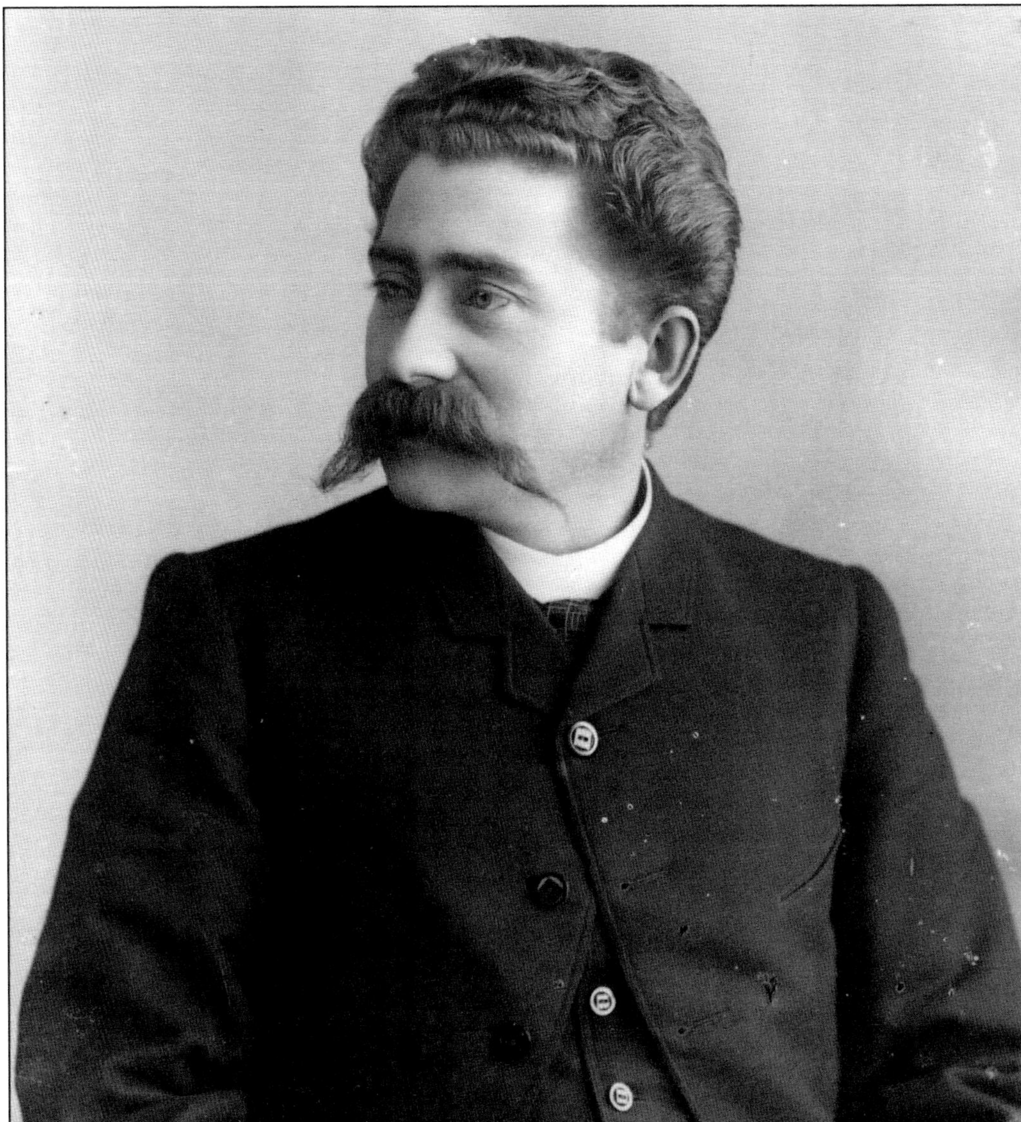

Born in Pennsylvania, Andrew W. Wolever (1852–1936) came to Indiana in 1867, moving to Lafayette in 1869 to learn photography from his brother, Peter Wolever. By 1874, Andrew had moved to Delphi and purchased the photography business of James M. Boltz, including his glass-plate negatives. For the next six decades, Wolever skillfully created the visual record of Delphi and the surrounding area. He was mayor of Delphi from 1887 to 1891 and respected by all as a friendly and honest man. Wolever was particularly active in the Odd Fellows and the Knights of Pythias lodges. He retired in 1933 and passed away in 1936 at the age of 84. (Courtesy C. E. Gerard collection.)

On the Cover: Labor Day in 1919 was celebrated as a "welcome home" event for those men and women who had served in the World War. The courthouse, completed two years earlier, was decked out in banners and flags, as were most buildings and residences in Delphi. The band, representing different branches of service, stands in front of the Soldiers and Sailors Monument erected in 1893 to memorialize the fallen. (Photograph by Andrew Wolever, courtesy C. E. Gerard collection.)

IMAGES
of America

DELPHI

Anita L. Werling and Bonnie J. Maxwell for
the Delphi Preservation Society, Inc.

ARCADIA
PUBLISHING

ISBN 978-0-7385-8437-9

Published by Arcadia Publishing
Charleston, South Carolina

Printed in the United States of America

Library of Congress Control Number: 2009943819

For all general information contact Arcadia Publishing at:
Telephone 843-853-2070
Fax 843-853-0044
E-mail sales@arcadiapublishing.com
For customer service and orders:
Toll-Free 1-888-313-2665

Visit us on the Internet at www.arcadiapublishing.com

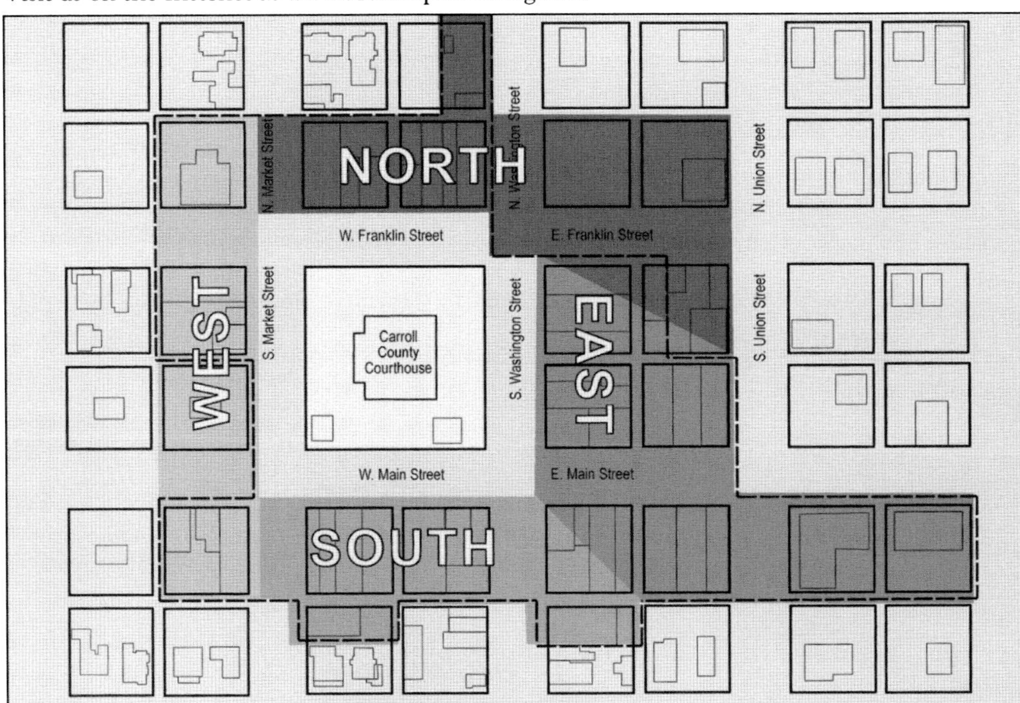

In 2010, the Delphi Courthouse Square and the commercial blocks surrounding it have been designated as a historic district on the National Register of Historic Places. This book celebrates Delphi's architectural treasures and its unique cultural heritage. The district boundaries are indicated by a dotted line. It all begins at the center with the three courthouses that have graced the square. These are presented in the first chapter. Moving around the square, the shaded areas each have a chapter highlighting their buildings, merchants, and activities through the decades. This book is dedicated to those who have built, owned, and maintained through the years the extraordinary buildings in Delphi's Courthouse Square Historic District. (Map by Anita L. Werling.)

Contents

ACKNOWLEDGMENTS

Charles E. Gerard (1949–2005) was a Carroll County historian, photographer, and writer. He was active with several local historical groups, including the Delphi Preservation Society. Unless noted otherwise, the photographs in this book are from his print and negative collection. The majority are prints he made from the Boltz-Wolever glass photographic plates, which were in the possession of the Bradshaw Insurance Company and made available to Gerard and Michael Griffey for their 1977 *Carroll County Sesquicentennial Publication*. Those plates were subsequently donated by William Bradshaw to the Carroll County Historical Society and made available through their photograph archive at www.carrollcountymuseum.org. Gerard donated his photograph collection as well as his extensive historical archives to the Delphi Preservation Society prior to his death.

Delphi has had an extraordinary number of professional photographers since the earliest times—at least 20 in the 1800s alone. James W. Boltz took many of the earliest surviving views before he sold the business to Andrew W. Wolever in 1874. Some of Boltz's oldest plates date from the late 1850s and survive along with Wolever's vast output of 60 years.

Special appreciation goes to Mark Smith, a friend and contemporary of Gerard, who shares the passion for local history. He generously lent his files of research materials compiled over several years. Mark's special bent is exploration of the family relationships among the people of the area, particularly merchants and others from the heyday of the Wabash and Erie Canal.

Some local histories are noted in the bibliography, but work of the late Robert G. Bradshaw was also extremely helpful. Photographs and information were shared by William Bradshaw (Bradshaw Insurance); Richard and Karen Bradshaw (Delphi Body Works); Gail Baker Seest (Kerlin and Gregg families); Robert and Lynda Brooks and Claudann Brooks Burks (House on the Square); Doris Shepard (John Lathrope); Julie Smith Pyle (William C. Smith's writings); Peg Minnicus (Carroll County REMC, a Touchstone Energy Corporation); Sandy Flora (Carroll County Abstract and Title); William and Thomas Freeman (Globe Valve); Mary Ann Burton (recorder's office); Dan McCain (Carroll County Wabash and Erie Canal Association); and the Indiana Historical Society. Thanks go to the Delphi Public Library for assistance and to Carol Wellnitz for proofreading.

INTRODUCTION

Delphi, Indiana, the center of government of Carroll County, was first settled in 1824 by the Henry Robinson family. Delphi was platted in 1828 by Gen. Samuel Milroy on land donated by William Wilson, and the county was established that same year. Located in the valley framed by the Wabash River and Deer Creek, the first settlers came via the Federal Land Office at Crawfordsville. Pioneers immigrated by foot, horseback, boat, and wagon. Stagecoach and canal travel began a bit later. Indiana's first "state highway" was laid out along the Wabash River from the National Road at Terre Haute to Fort Wayne in 1826 and guided settlers to the area.

Delphi was formally established as a town in 1835 and incorporated as a city in 1866. Early settlers cleared land and constructed needed dwellings. They also established all types of mills for grinding grain, processing wood, and making paper. Merchants opened shops downtown and began building the two- and three-story brick buildings still found there today. Blacksmiths, wagon makers, doctors, lawyers, bankers, druggists, grocers, saloonkeepers, and merchants of all kinds arrived. County and town governments were organized, elections took place, and government buildings were constructed.

The Wabash and Erie Canal was completed from Fort Wayne to Delphi in 1840. By 1843, it connected Delphi with Toledo on Lake Erie and opened the area to commerce with the east. The canal was finally completed to Evansville in 1853, but its heyday was interrupted by the spread of railroads. Rail transport provided stiff competition in cost, availability, and reliability beginning in the 1850s.

Two rail systems served Delphi in addition to the electric interurban railway. Direct connections to Lafayette, Logansport, Monticello, and Frankfort were also established through the development of roads and highways. Local roads linked the rest of Carroll County to Delphi to allow access to government, markets, and goods. Now the Hoosier Heartland Highway is being built from Fort Wayne to Lafayette, introducing another era of change.

As the downtown commercial area thrived, the early, simple dwellings gave way to elaborate homes not far from the courthouse square. Many of those remain and are well maintained, contributing to the wealth of fine architecture. A number of churches were established as well, and those historic buildings still stand.

While not centrally located in Carroll County, Delphi has benefited from being the county seat of government and being a transportation nexus. Camden, Flora, and Burlington continue to be important centers, but many of the smaller villages that developed because of the early railroad or the canal have nearly ceased existence. The majority of the county remains rural and agricultural and is a leading producer of corn, soybeans, and pork.

The Delphi Preservation Society (DPS) is dedicated to encouraging the preservation of historic architecture in the Greater Delphi area. The Society owns the 1865 Assion-Ruffing City Hall building on the east side of the courthouse square. The structure's façade has been restored, and plans are in place to renovate the 1882 Lathrope and Ruffing Opera House on the third floor.

The goal is to provide a venue that will allow the performing arts to return to the heart of Delphi. DPS presents programs about the architectural and cultural history of Delphi, provides tours of the opera house, and leads guided architectural walks. During the Old Settlers Festival, Delphi Public Library's Red Brick Theatre and Stargazers groups, as well as other groups, have provided entertainment in the opera house. Downstairs in one of the retail bays, Carroll County artists and other guest contributors are featured in the Opera House Gallery of Contemporary Art.

After decades of planning and development, the Carroll County Wabash and Erie Canal Association opened their Interpretive Center on North Washington Street at Canal Park in 2003. The interpretive center provides displays on canal development, travel, and life as well as early local industries. Its facility also provides rooms that are used for weddings, meetings, and other events. In 2009, they inaugurated their replica canal boat *The Delphi*, which offers rides and tours on the watered canal. The relocated and restored Reed Case House, several pioneer cabins, a playground canal boat, interpretive exhibits, and canal lock and lime kiln reproductions provide an educational and entertaining experience. Pedestrian and bicycle trails utilize the canal towpath and relocated historic bridges. Delphi has a fine network of six city parks that connect to the trail system. Rental bicycles and carriage rides are available at Canal Park during the warmer months.

The Carroll County Historical Museum in the courthouse is operated by the historical society. It exhibits a large collection of local artifacts and memorabilia gathered over the last decades. It also houses a vast archive of genealogical and historical data. During Old Settlers, the society sponsors early craft demonstrations and old-fashioned musical events. Delphi recognizes its heritage with several annual events. Carroll County Old Settlers is celebrated the second weekend of August each year. The first meeting was held in 1855 to listen to and make note of the stories related by the county's first settlers, and meetings have been held annually since then. Besides the Old Settlers Association meeting and its Heritage Award presentations, the festival features many informative and entertaining programs put on by various groups, an art show, food and information booths, community dinners, and a carnival.

The Heritage Transportation Festival is held each Father's Day weekend and features exhibits, demonstrations, and events relating to all forms of historic and current transportation. It includes events downtown, at Canal Park, and at the Delphi Airport as well as guided tours on the interurban trolley.

Canal Days are celebrated each Fourth of July weekend with numerous events at Canal Park. Demonstrations of pioneer crafts, reenactments of education in a one-room school, and tours of the Reed Case house and log cabins are featured. Christmas at Canal Park is another favorite weekend in December, showing aspects of Christmas celebration from the past.

These festivals and events are supported not only by the organizations mentioned above, but also by the City of Delphi, Delphi Main Street, Delphi Chamber of Commerce, and numerous service groups. Carroll County is recognized for the vast outpouring of volunteer support that makes all this possible. They are also supported by downtown merchants, including a cluster of galleries, antique shops, gift and flower shops, and restaurants.

Surrounding communities in Carroll County also have festivals, notable architecture, and attractions of their own. The county has maintained and restored a large number of historic bridges. The Deer Creek Valley Rural Historic District east of Delphi holds many architectural gems, including the restored 1898 Wilson Bridge. The Cutler area in southeastern Carroll County is home to Adams Mill—an 1845 gristmill on scenic Wildcat Creek. Adjacent to the mill is the Adams Mill covered bridge, and the Lancaster covered bridge is not far away. To the north of Delphi is French Post Park, the site of an early French trading post, which is just across the Wabash River from Lockport, a busy settlement in canal days.

This book is meant to supply information about Delphi's downtown and the surrounding area as documented in photographs from the 1850s to the 1950s.

One

THE COURTHOUSE SQUARE

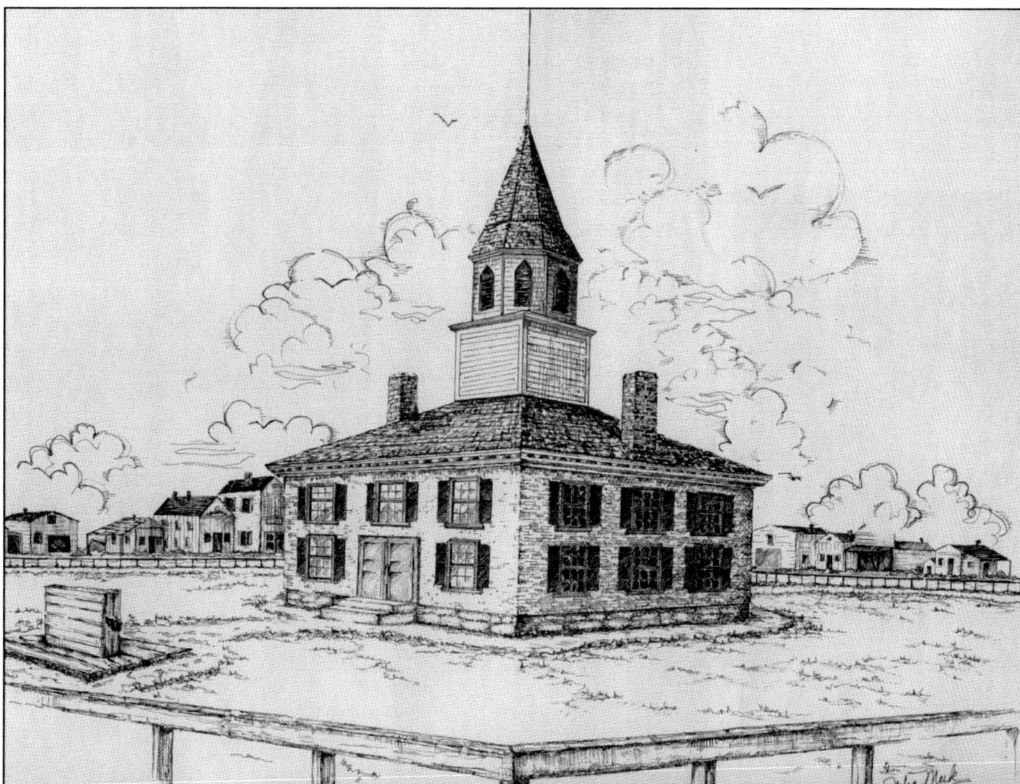

Delphi was platted in 1828 by Samuel Milroy on 100 acres of land donated by William Wilson for the "seat of justice" in Carroll County, Indiana. In 1832, construction began on a 50-foot-square, two-story brick courthouse with a stone foundation, four-sided shingle roof, and octagonal bell tower. Built by John Dollason for $3,500, the courthouse is depicted in Julia Meek's drawing commissioned by C. E. Gerard in 1985.

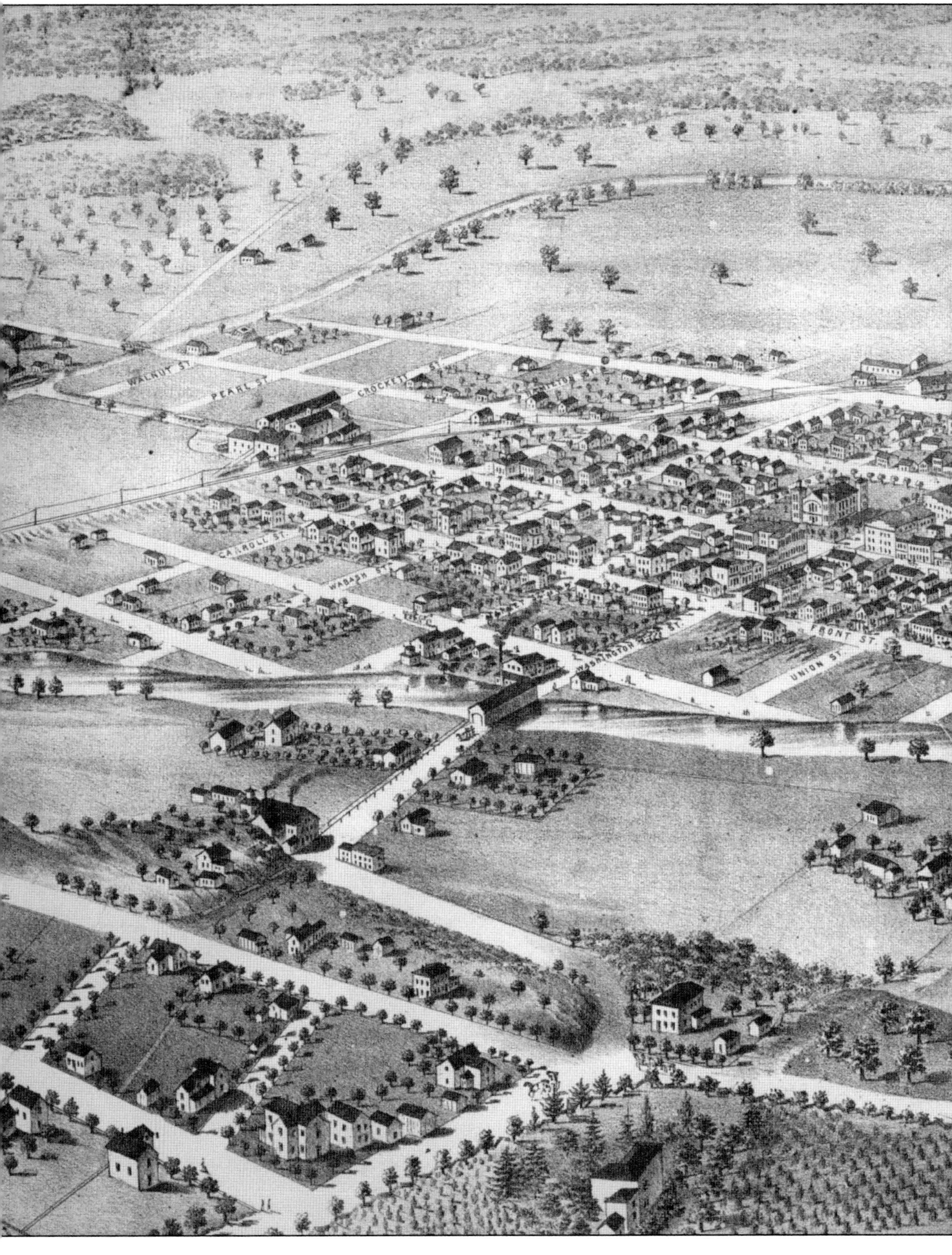
WALNUT ST.
PEARL ST.
CROCKETT ST.
CARROLL ST.
WABASH ST.
WASHINGTON ST.
FRONT ST.
UNION ST.

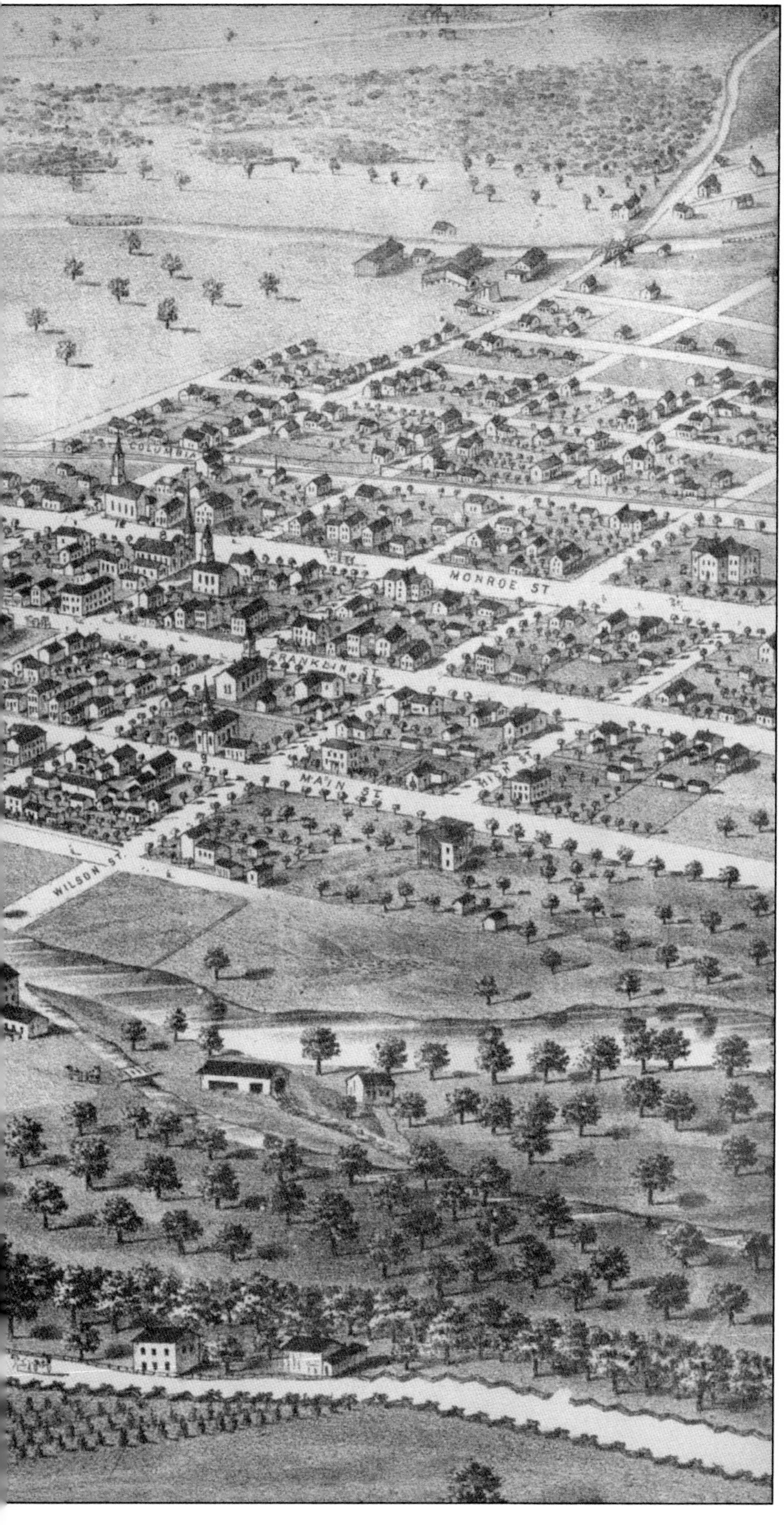

Panoramic lithographs of cities and towns were in vogue in the mid-1800s to early 1900s. In June 1868, agent T. M. Fowler was soliciting the 100 subscriptions necessary to publish Albert Ruger's 1868 panoramic drawing of Delphi. This detail from Ruger's birds-eye view shows a bustling commercial block surrounding the central courthouse square with tall brick buildings framing two sides. The Wabash River is toward the top, the Wabash and Erie Canal upper middle, and Deer Creek toward the bottom. On the left at Main Street are the Spears and Case grain elevator and warehouse connected to the canal by a side-slip. The Rinehart paper mill is visible west of the canal. The Wabash Railway depot is above and left of the courthouse. Mills and factories dot the landscape around the canal and Deer Creek. Six churches are visible along with the public school. Fine residences are built on Front Street, the south hill, and just to the east of the town. The population in 1868 is about 2,000 compared with about 3,000 today.

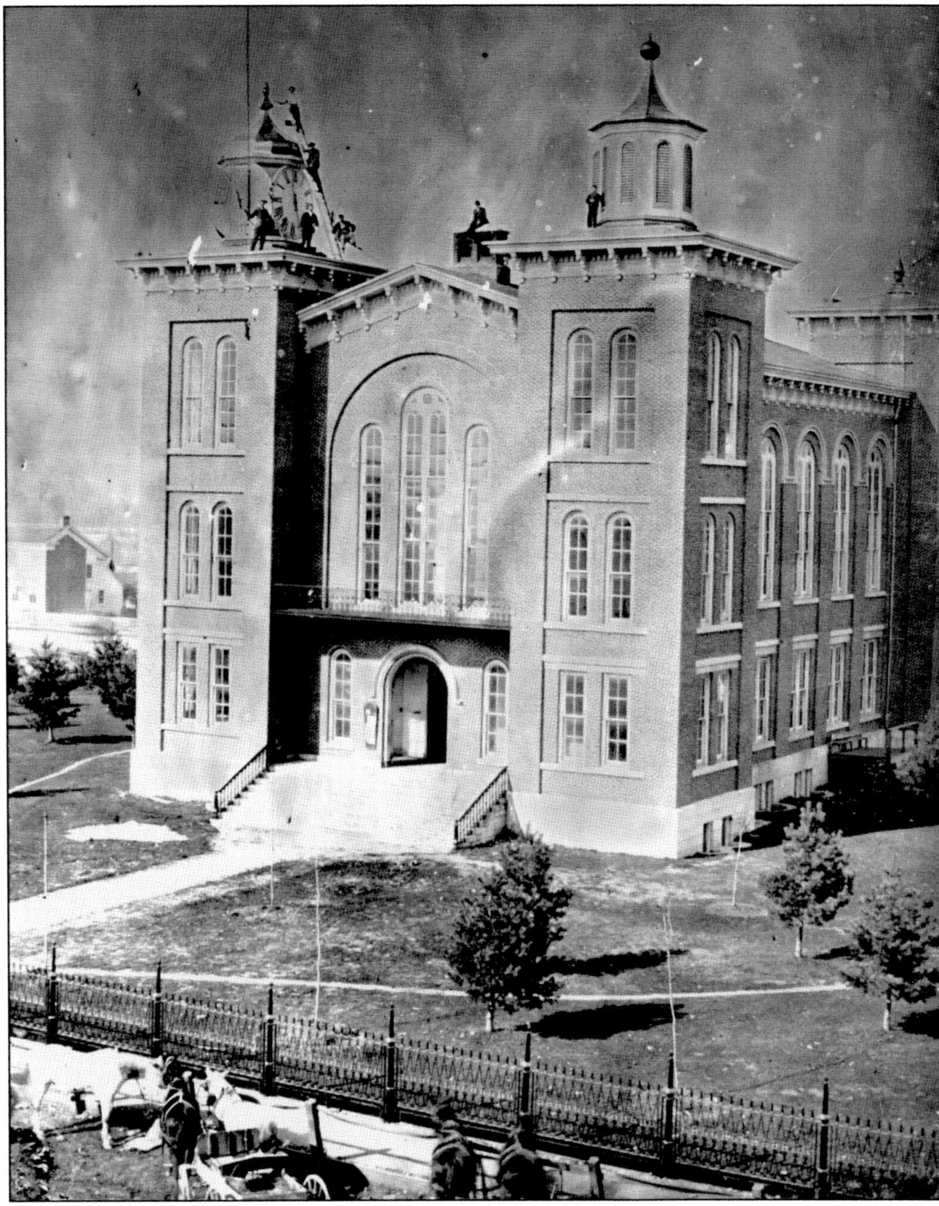

Located between the Wabash River and Deer Creek, Delphi was connected to Logansport, Lafayette, Frankfort, and other towns by river, plank roads, and stagecoach routes. In the late 1830s, the Wabash and Erie Canal was dug, ensuring more reliable shipping. By the mid-1850s the first railroad was built, and the bustling county had outgrown its courthouse. In 1856, the commissioners ordered that a new courthouse be built. Designed by M. J. McBird of Logansport, the second courthouse had a base of 65 feet by 95 feet with 80-foot clock and bell towers in front. Two rear towers housed jury, witness, and sheriff rooms. The large second floor courtroom had an ornate ribbed ceiling with pendants. The first floor housed offices for the clerk, treasurer, and recorder with storage vaults for public documents. Four prisoner cells and a cistern were in the basement. The red-brick-and-limestone Italianate structure was completed by Wood and Rodifer in 1859. This remarkable photograph from about 1860 shows the completed courthouse surrounded by landscaped grounds and an iron fence.

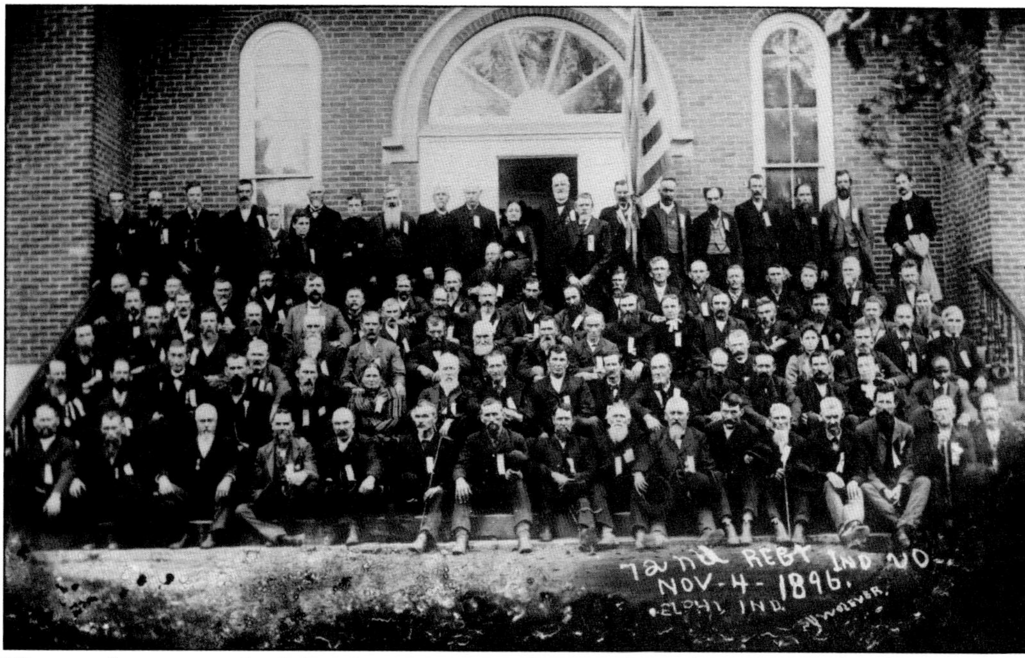

The courthouse was a backdrop for many group photographs such as this one dated November 4, 1896, of surviving members of the 72nd Regiment of the Indiana Volunteers who fought in the Civil War. Indiana provided more than 200,000 volunteers to the conflict, nearly 75 percent of its eligible population. Of these, more than 24,000 died, about 200 from Carroll County.

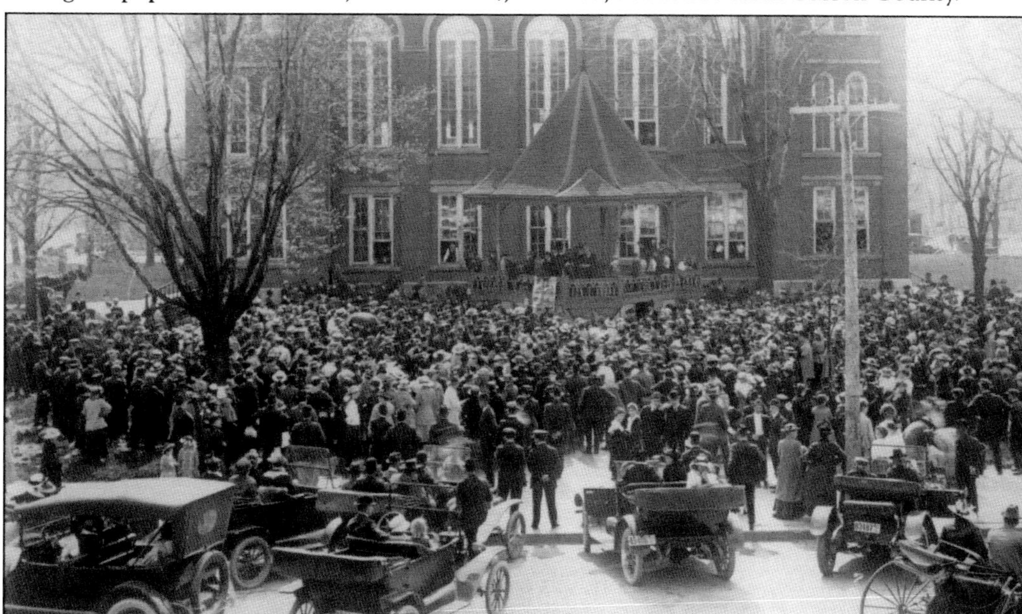

William Jennings Bryan campaigned in Delphi in all three presidential bids. Bryan is speaking from the bandstand as throngs of people gather on the lawn of the courthouse in this 1906 stop. Gone are the iron fence and hitching rail surrounding the courthouse. The streets were paved in 1905 following the construction of concrete sidewalks. Only one carriage is seen in the foreground as automobiles gained in numbers in Delphi.

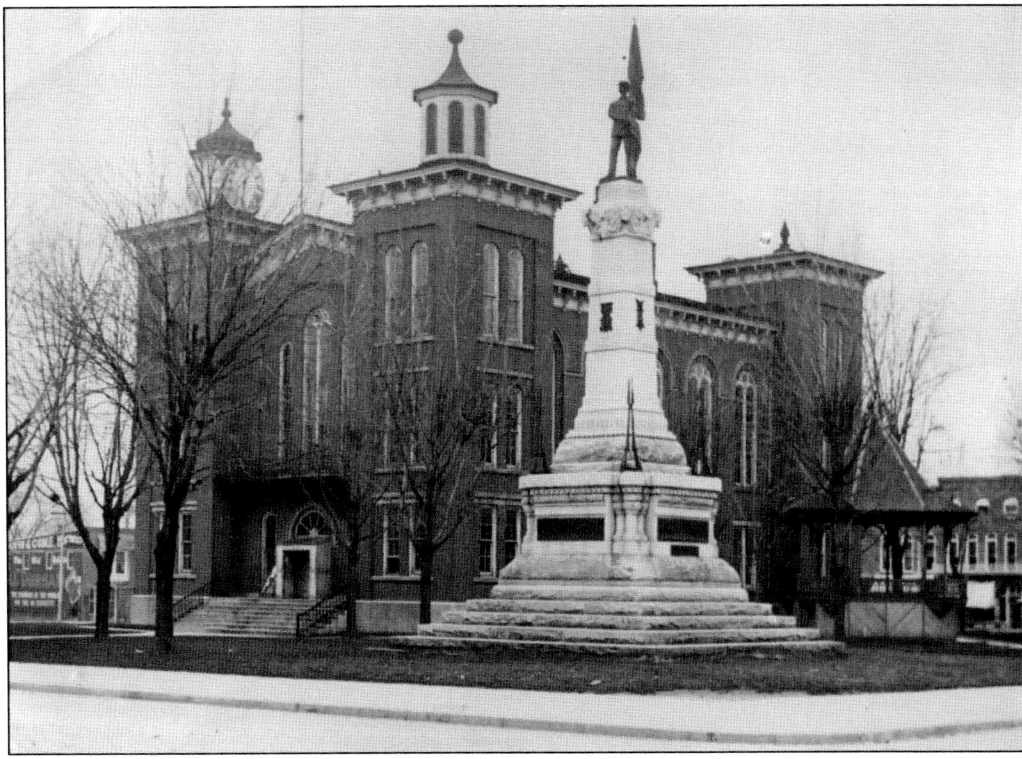

The iconic Soldiers and Sailors Monument was unveiled on July 27, 1893. After a petition campaign in 1889, the commissioners authorized a 2¢ levy to construct a monument commemorating fallen soldiers. Created by A. A. McKain of Indianapolis at a cost of $11,990, the monument was erected by Delphi contractors Hannum and Conners. A bronze statue of a color bearer stands on top of the 51-foot base of Vermont marble.

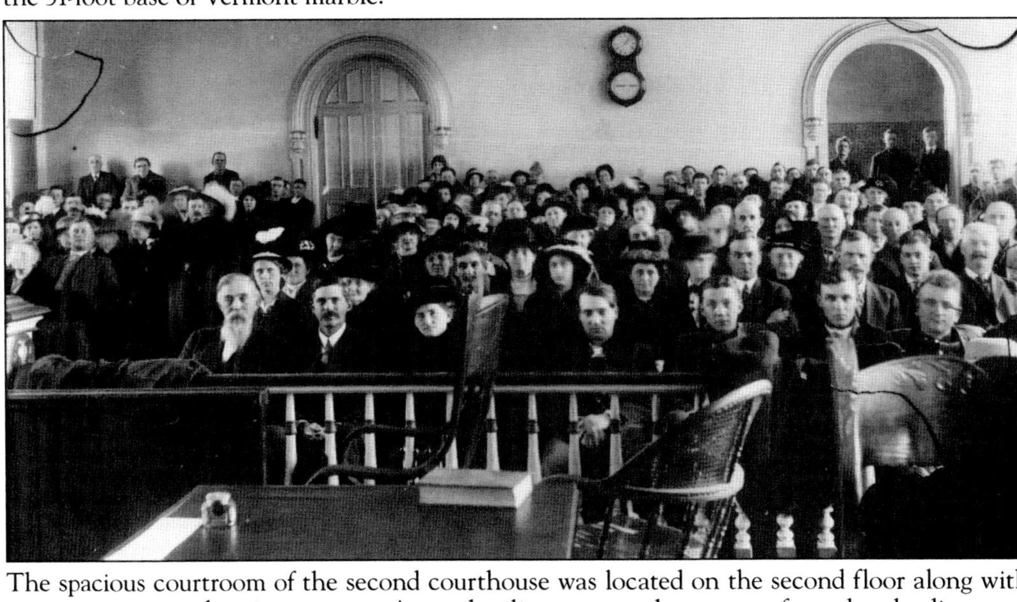

The spacious courtroom of the second courthouse was located on the second floor along with two jury rooms and a witness room. A wood railing separated spectators from the pleading area, judge's bench, and jury box. The courtroom was also used for community meetings.

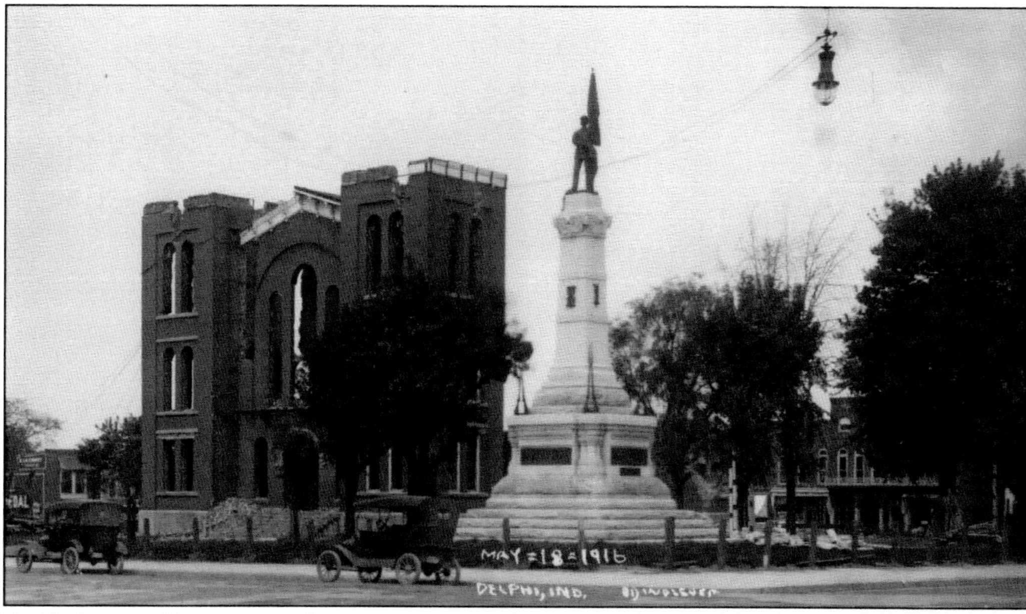

By 1916, Carroll County had once more outgrown its courthouse. The demolition of the second courthouse is nearing completion in this May 18 photograph. It is one in a series taken by Wolever documenting the process as the courthouse walls are reduced to rubble. The laying of the cornerstone for the third and present courthouse is shown in the photograph below taken September 4, 1916. It was a day of great celebration with thousands of people crowding the streets and grounds. Grand marshall Harry Haugh and Mayor W. C. Smith led a parade 12 blocks long. Having performed at the first two courthouses, John Lathrope directed the Delphi band in the procession. The Bedford cornerstone block, weighing 1,400 pounds, was lowered into place containing a box with photographs and histories of the county and its organizations.

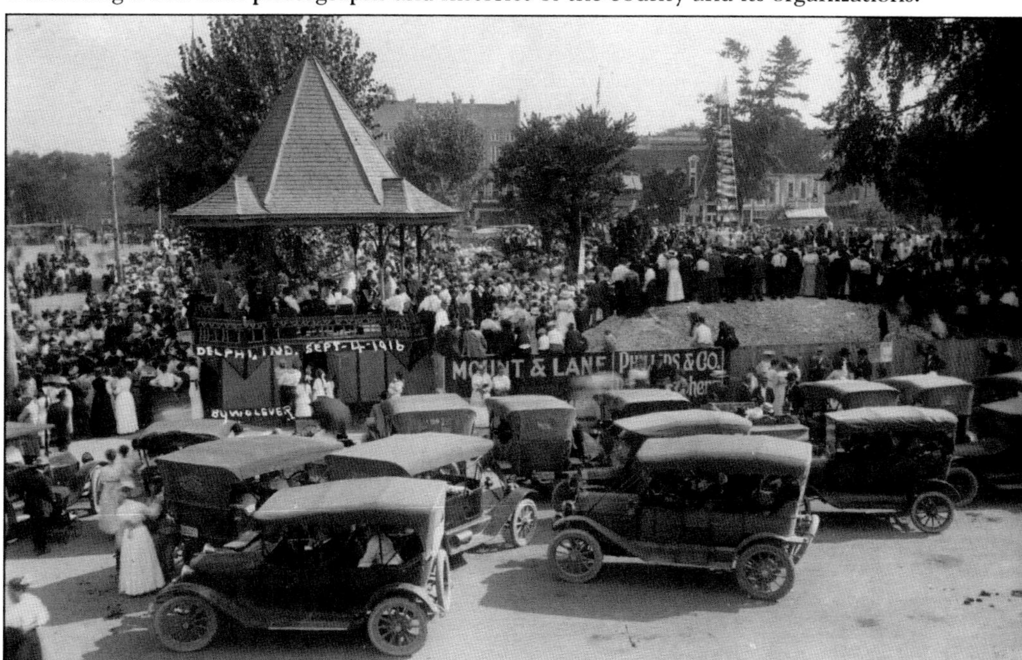

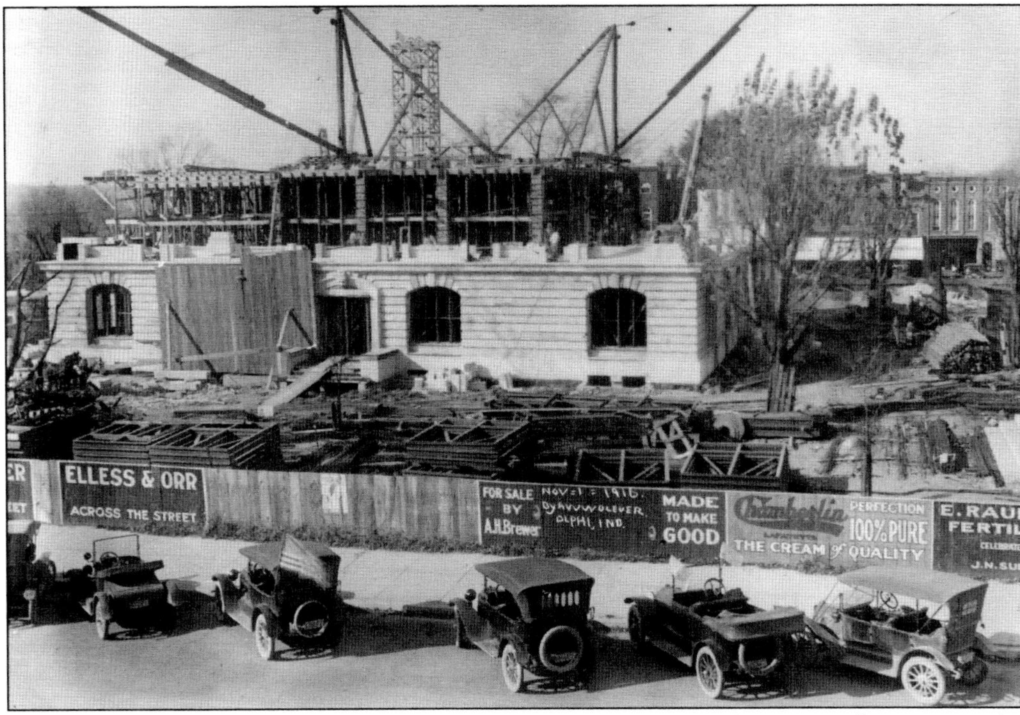

Construction of the new courthouse was well documented by Wolever as well. By November 1, 1916, just two months after the laying of the cornerstone, the progress above is amazing. By December 6, 1916, the frieze and its entablature are being completed on the south side of the courthouse. Designed by Elmer E. Dunlap, the classical revival limestone structure was built at a cost of $171,000. Of note are the businesses advertising on the construction fence. The courthouse was completed and open for public use in 1917.

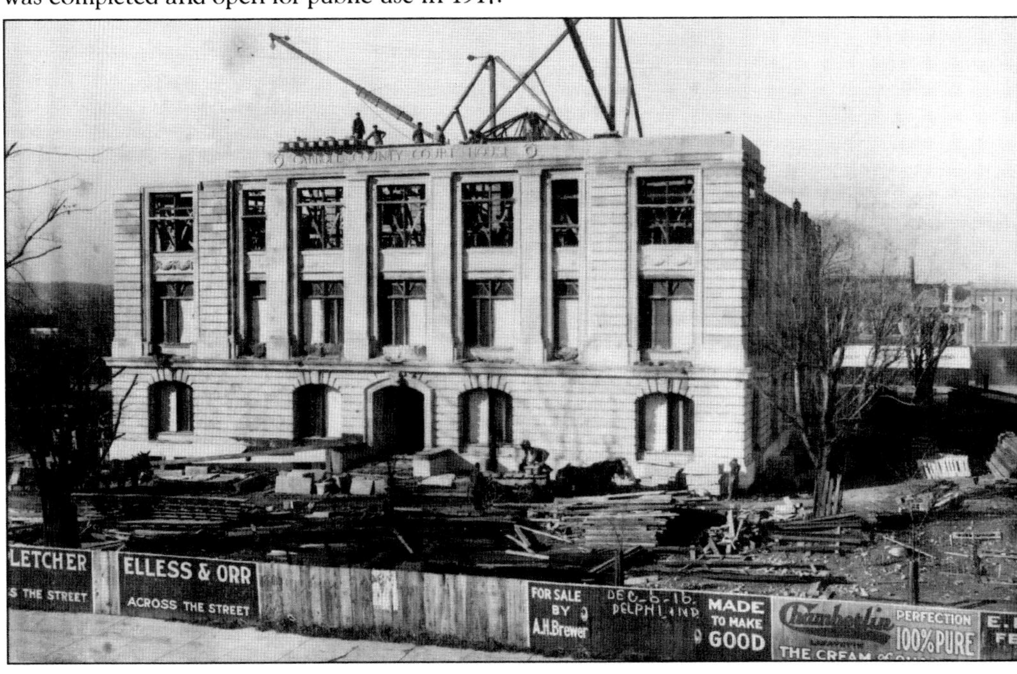

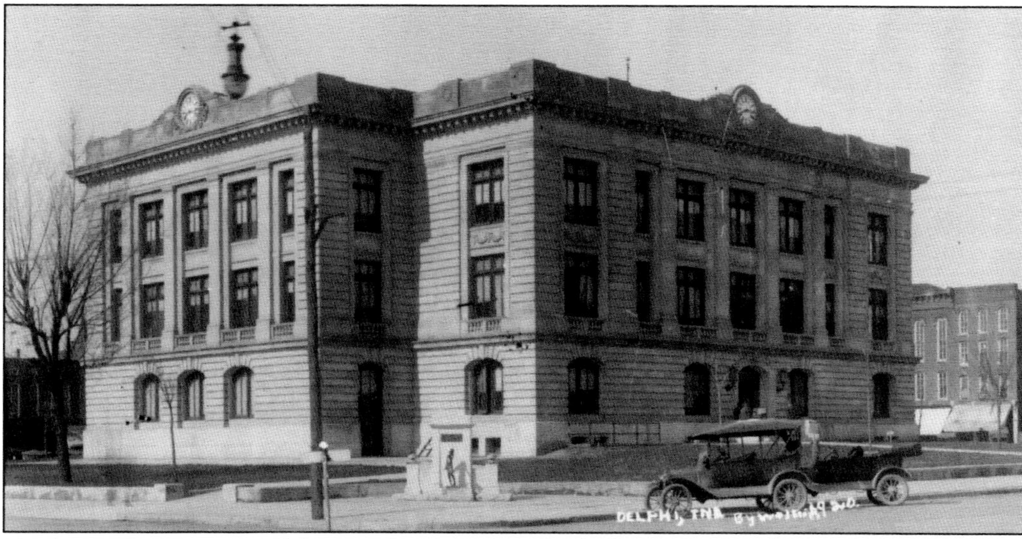

On the southwest corner of the courthouse square stands the "Water Maiden" or Murphy Fountain. The monument is built of Vermont marble, and the maiden is cast in bronze. The City of Delphi commissioned the monument in 1918 with $3,300 donated by Mitchell and Clara Murphy whose drugstore operated at 112 West Main Street from the late 1870s until 1911.

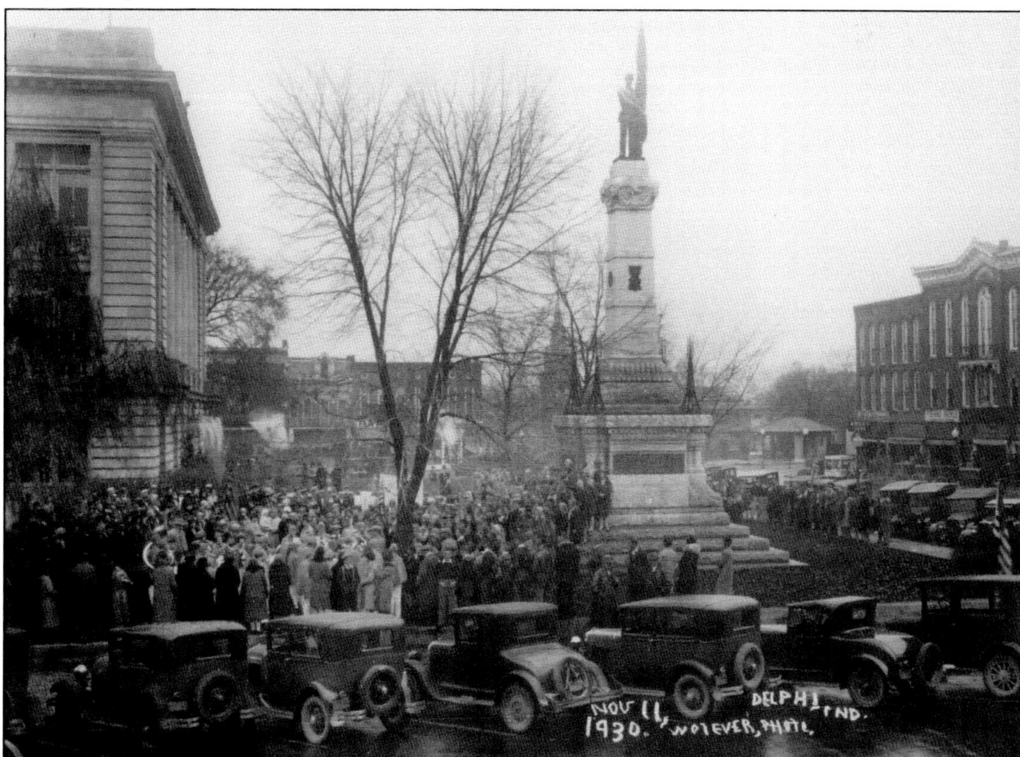

Veterans Day was, and is today, commemorated with gatherings on the square at the Soldiers and Sailors Monument to honor the fallen and those who have given service. To the right of the monument in this 1930 photograph is a rare glimpse of the filling station that once stood on the corner of East Franklin and South Washington Streets.

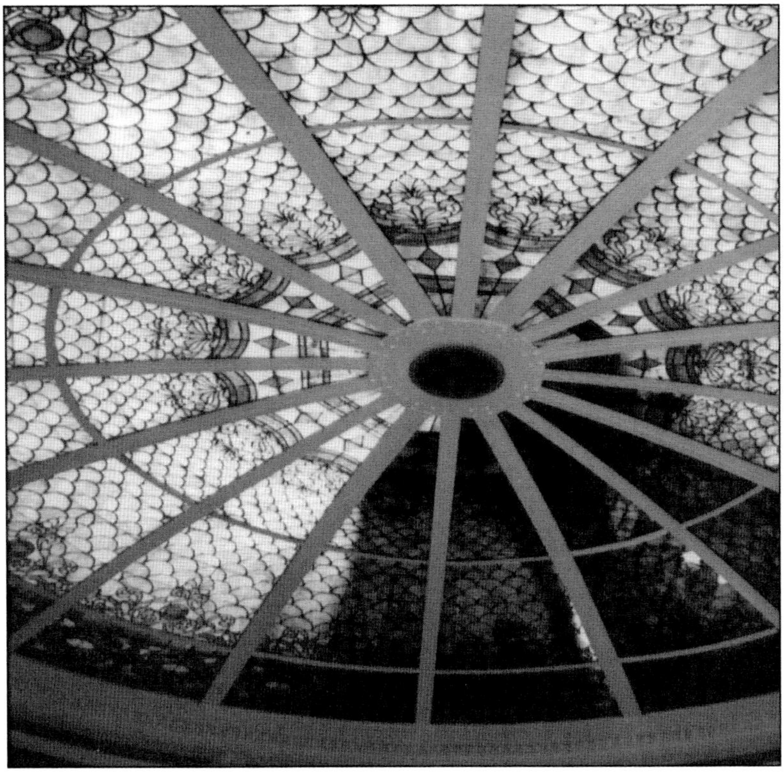

A beautiful stained-glass dome overarches the courthouse rotunda, which features a mosaic floor of hexagonal tiles surrounded by marbleized pillars. Curving marble stairs lead to the second and third floors. Offices are richly adorned with oak woodwork. The third-floor Circuit Courtroom features stained-glass panels between oak beams. A treasure of Carroll County, the courthouse was placed on the National Register of Historic Places in 2003.

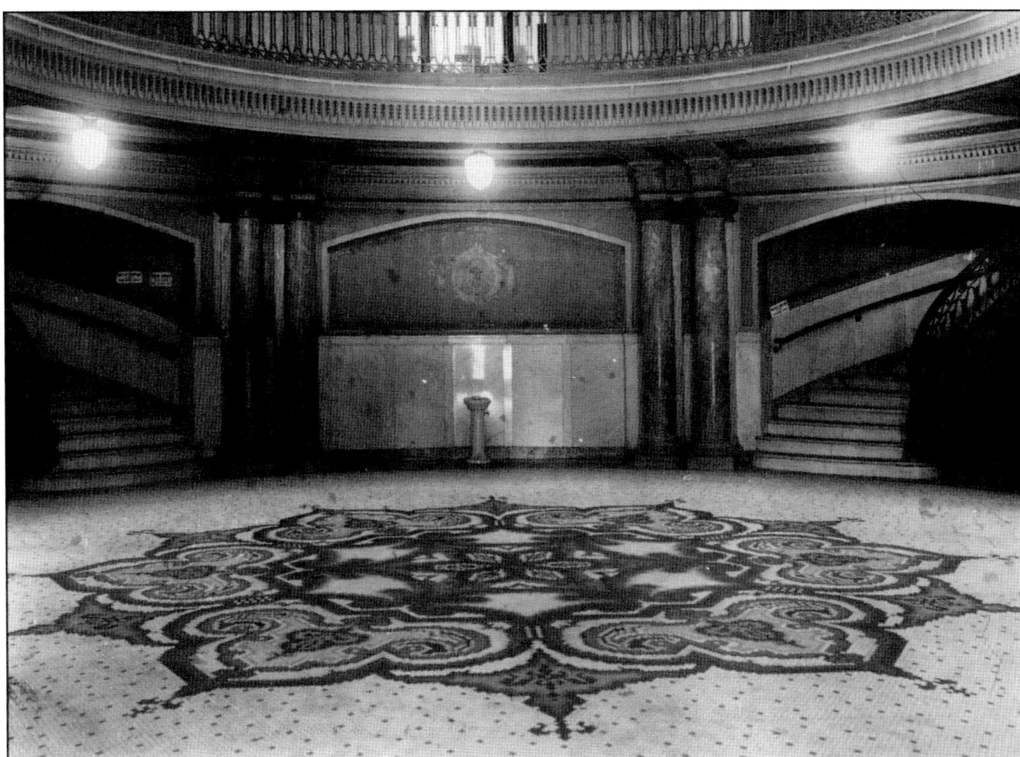

Two

North of the Square

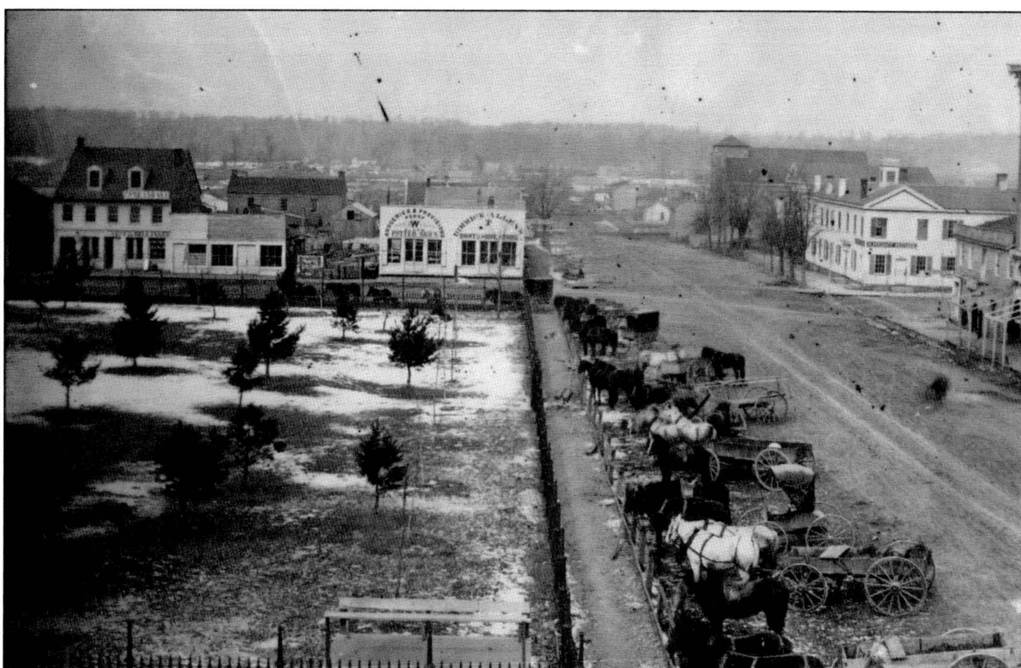

The north side of the square consists of frame buildings in this 1867 J. M. Boltz image. Not visible is Griffith's Livery to the west. Neff's Alhambra Saloon and Dillinger's Cigar Store are left. Behind them is the two-story jail. Potter Brothers Groceries and Provisions and Dimmick and Allen's Boot and Shoe Store are on the corner of Washington and Franklin Streets. Across the street is the Knight House and farther north is St. Joseph's Catholic Church.

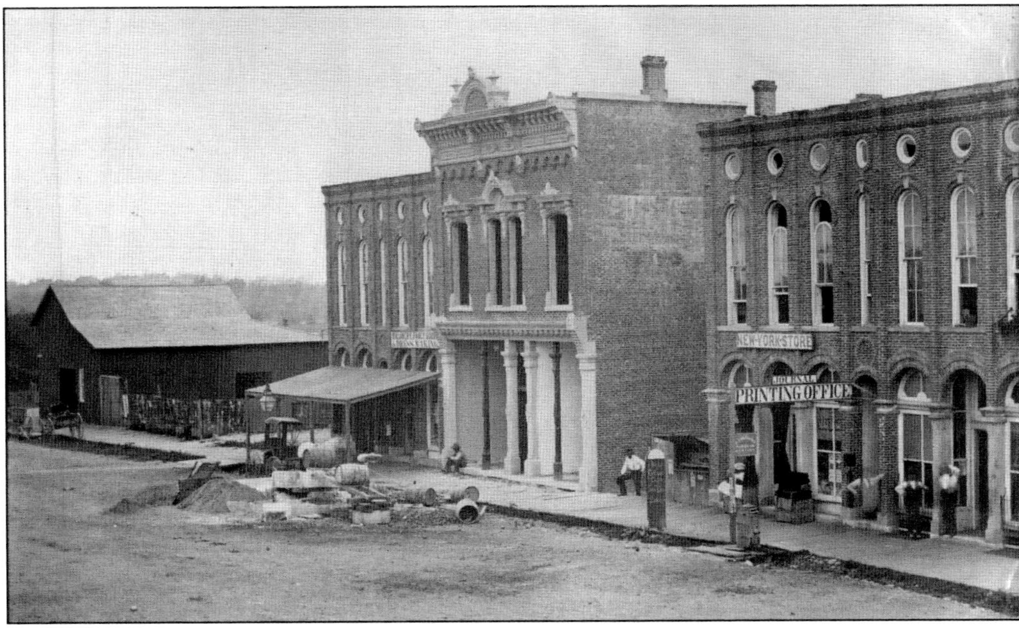

In 1871, a devastating fire burned nearly the entire block north of the square. By 1875, several brick buildings had replaced structures destroyed in the fire. On the corner (right) is Dimmick and Allen's again. The Journal Printing Office is upstairs along with surgeon and dentist S. S. Mathers. The New York Store has opened in Bradshaw's west bay and will become a fixture of the north side of the square. Still under construction in the middle is the building of George and Marx Carll. In Christian Neff's building is Haisley's Millinery with the Nipper Saloon in the west bay. Past the alley is the Griffith Livery and Sale Stable, the sole survivor of the fire. Griffith's Livery was purchased by Swatts and Metsker in 1896, as seen below in this late-1890s photograph.

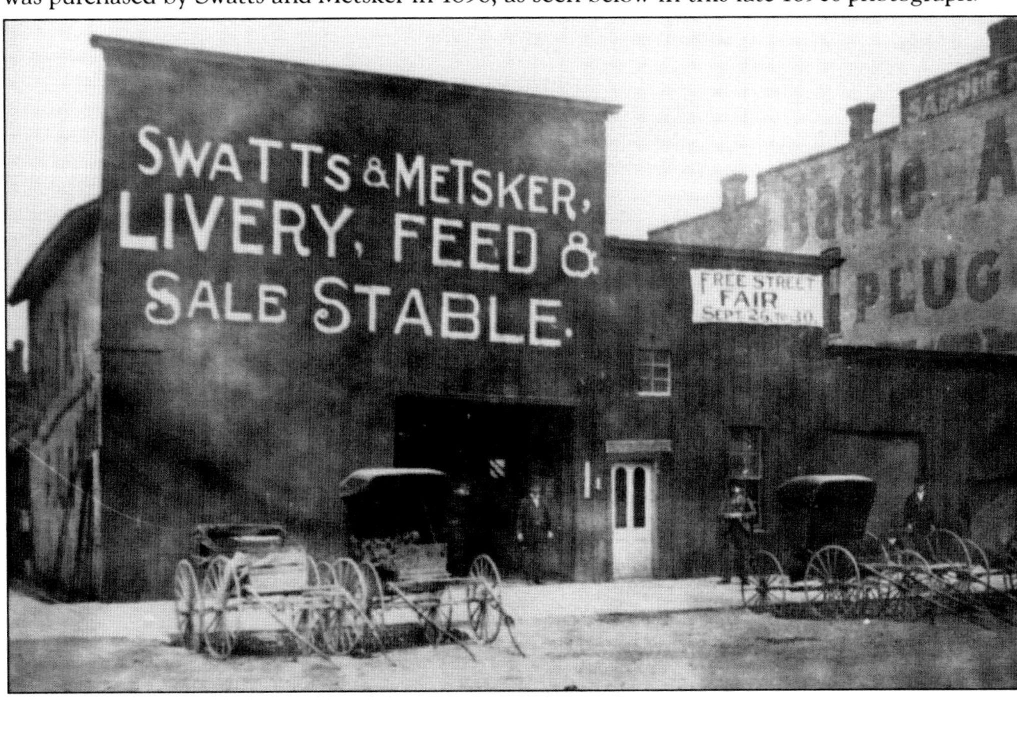

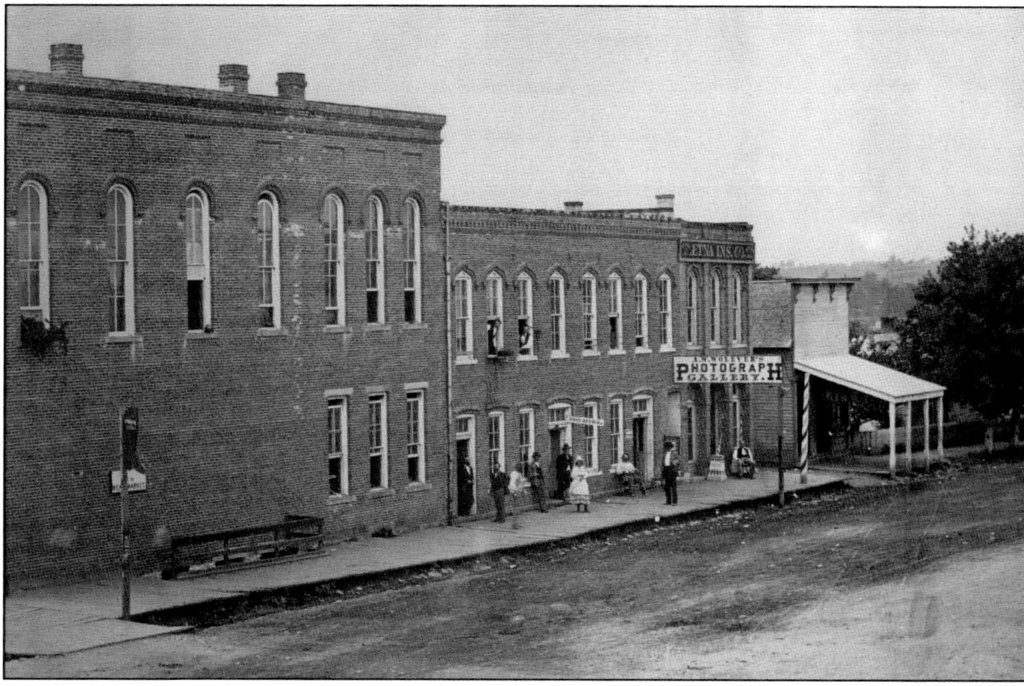

Turning the corner from Franklin Street onto North Washington Street, an exterior stair leads down to Stewart's Meat Market. The post office is located in the next building along with the United States Express Company. A. W. Wolever's Photograph Gallery and Aetna Insurance Company are upstairs. Next to the alley is a barbershop. City Bakery, later replaced by a saloon, is in the two-story frame building that survives today as Sassy's Spa and Hair Salon.

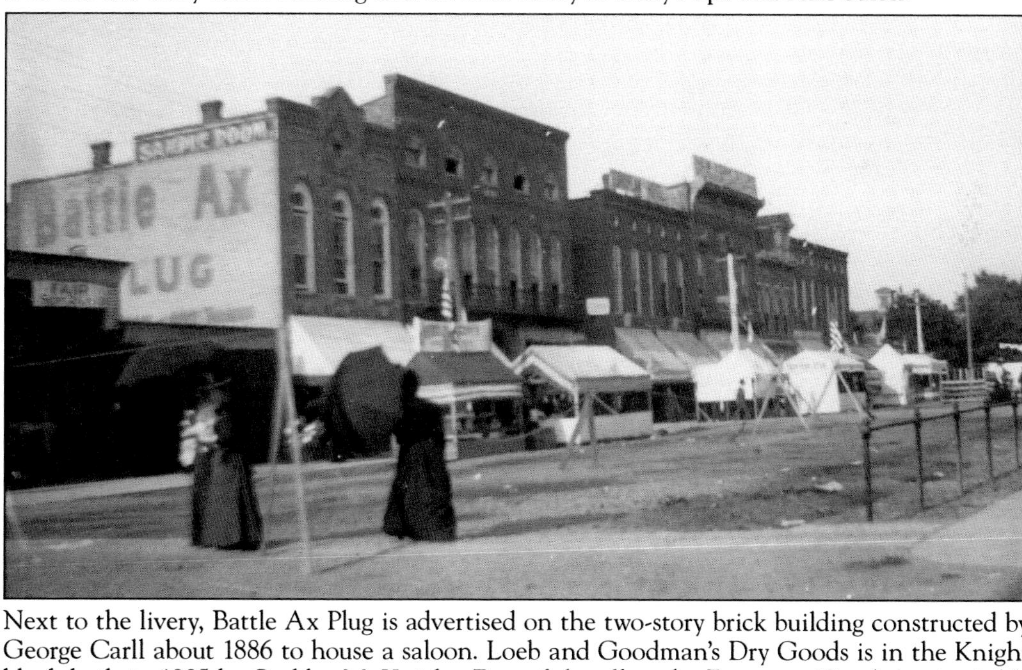

Next to the livery, Battle Ax Plug is advertised on the two-story brick building constructed by George Carll about 1886 to house a saloon. Loeb and Goodman's Dry Goods is in the Knight block built in 1885 by Corbley M. Knight. East of the alley, the European Hotel sign is visible next to the New York Store. The Free Street Fair is taking shape on the square.

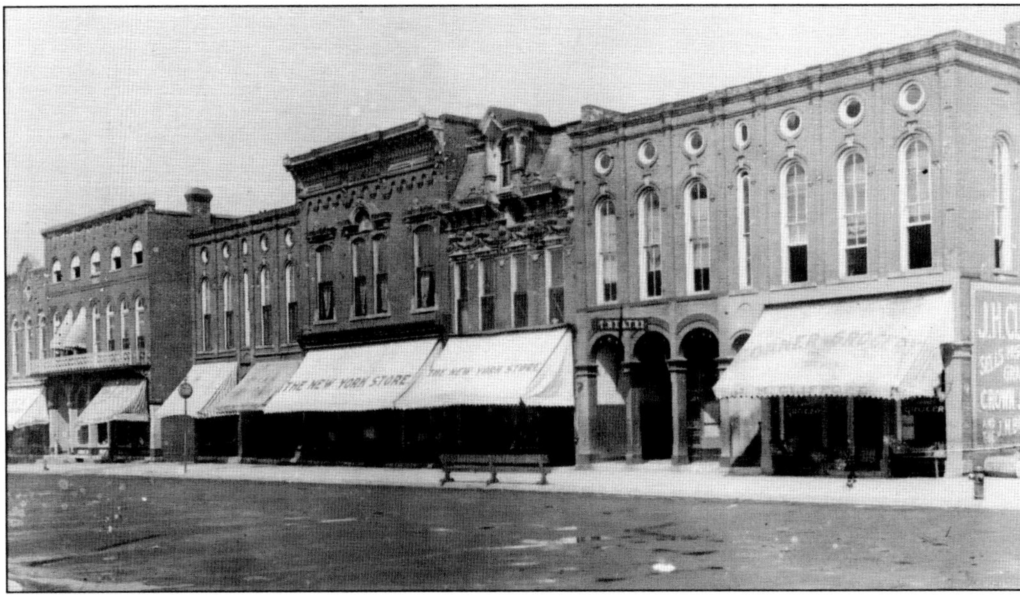

Paved streets and concrete sidewalks are apparent in this photograph from the early 1900s. At left stands the two-story brick Michael Ryan block, built in 1899. Gerard's Livery, Turner Grocery, Rohde Billiards, and the Lew Wallis Grocery complete the half block. East of the alley is a millinery store and McCain's Jewelry. The New York Store has expanded, taking in the ornate structure built for Martha Haisley and Bella Barnes in about 1880. The Bradshaw building has the Star Theatre, and the Clifford Market is on the corner. By the early 1930s, the livery has become the Auto Hotel (below, left) next to Art's Place, a lunchroom and recreation hall maintained by Art Rider. Concrete block has replaced the Italianate façade in the middle building housing Delphi Sheet Metal and Furnace. Will Cowdin Plumbing and Heating and the City Meat Market are located in the Knight block with Leavell and Bates Loans on the second floor.

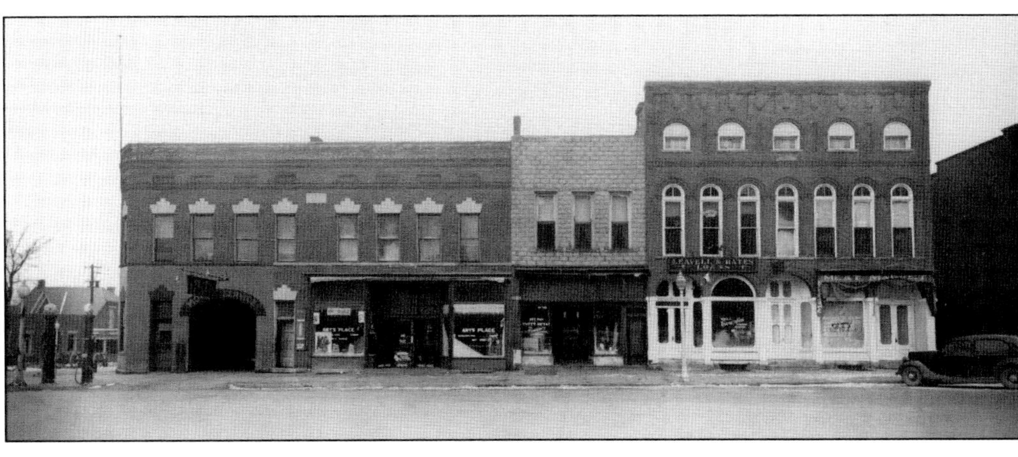

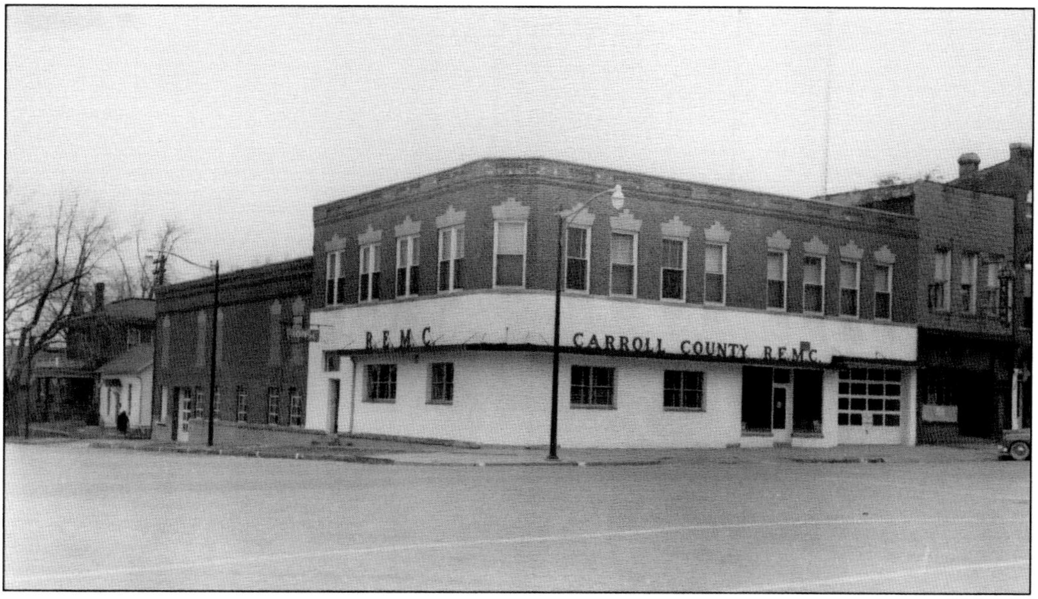

At the end of 1950, Carroll County REMC was located on the corner of Market and Franklin Streets. Its auditorium was used for many meetings and other events, and the Moose Lodge was on the top floor in 1946–1964. The Carroll County Economic Development Corporation and Carroll County Chamber of Commerce are presently housed upstairs. Next door was Ben's Tavern. Below is Will Cowdin's Plumbing and Heating (left). Cowdin operated from this location for more than 60 years followed by the present Ives Law Offices. Robert Pearson's appliance stores are on both sides of the alley. McCain's Jewelry was situated in this storefront for decades, first run by Luther McCain and then by his son, Tom. Gerald Fielding provides this service today. The Roxy Theater was next, until 1974, and to its east are the Penguin Café, Darraugh's Clothing, and Clifford's Grocery. (Courtesy Carroll County REMC.)

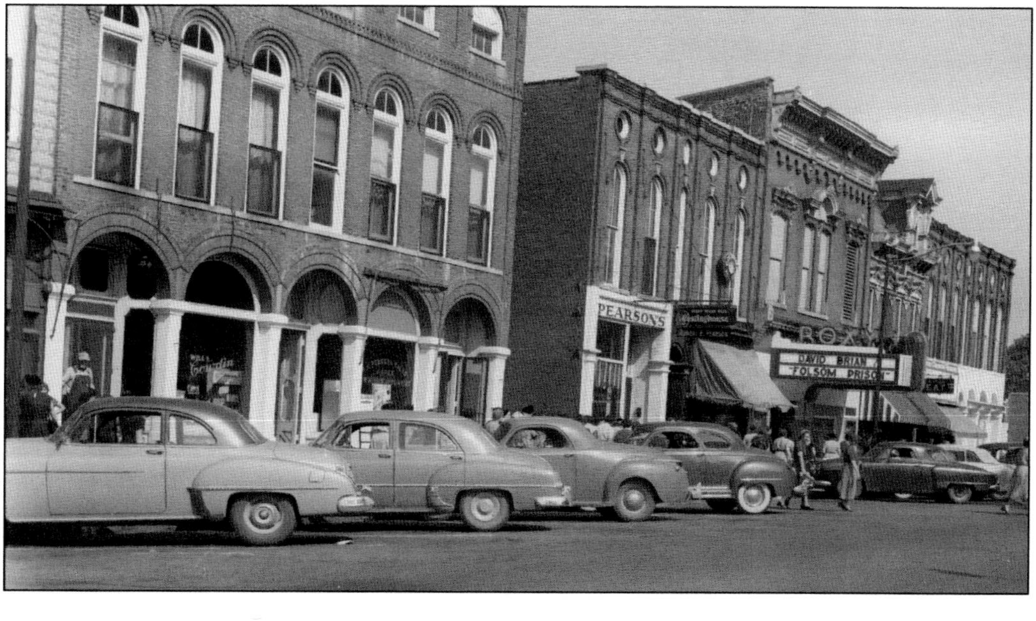

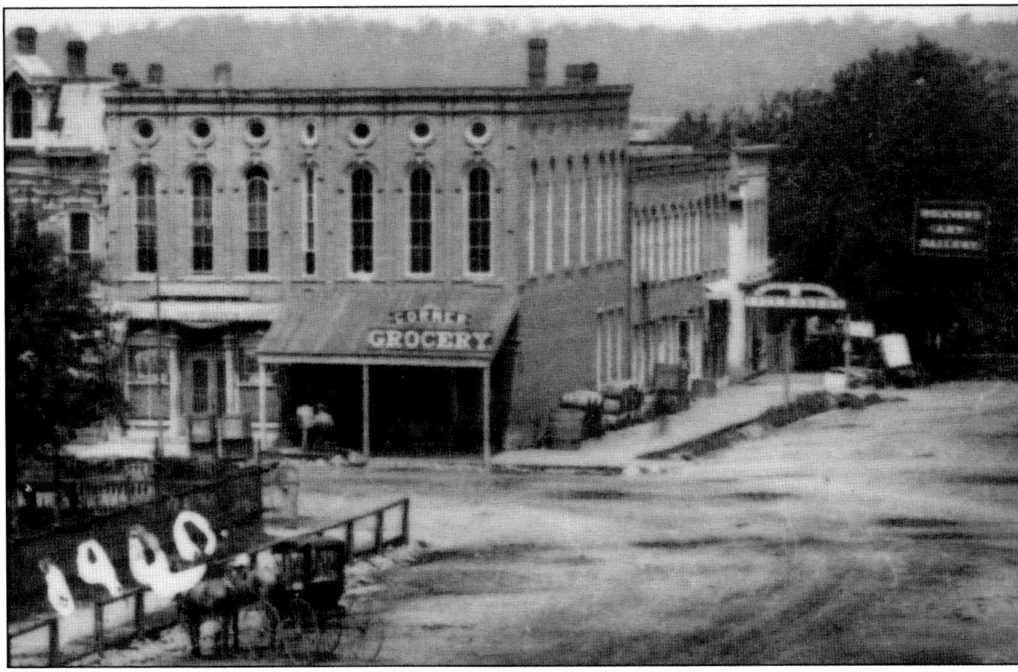

This detail from a 1900 photograph of the west side of North Washington Street shows Clifford's Grocery, Wolever, and City Bakery. Taken about the same time in front of Wolever's studio, the photograph below shows the sign for the Citizen Printing Office located on the second floor. The *Citizen*, a weekly newspaper, was published beginning in 1848. A poster in the window to the right of the stairway advertises a play in the Delphi Opera House on Wednesday, May 30, dating this to 1888 or 1894.

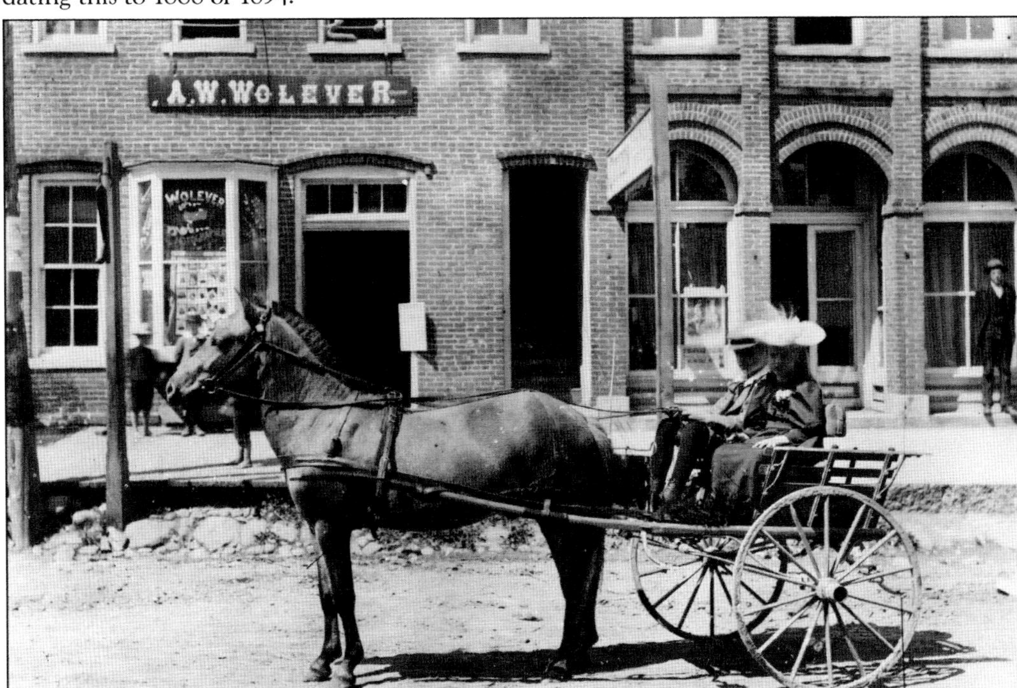

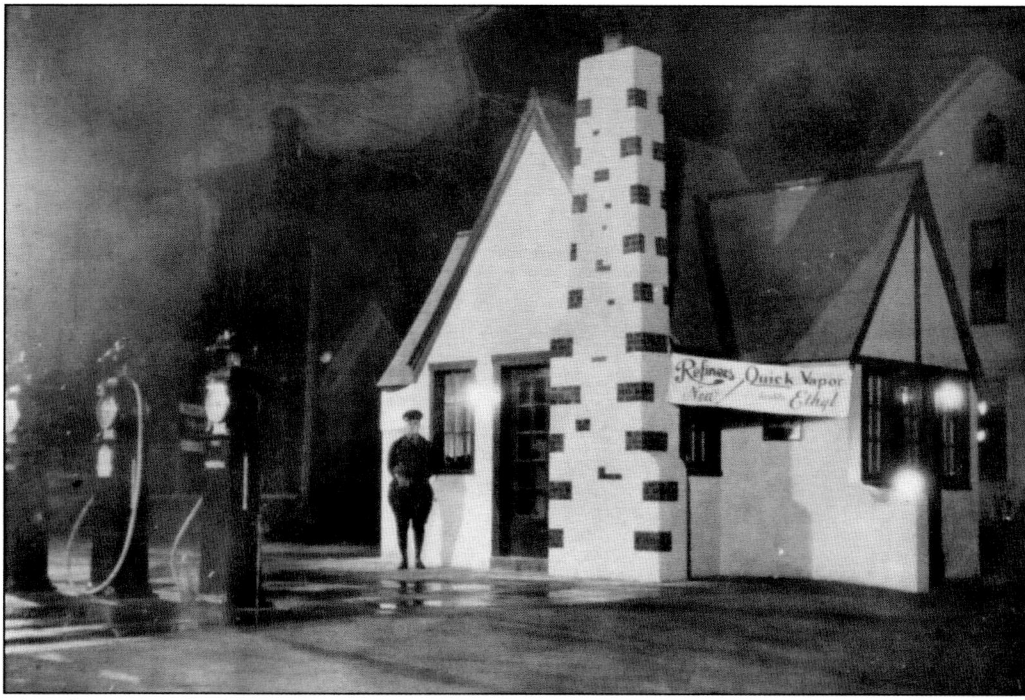

This diminutive building with Tudor details was erected in 1930 as Davies Service Station on the southwest corner of North Washington and Monroe Streets. With its details intact, it is now home to Mitchell's Mexican Grill.

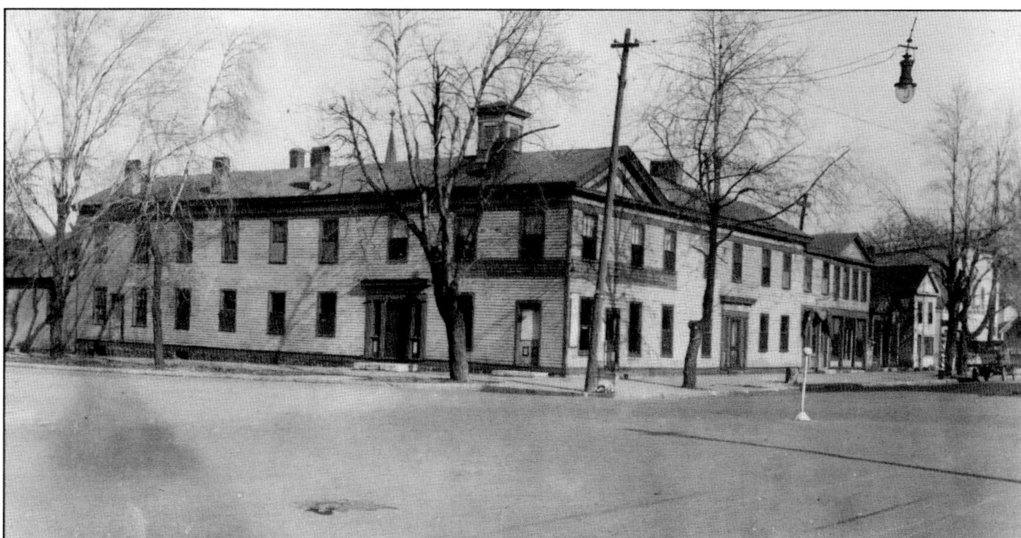

The City Hotel, on the northeast corner of Franklin and Washington Streets, had many names and proprietors during its 80-year history. It was also known as the New Buford, Knight, Delphi, and MacDonald Hotel. It was built in 1844 by William H. Buford to increase accommodations offered at his previous Buford House located across the street to the south. Other owners included Corbley Knight and Harry Sharp. This photograph was taken shortly before it was torn down in 1924 to accommodate a gas station. That was later removed, and the space now provides parking for Regions Bank.

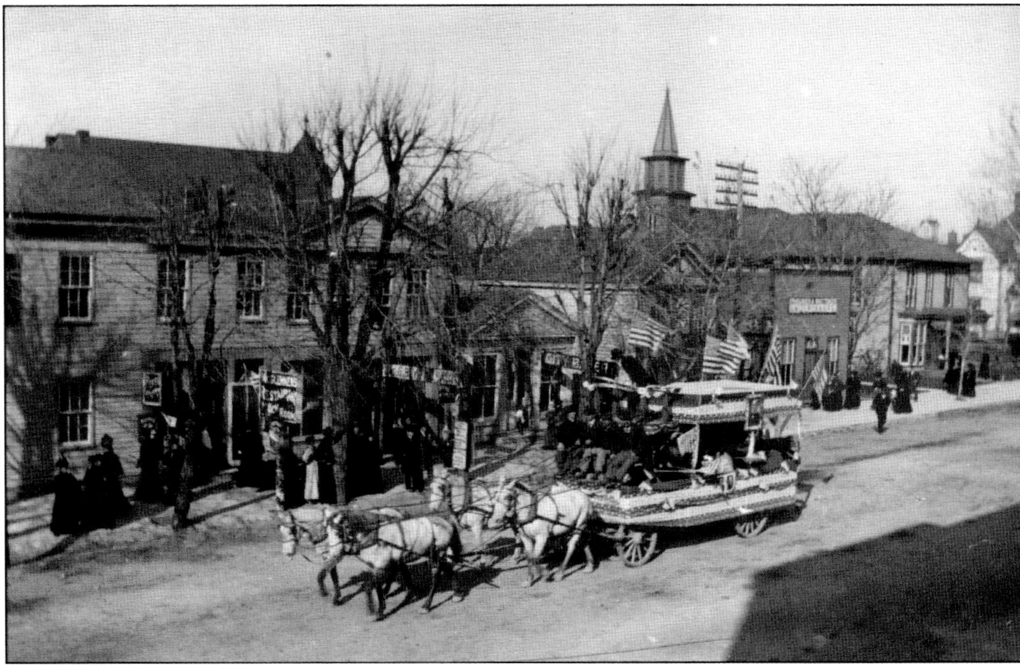

A parade down East Franklin Street in 1896 celebrates the visit of William Jennings Bryan during his first campaign for president. In the hotel building (left) is McGlennen's Bakery and Restaurant. Farther east is Hinkle's Bakery and the meat market owned by Stranahan then Hall. Bragunier and Whittaker Undertakers are farther east with Emrick Creamery on the corner. The photograph below, taken in front of the restaurant in the 1890s, includes many prominent Delphi men. Henderson Dunkle, Carroll County treasurer and then auditor for many years, is seated in the middle (with cane). To his right is undertaker John Bragunier. Standing in the doorway is William Stewart, county treasurer.

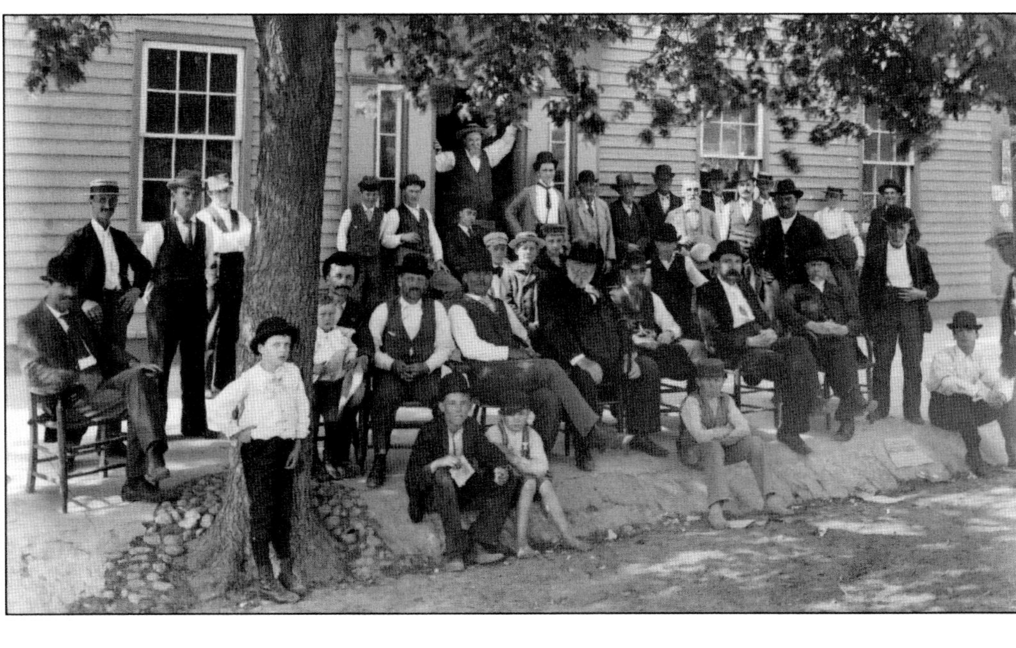

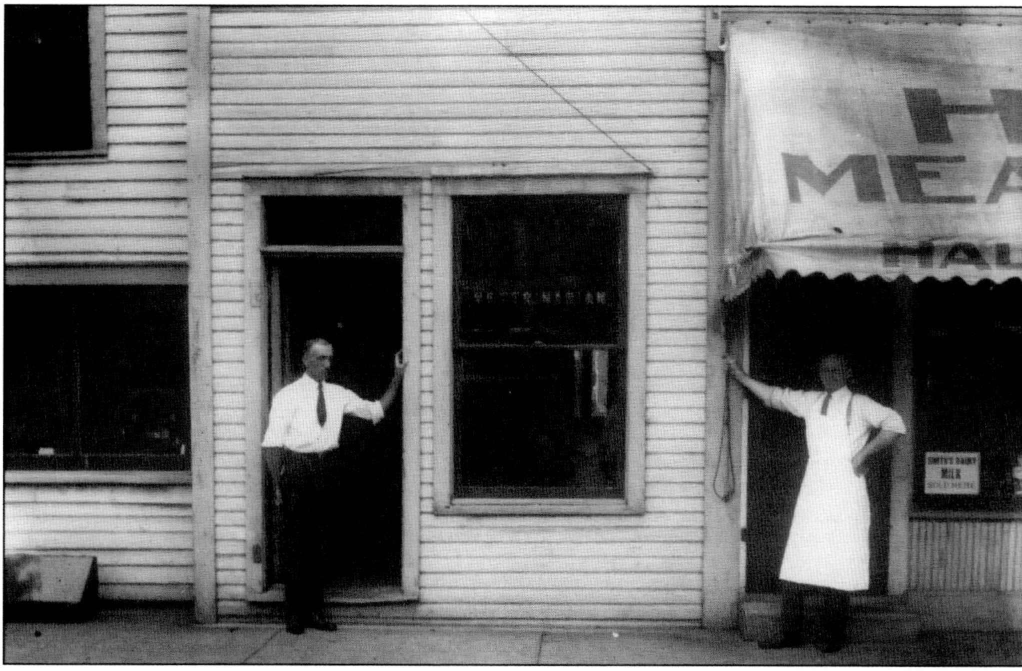

Veterinarian Clarence Hoover and butcher George Hall are on the north side of East Franklin Street in the early 1900s. The sign "Smith's Dairy Milk Sold Here" touts a local dairy. In the 1940s, George's son, Robert Hall, moved the meat market and grocery to the corner of Union and Franklin Streets where it continues today as Wallmann's Quality Foods.

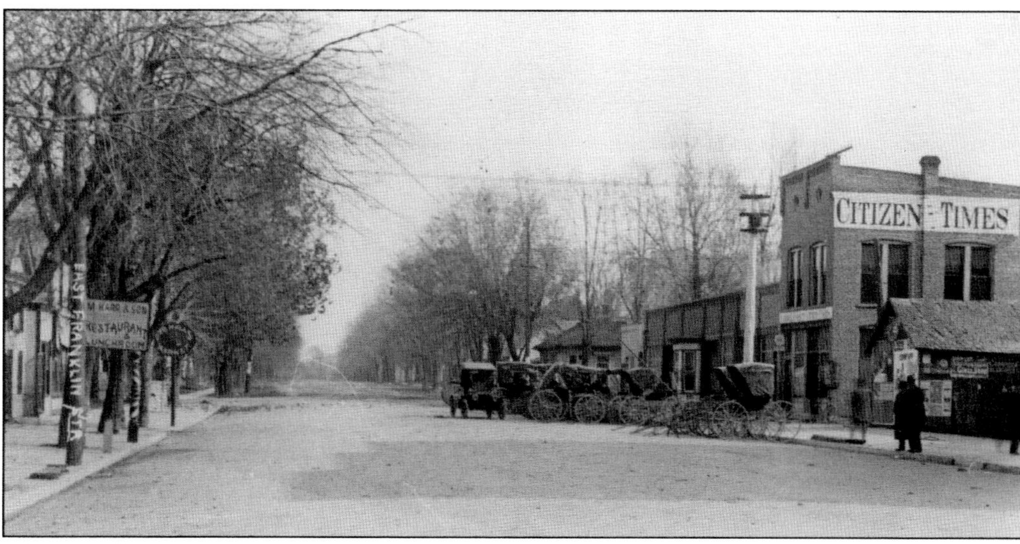

The *Carroll County Citizen Times*—edited by A. B. Crampton, his daughter, Mindwell, and son-in-law, Henry Wilson—built on the south side of East Franklin Street in 1903. It was later the *Delphi Citizen*, run by the Myron Johnson family. After a series of mergers, the Delphi office of the *Carroll County Comet* is there today, run by the third generation of the Moss family. Since 1920, Morrow's Shoe Shop has been to its immediate left. Gresham Livery occupied much of the east quarter block from 1867 to 1908. Samuel Gresham and his son, Edward H., each served as sheriff.

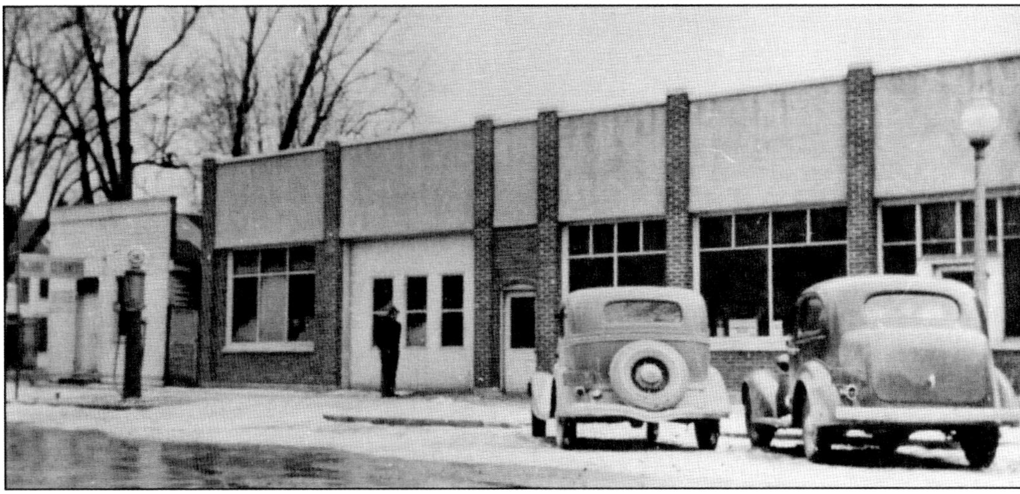

In the 1940s, the southeast corner of Union and East Franklin Streets has a cleaner (left), but from the 1860s to the 1930s, the small building housed Doctors F. A. and J. J. Shultz—father and son. The Farm Bureau and Carroll County REMC, beginning operation here in 1935, shared the next building. These buildings were replaced decades ago with parking and office buildings currently occupied by law offices and a title company.

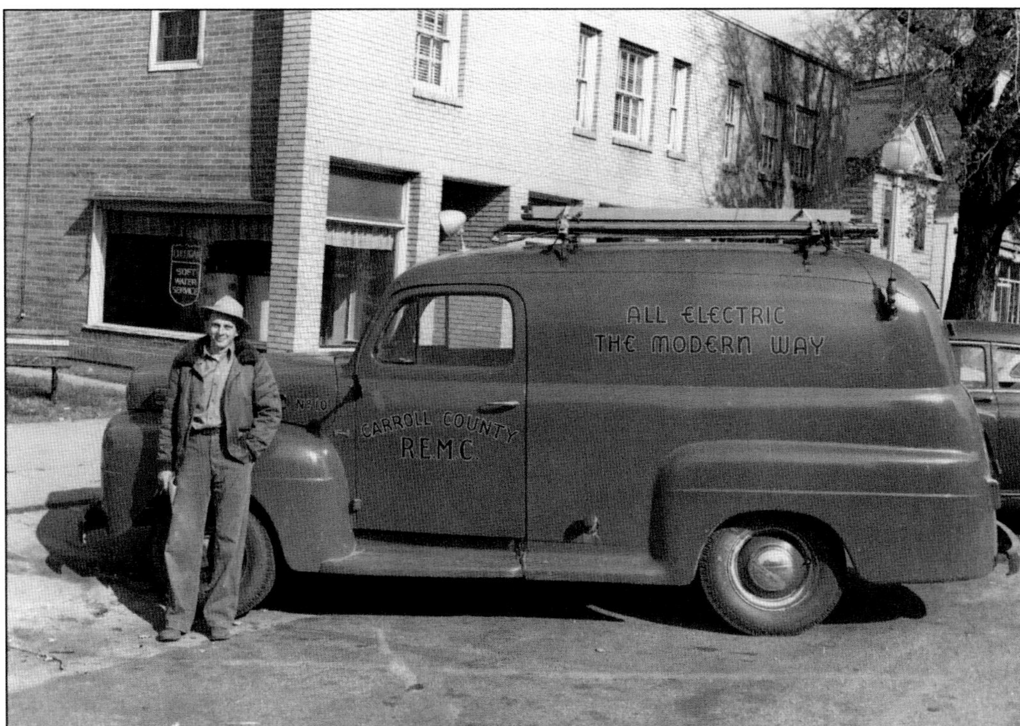

Herb Isaacs stands in front of a Carroll County REMC truck in the early 1940s. The brick building also housed Culligan Soft Water Service and the finance and insurance office of Yantis Wells. REMC moved from across the street in 1943 to this building west of the alley. In 1950, they moved to their current location on West Franklin Street. Young's Culligan moved to East Main Street, where it remains today. (Courtesy Carroll County REMC.)

Three

EAST OF THE SQUARE

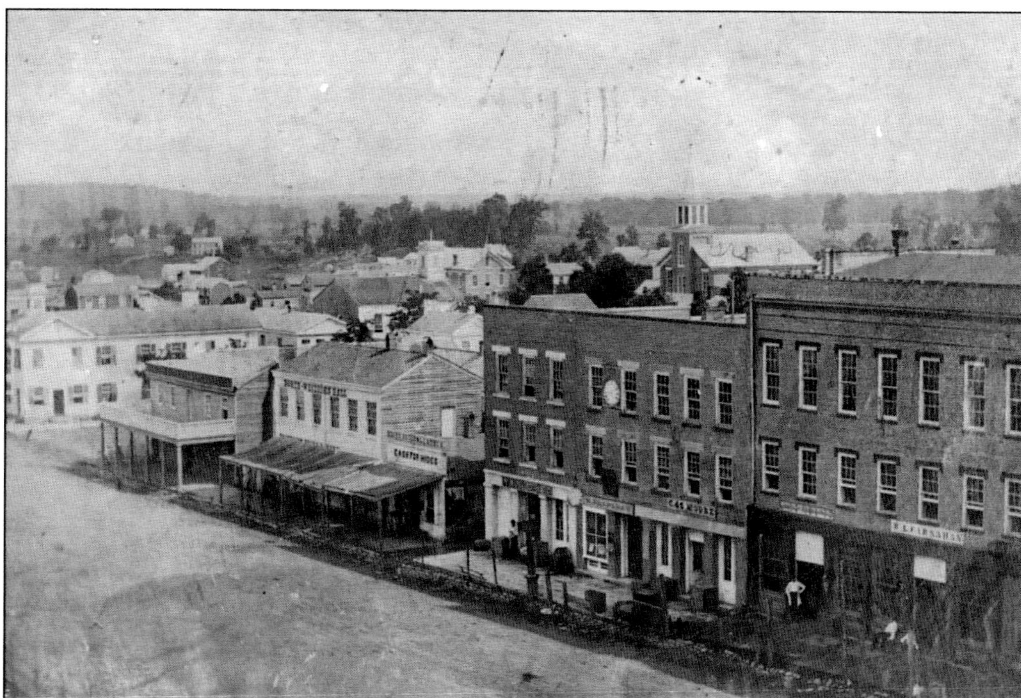

The 1860 photograph shows the Buford House (left) and Joseph Assion's grocery, bakery, and saloon in Northwestern Hall as well as John Brookbank's shoe shop. All buildings are already brick south of the alley. William Bolles' general store, William Bradshaw Jewelry, and C. and G. Moore's general store are in the 1851 Bolles-Stewart block. Wise and Sons Dry Goods, W. L. Carnahan Boots, and Spears and Case Bank occupy the 1855 Spears and Case block.

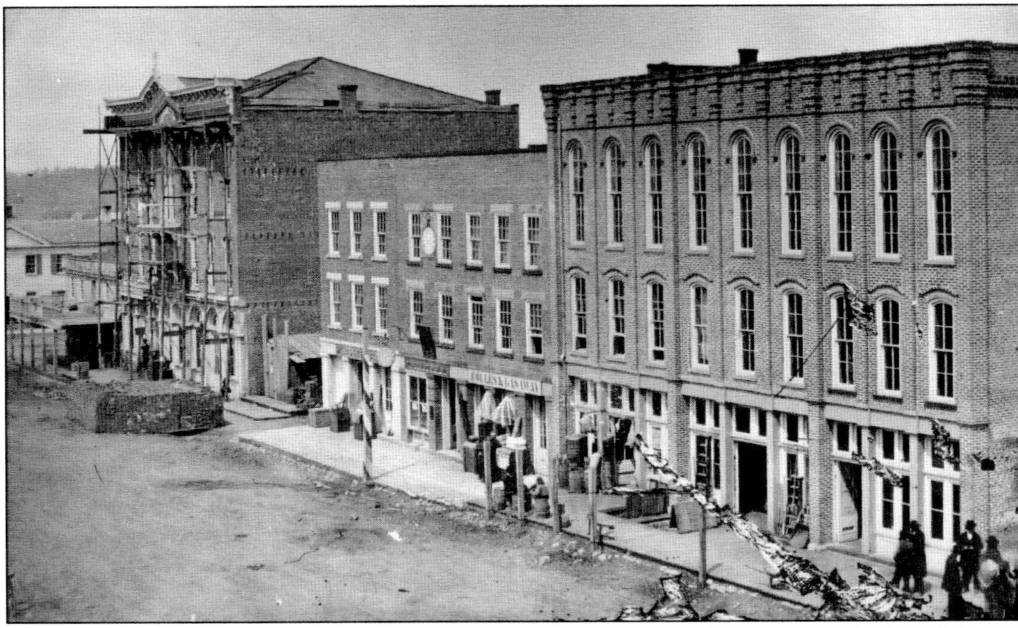

By 1865, the only frame building remaining is at left. The three-story, three-bay Assion-Ruffing City Hall replaced Northwestern Hall. The square of bricks in the street will become the Brookbank building. South of the alley, Bolles and Gasaway general store and Palmer and Denniston Hardware had arrived. The Spears and Case façade was completely redone in 1865, mirroring the 1863 Moore block diagonally opposite.

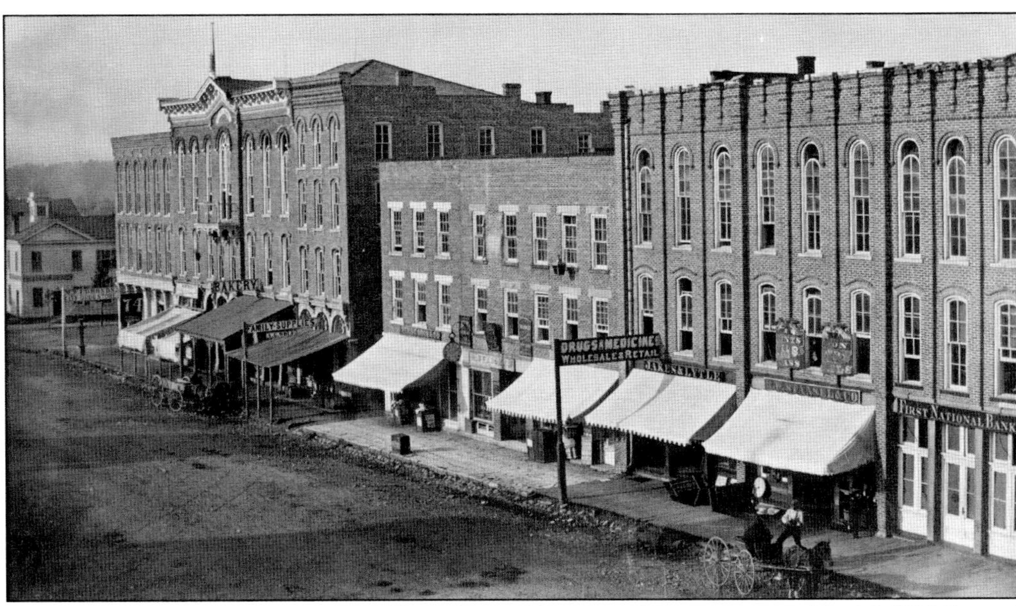

In 1875, the corner building, erected by John Ruffing in 1870, was occupied by M. W. Edmonds Drugs, Wineman clothing store had the north bay, and Lathrope's Bakery had the south part of the Assion-Ruffing building. A. G. Wolf is in the Brookbank building on the alley, completed in 1867. South of the alley is Henry Gros Jeweler and William Bradshaw Insurance. Jakes and Lytle Drugs, W. H. Stansel Hardware, and the First National Bank are in the Spears and Case block.

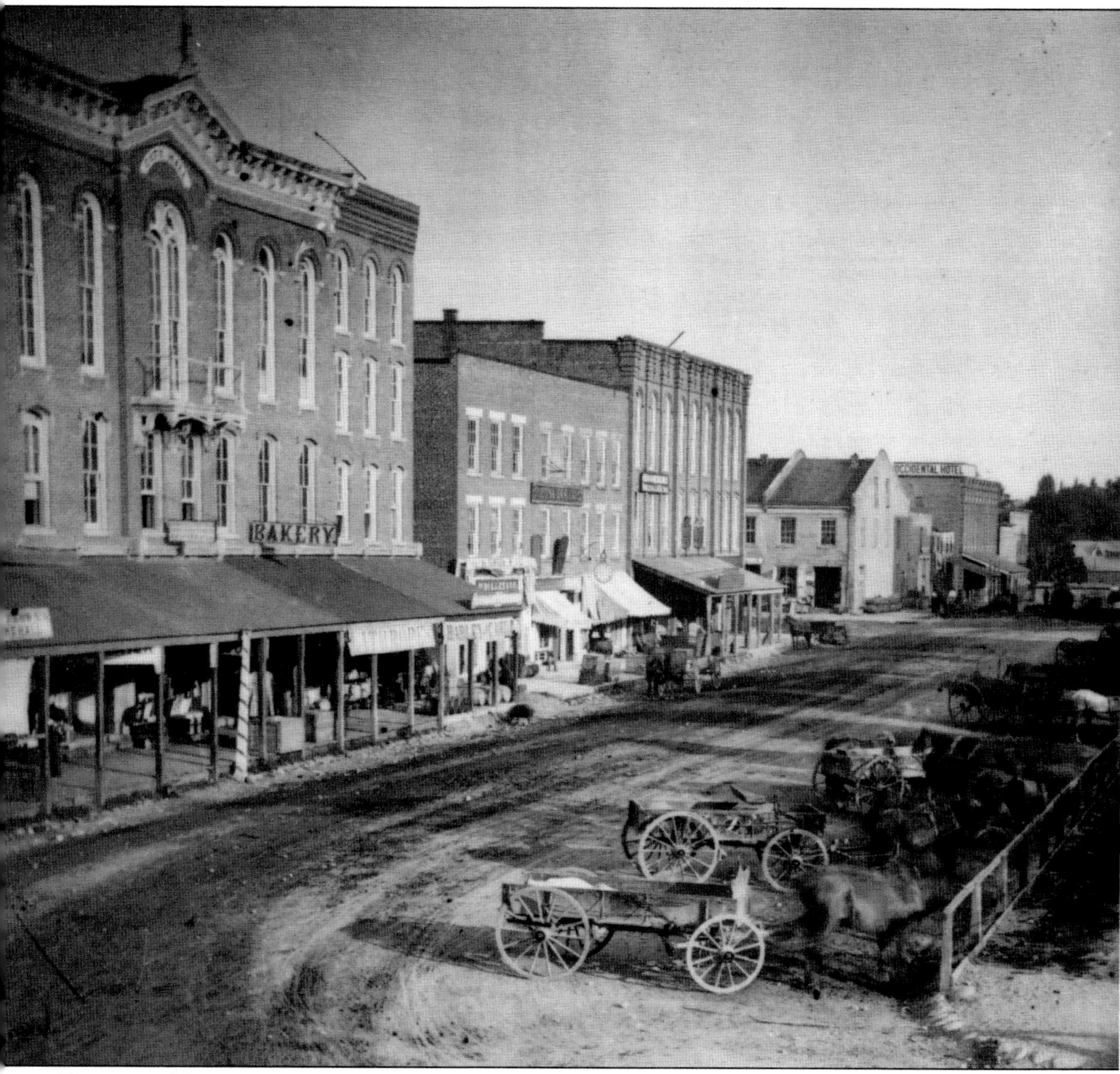

Wagons and horses line the hitching rail on the east side of the square while owners conduct business in the courthouse, buy provisions at the stores, get a meal at a lunchroom, do banking, or perhaps buy a new wagon. In this view from the late 1870s, a uniform awning now covers the fronts of the commercial buildings. Edward Brown runs a clothing store in the Ruffing building (left). Next to Lathrope is Harley and Carll's Grocery with a pig rooting in the dirt. The four-story hotel building was known by various names, including Greenup, European, and Crosby. Gros remains next to Bradshaw Insurance Company, which has been in continuous operation from 1851 to the present. On the corner of South Washington and East Main Streets is the Pigman building, and beyond it the Occidental Hotel, built in the mid-1860s, can be seen. The latter was also known as the Clifton, Iona, and Sabin, later becoming the Masonic Temple.

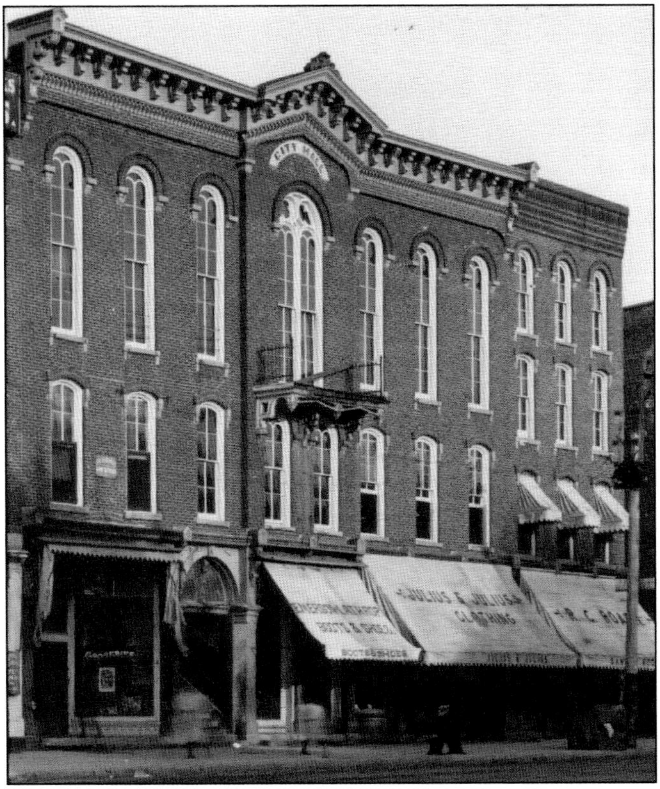

The Assion-Ruffing City Hall (left) is a commanding Italianate building placed on the National Register of Historic Places in 1998. Completed in 1865, the third-floor grand hall first opened with a dance for returning soldiers. In 1882, John Lathrope Jr. remodeled the third floor into the Lathrope and Ruffing Opera House. It was the center of entertainment in Delphi for many years, but closed by the fire marshal in 1914 for lack of a second exit. Today the building is home to the Delphi Preservation Society, which is working to restore the building and its third-floor auditorium as a performing arts venue, museum, and cultural center.

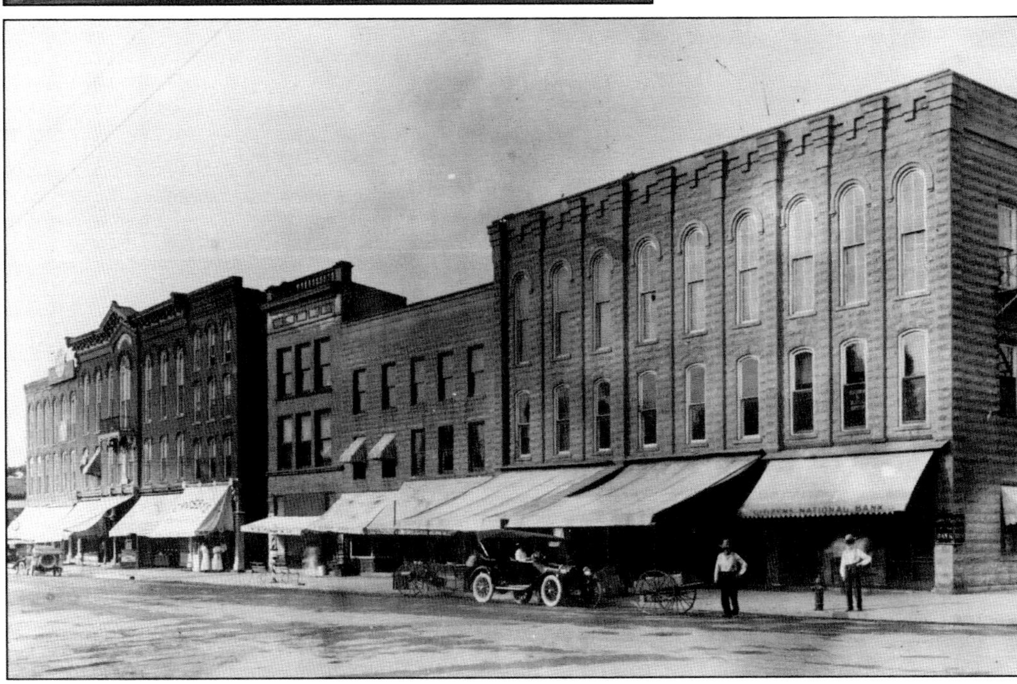

This photograph shows the cement coat resembling cut stone that was applied before 1906 to many buildings on the square. Sharp's Ice Cream is on the far corner followed by newcomers C. O. Julius Clothing, Crosby Hotel, Broadlick Five and Ten, and Citizens National Bank on the right.

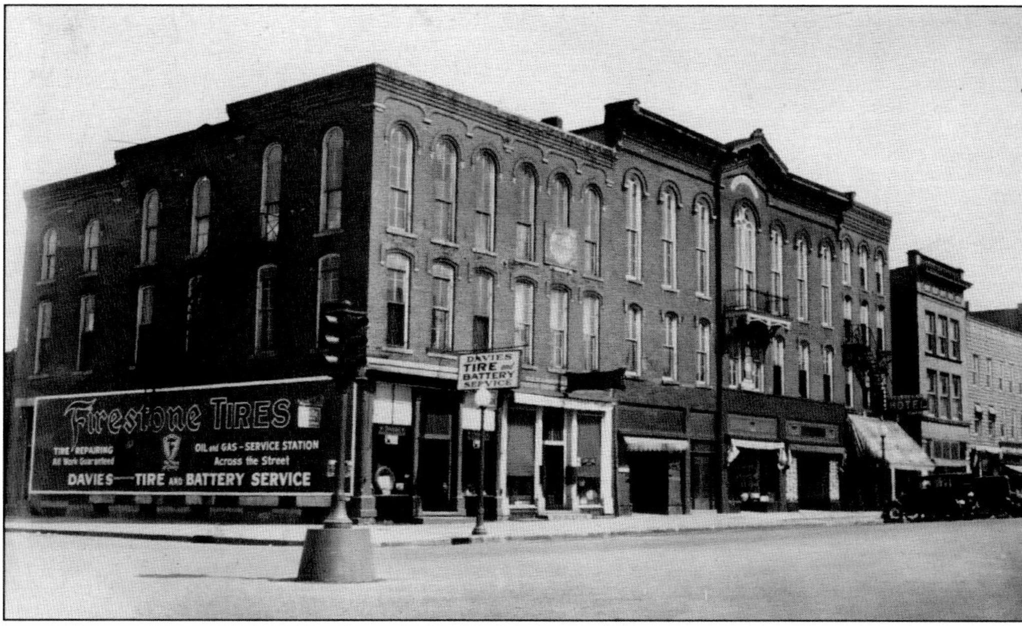

By the 1930s, the City Hall building had modern retail fronts and prismatic-glass tile transoms, replacing the cast-iron archways. Its merchants include Ruffing Music, McFarland Grocery, and C. O. Julius Clothing. Davies Tire and Battery Service on the corner was one of many new automotive stores. Margowski Drugs and Wallpaper is next. On the alley are the hotel and café and beyond is Goff's Five and Ten.

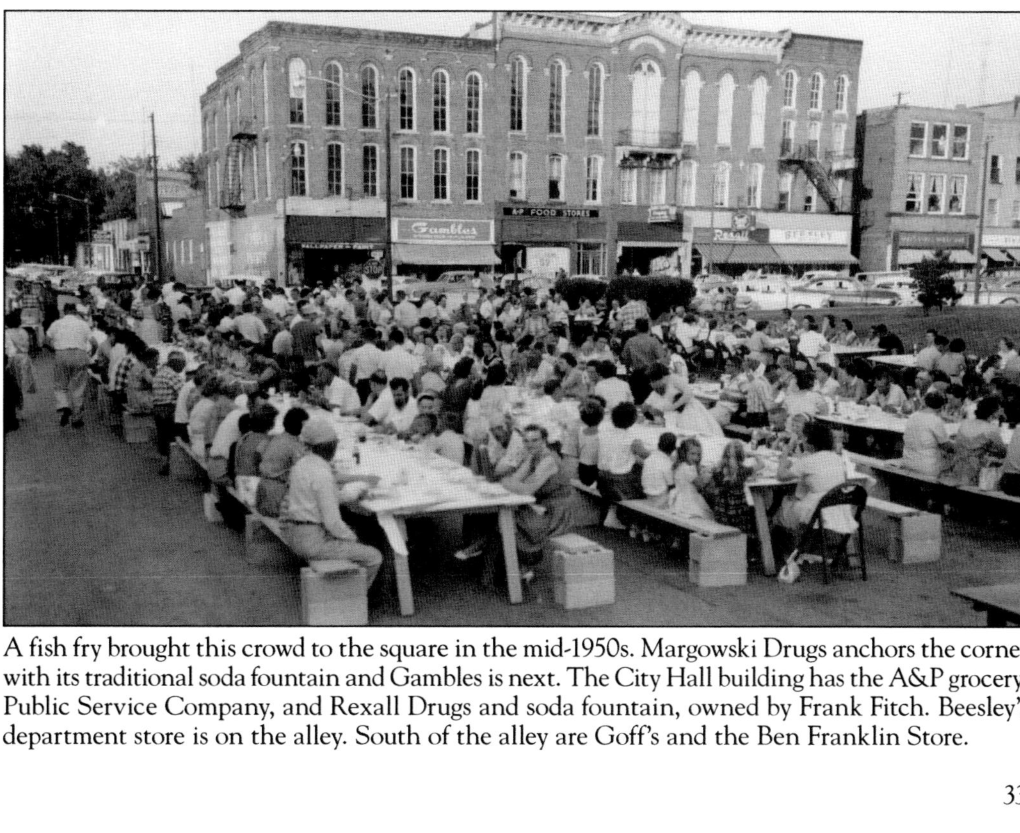

A fish fry brought this crowd to the square in the mid-1950s. Margowski Drugs anchors the corner with its traditional soda fountain and Gambles is next. The City Hall building has the A&P grocery, Public Service Company, and Rexall Drugs and soda fountain, owned by Frank Fitch. Beesley's department store is on the alley. South of the alley are Goff's and the Ben Franklin Store.

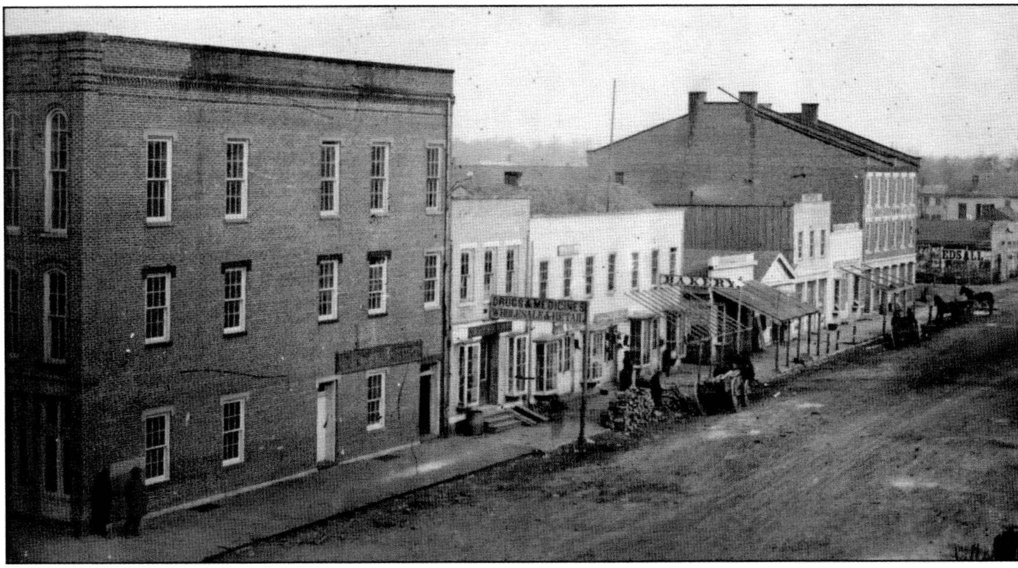

On East Main Street, about 1868, Spears and Case (left) and the Bowen Bank buildings are the brick bookends. The frame buildings between are occupied by Stewart Drugs, Dixon and Callahan Shoemakers, Lathrope's Bakery, Ottmar Boots and Shoes, Givens and Graham Bakery, Nicholas Smith Stoves, and Best and Barclay Tailors. Across Union Street to the top is R. H. Graham Furniture.

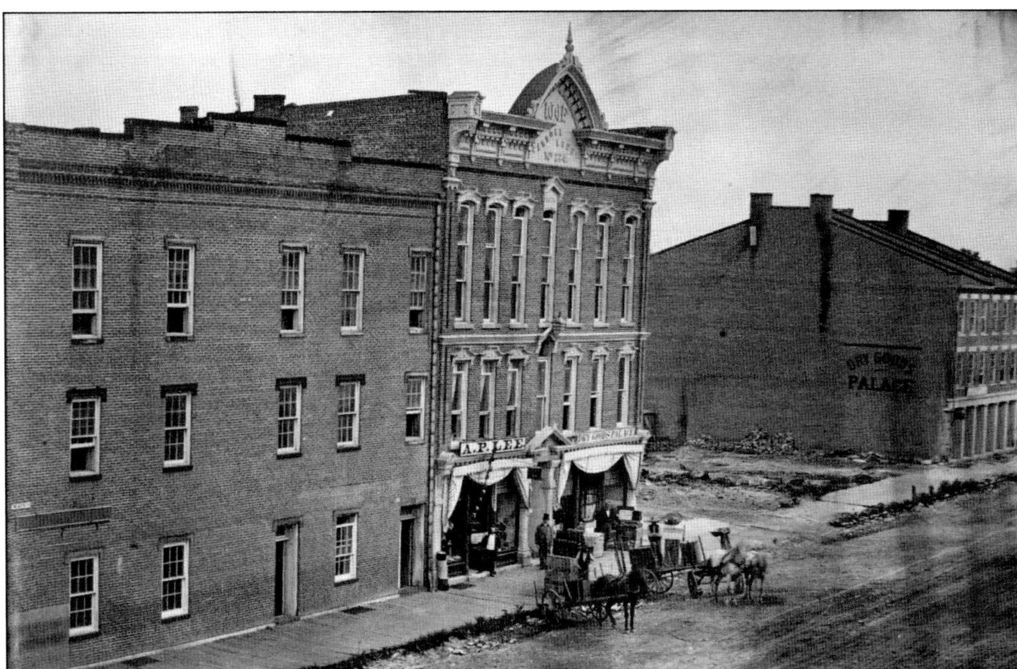

Carroll Lodge No. 174 of the Independent Order of Odd Fellows (IOOF) is the dominant building on the north side of East Main Street in this 1875 photograph. William Bradshaw, W. F. Lytle, and Charles Brough formed the committee that bought the ground and built the Italianate lodge, incurring a $6,600 debt soon retired from expanded membership. A. P. Lee Hats and Ramey's Dry Goods Palace occupy the retail bays. Earlier frame buildings have all been razed.

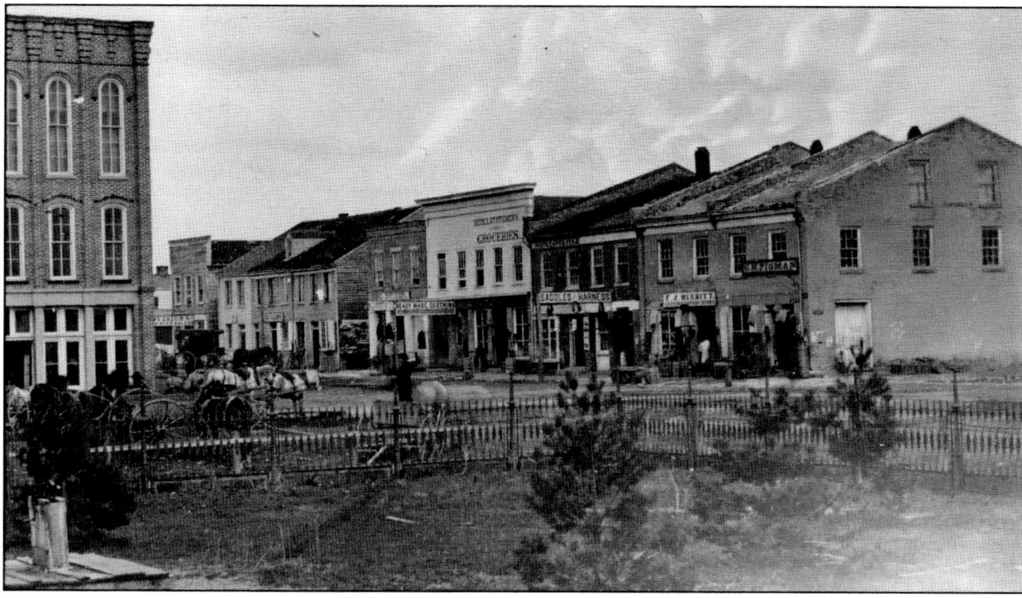

On the south side of East Main Street is the 1840s G. W. Pigman brick (right) with his general store and F. J. Merritt Groceries and Provisions. Next to it is McIntosh Saddles and Harness and the City drugstore. Tailor M. Wellhouse occupies the 1850s brick on the alley, the only building shown that survives today. East of the alley is the Assion Saloon and Louis Biersdorf's Meat Market.

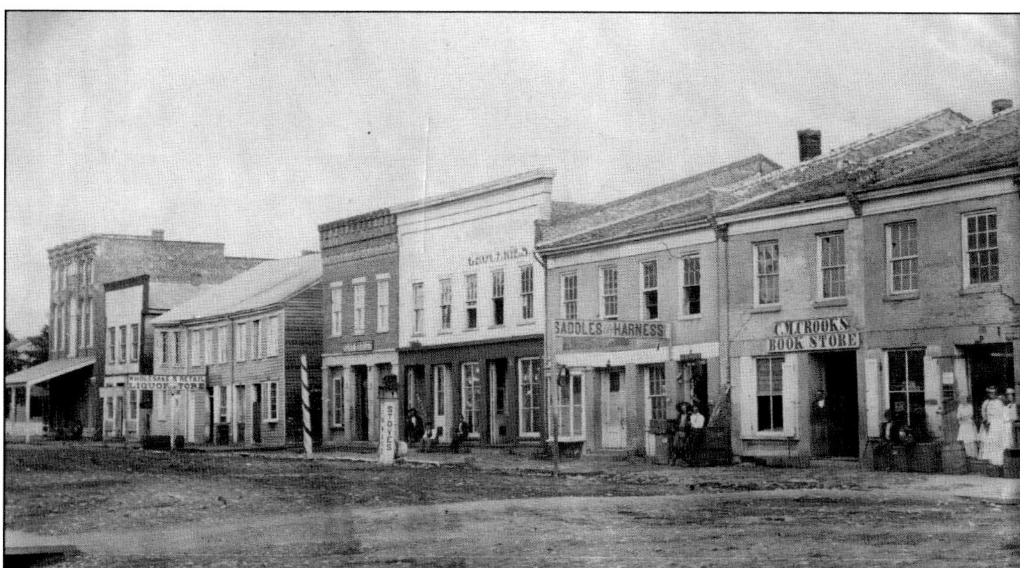

In this 1875 photograph, the Niewerth building (left), constructed in 1874, anchors the south side of East Main at Union Street. The Italianate structure was placed on the National Register of Historic Places in 1984. It was Hamling's Tavern and poolroom for several decades, and some say brothel above. On the near corner, the Pigman building has a grocery with C. M. Crooks Book Store occupying the east bay.

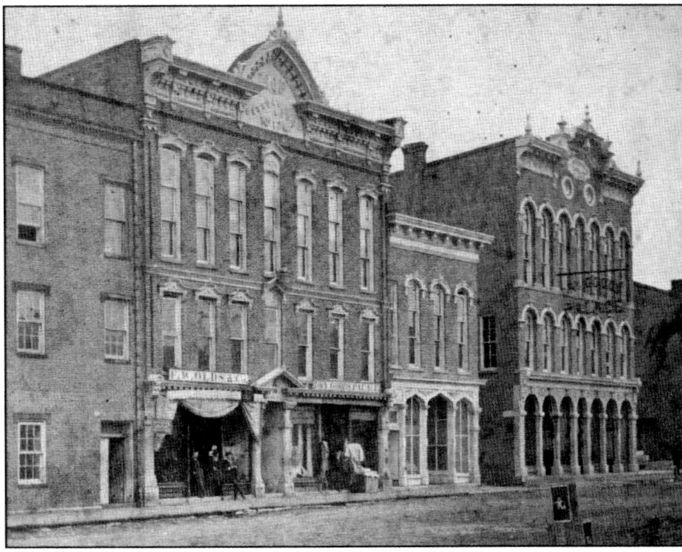

This stereopticon image from about 1880 shows F. W. Olds Clothing and Ramey Dry Goods Palace in the IOOF building next to a two-story Italianate structure built by Anthony Hanrahan about 1876 for a saloon. Next, George and John Carll's Centennial block (completed 1878) had a third-floor hall or opera house, which was used for meetings and performances. A saloon was part of its first floor until the early 1900s. Below, by the 1920s, Carroll Lodge houses Sanitary Barbershop and Baths and Wingerd's Grocery. Carroll County Loan and Trust is in the building next door. To the east are Yantis Wells Grocery and Goff's Novelty Store. The Sugar Shack and Blythe Furniture are located in the three-story Italianate building, built by A. H. Bowen in the late 1870s, next to the Bowen Bank.

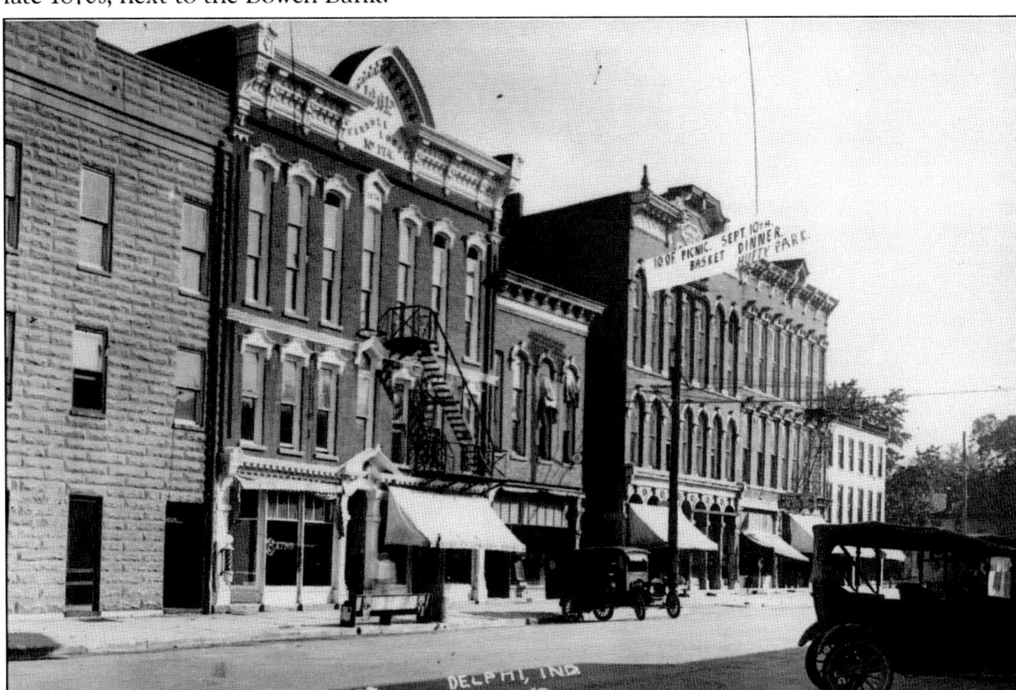

Abner H. Bowen (1814–1890) and his brother, Nathaniel W. Bowen, came to Delphi in 1837 at the start of the canal era. Abner was the sole owner after Nathaniel died in 1848. Bowen family interests included grain and produce, papermaking, dry goods, wool, banking, and real estate. The Bowen Bank financed many businesses in the area. Upon his death in 1890, Abner left a multimillion-dollar estate, which generated controversy for many years.

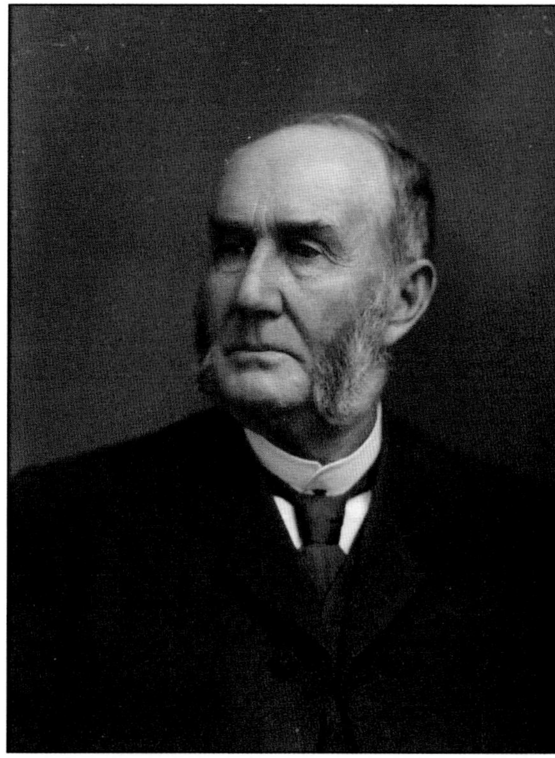

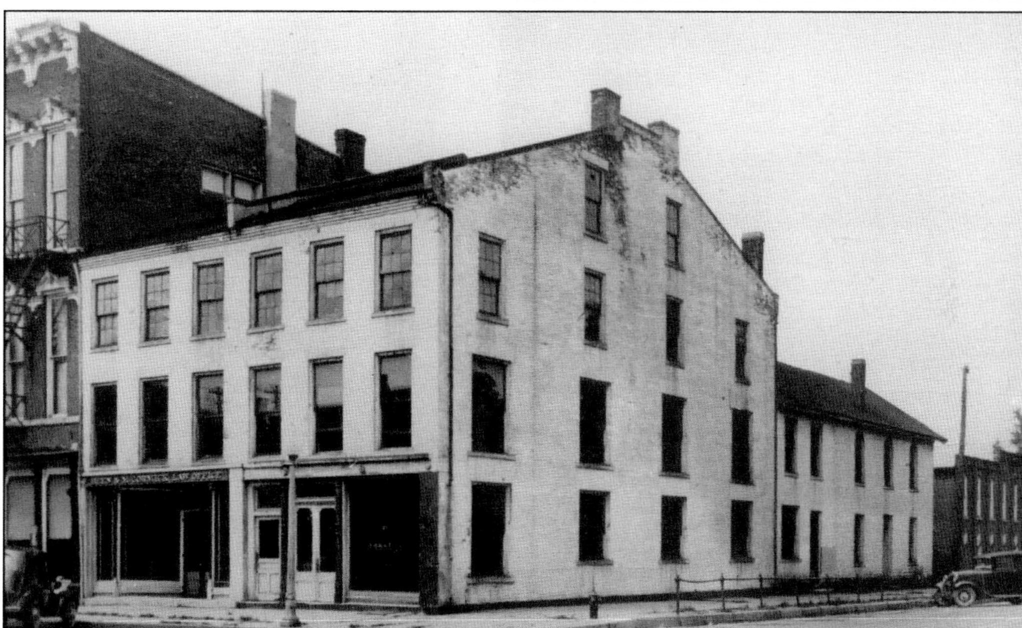

The Bowen brothers built this Federal-style, three-story building in 1845. It served as an office for their various businesses. The Bowen Bank was here until 1930. The eastern half was extensively remodeled in 1939 to house the Carroll Telephone Company, which had begun service in 1896. Three generations of the Walker family ran the business for decades. In 1981, the building was removed for a new telephone building.

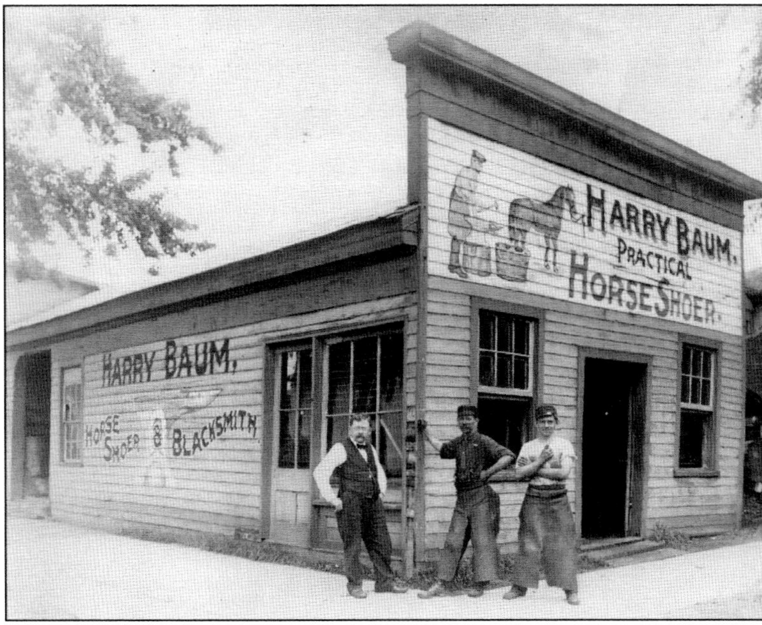

Located on the northeast corner of Union and East Main Streets was Harry Baum, Practical Horseshoer. Standing with Harry Baum (center) is Andrew W. Wolever (left) and an unidentified apprentice. Many other blacksmiths were at work in Delphi throughout its history, including Ramsey Finley, George Armitage, Israel Badorf, Josiah Dimmick, and Howard Landis.

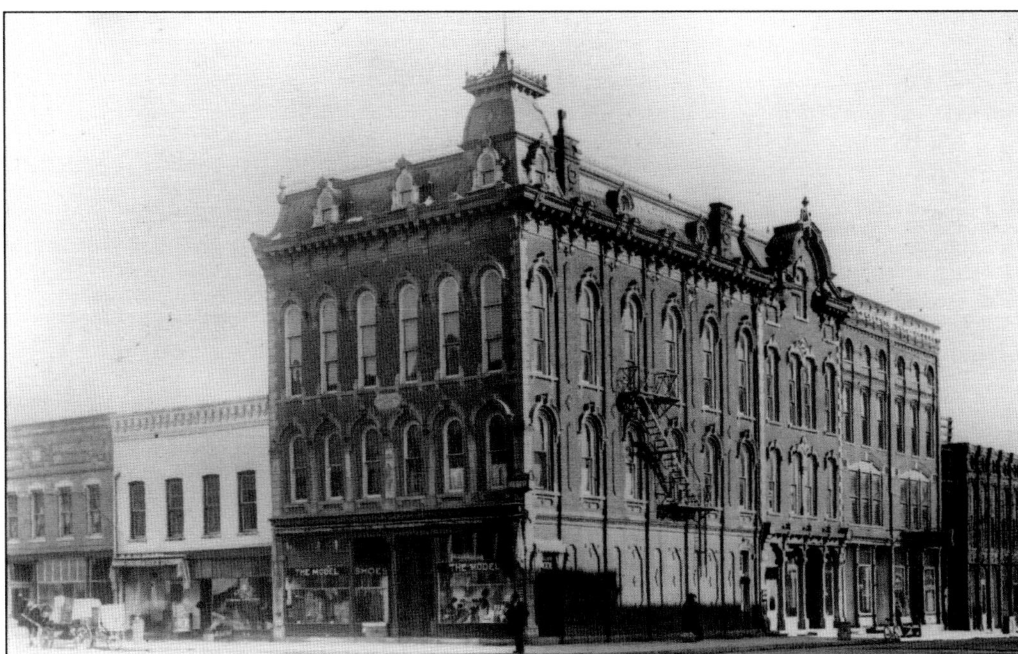

Shown here in the 1910s, the Second Empire–style IOOF Lodge No. 28 was erected on the corner of East Main and South Washington Streets in 1880. The Model clothing store occupies the retail bay. The two-story structure to its left houses Clay Pearson's clothing store and Charles Worley's (later Henry Crone's) market. The brick façade on the building to the far left was added in 1911.

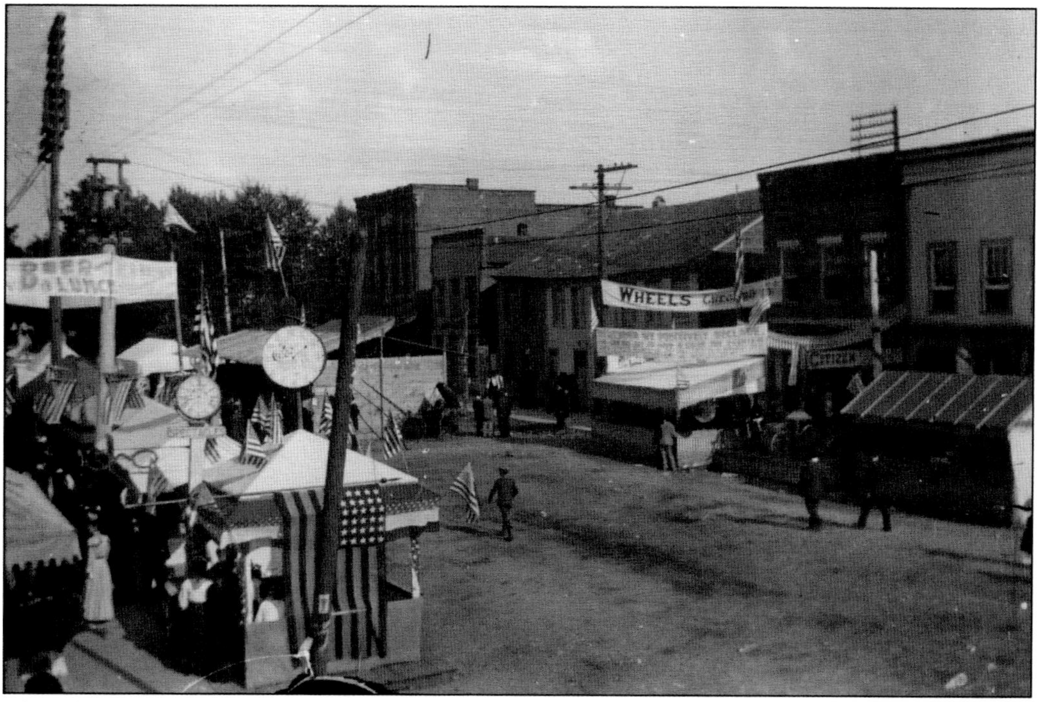

This photograph from the early 1900s shows the south side of East Main Street during a street fair. The Niewerth building (left) houses the Hamling Tavern. J. C. Fisher Wallpaper Hanger is located in the next building. The sagging frame structure is the Russ building, to be torn down in 1909. Right of the alley is the 1850s brick building currently housing the Sandwich Shop, located there since the 1940s.

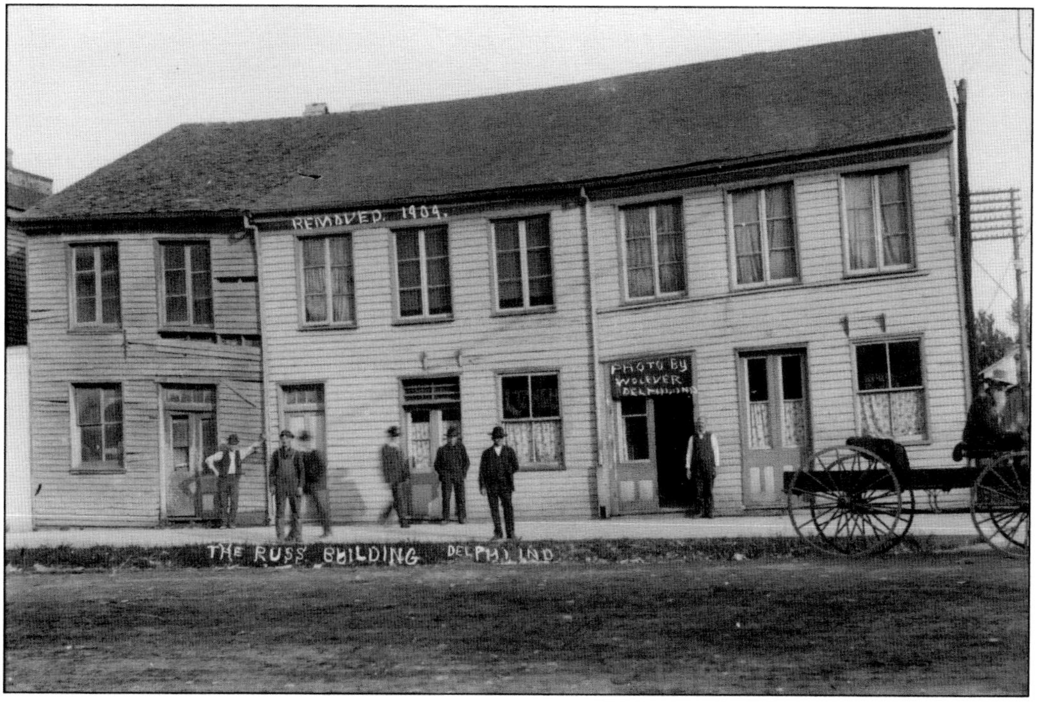

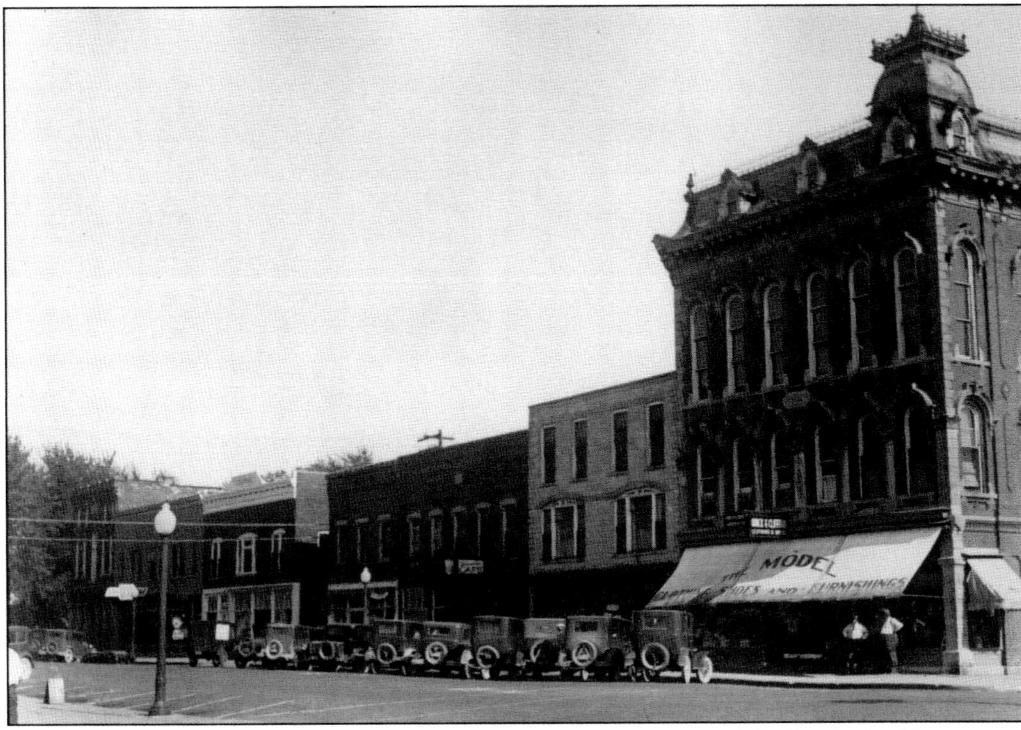

In the 1930s, the south side of East Main Street was a busy commercial block. The building second from left was completed in 1911 and housed Clawson Chevrolet. It was built by Ren Julien for his veterinary practice before he left to become State Veterinarian. The second building to the right of the alley is the Welcome Inn Café, which was located there for decades through 1942, when it moved to West Main Street.

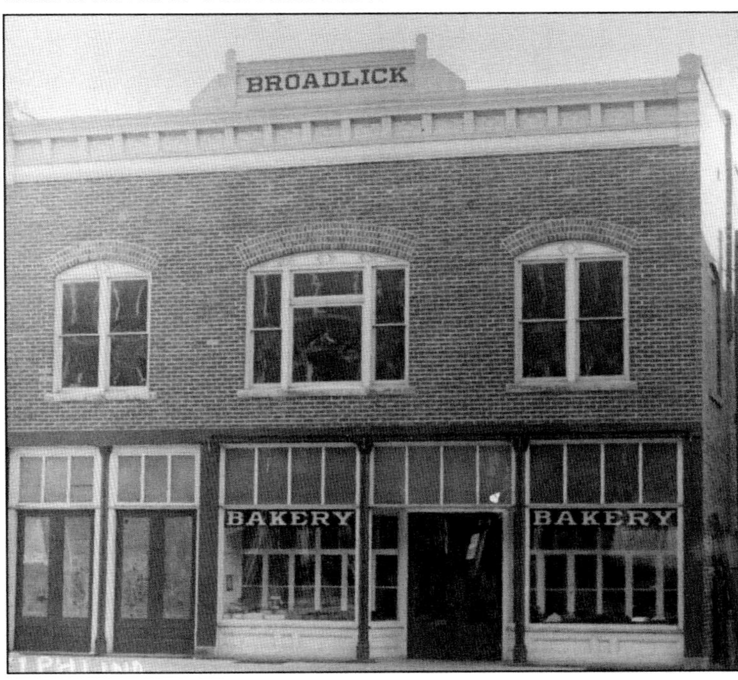

Broadlick Bakery was a fixture on East Main Street until 1930, when the building was sold to the *Delphi Journal*, a weekly publication printed from 1850 to 1966. In 1967, the *Journal-Citizen* was formed, and Myron Johnson acquired the printing shop, which became Oracle Press, later owned by Wayne Disinger. Bret and Sarah Hanaway acquired Oracle Press and operate Q Graphics printing today in the Gros building two doors west.

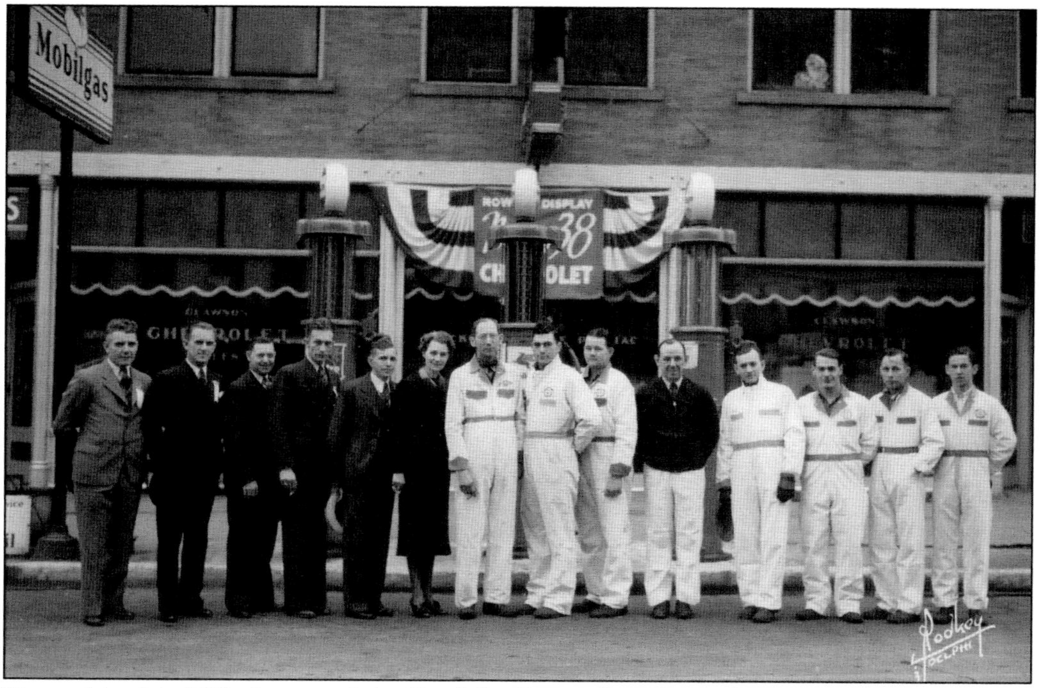

Pictured in this 1938 photograph by Frank Rodkey is the sales and service staff from Clawson Chevrolet. Gearold Clawson is second from left. The sales lot (below) was located on South Union Street behind the Niewerth building. The gingerbread gables of the former Lathrope residence can be seen behind the sales pavilion. NAPA Auto Parts and service bays are located in these spots today.

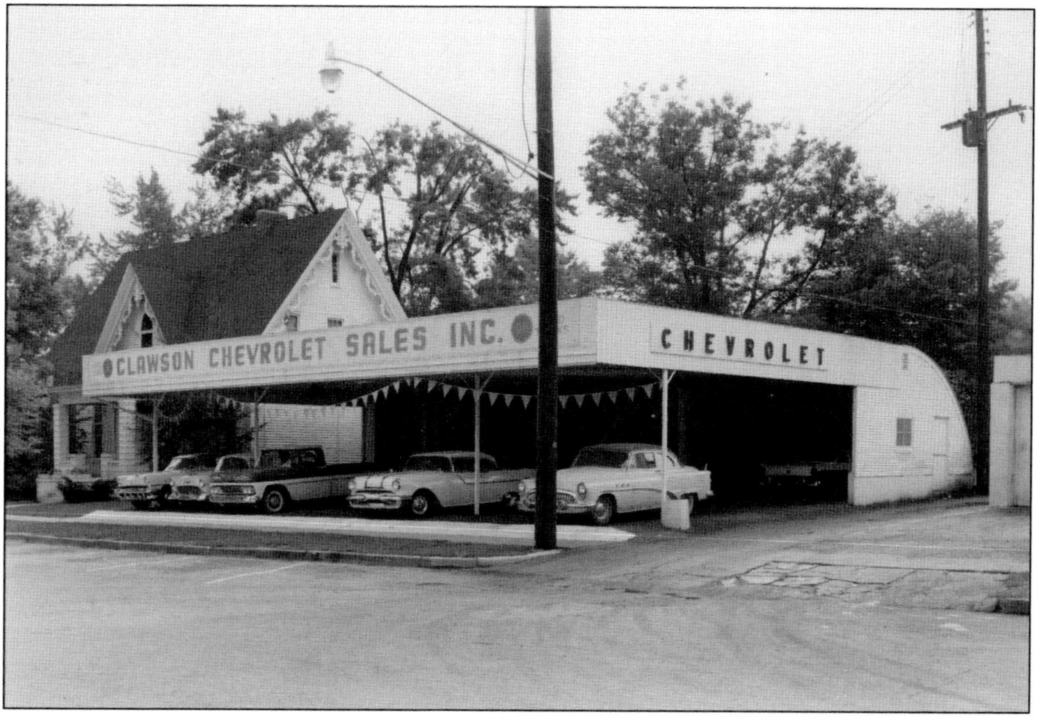

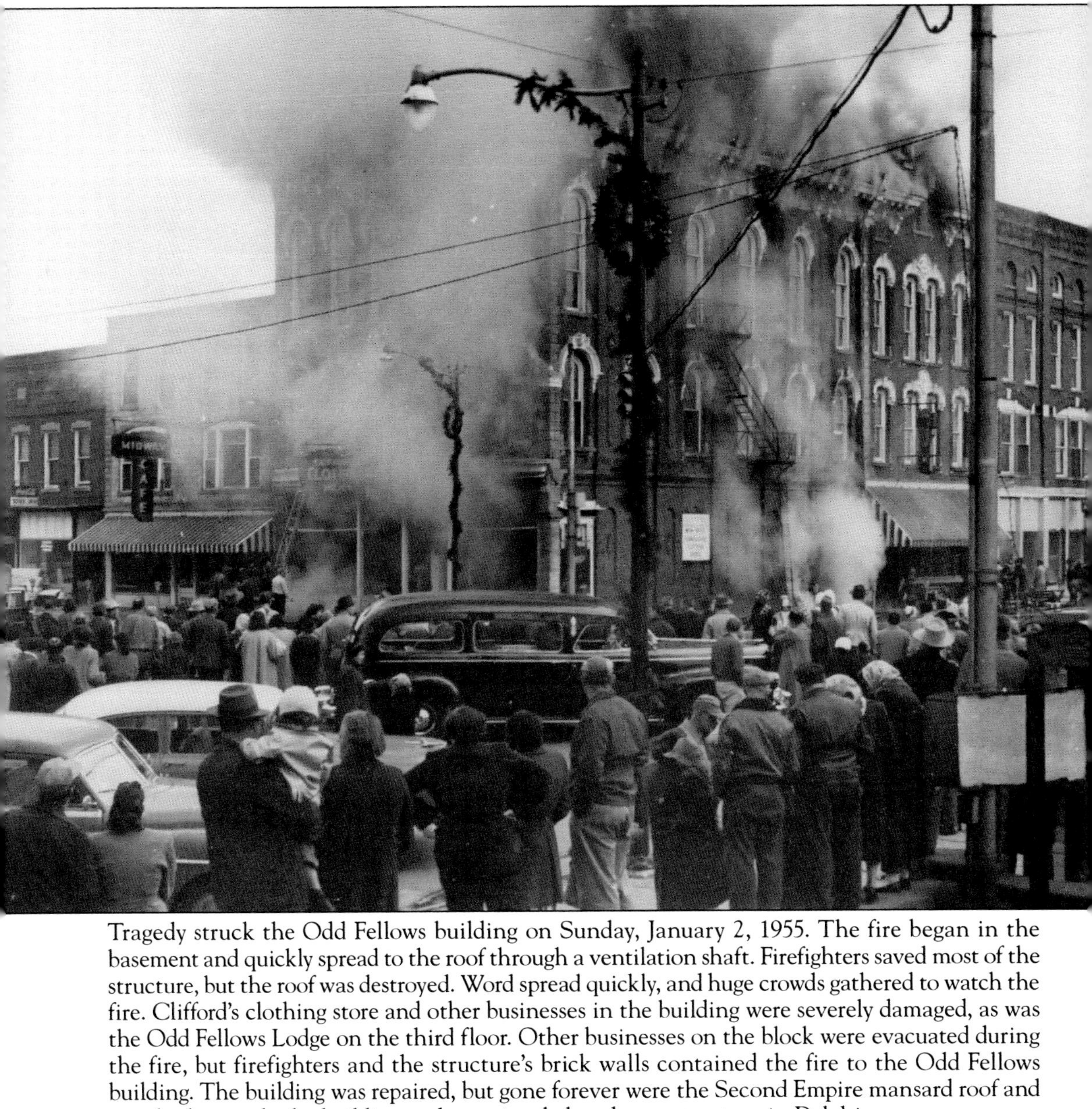

Tragedy struck the Odd Fellows building on Sunday, January 2, 1955. The fire began in the basement and quickly spread to the roof through a ventilation shaft. Firefighters saved most of the structure, but the roof was destroyed. Word spread quickly, and huge crowds gathered to watch the fire. Clifford's clothing store and other businesses in the building were severely damaged, as was the Odd Fellows Lodge on the third floor. Other businesses on the block were evacuated during the fire, but firefighters and the structure's brick walls contained the fire to the Odd Fellows building. The building was repaired, but gone forever were the Second Empire mansard roof and cupola that made the building such a uniquely handsome structure in Delphi.

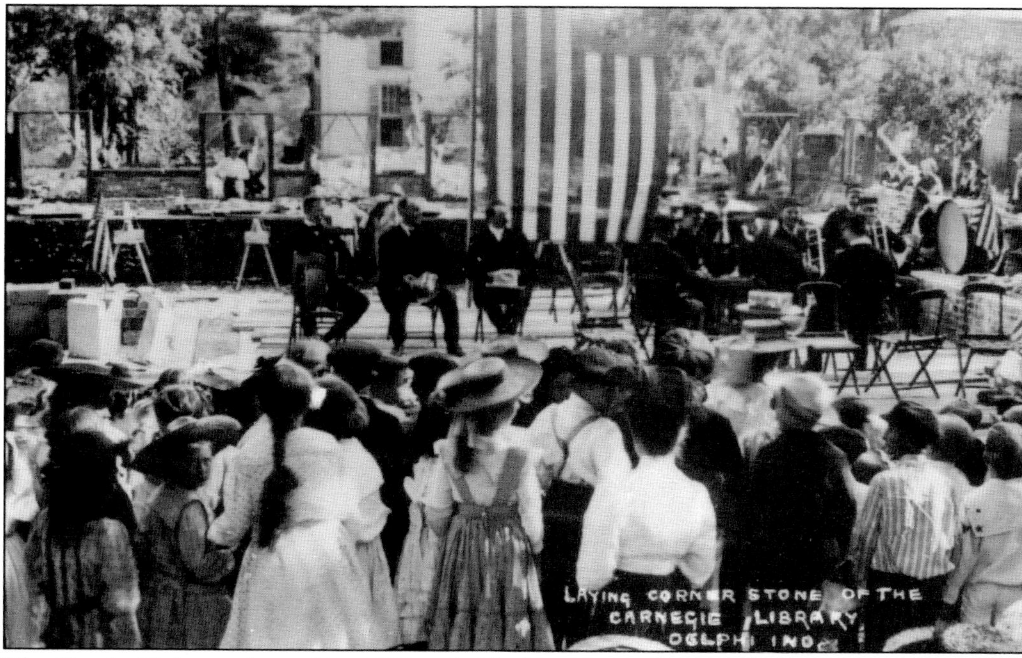

The Oracle Club was formed in 1886 with 25 charter members for the purpose of establishing a public library in Delphi. Books were collected, and the library was housed at the high school until 1904, when it was moved to the Bowen Bank building. In 1905, the library board asked the city council to appropriate $2,000 for a site, and they received a Carnegie grant of $10,000 to construct a public library. The cornerstone for the building was laid on September 1, 1905, at East Main and Indiana Streets as the Delphi City Band played for those in attendance. The Oracle Club continues today.

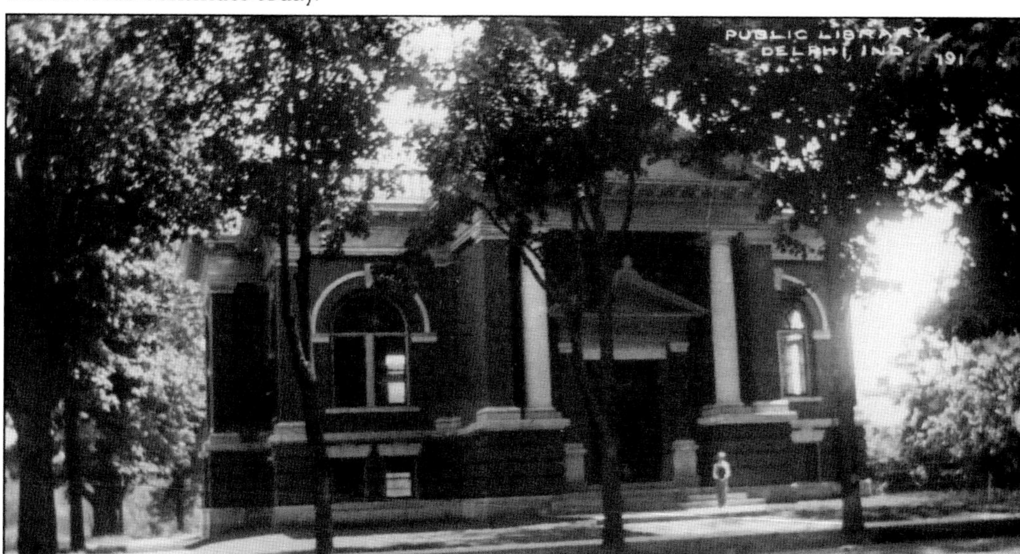

The neoclassical revival design of the Delphi Public Library and its red-brick-and-limestone façade blended well with the architecture of the downtown commercial district. The building was dedicated on June 19, 1906. In 1990, the library was nearly doubled in size with a tasteful addition that extended the useful life of the structure well into the future.

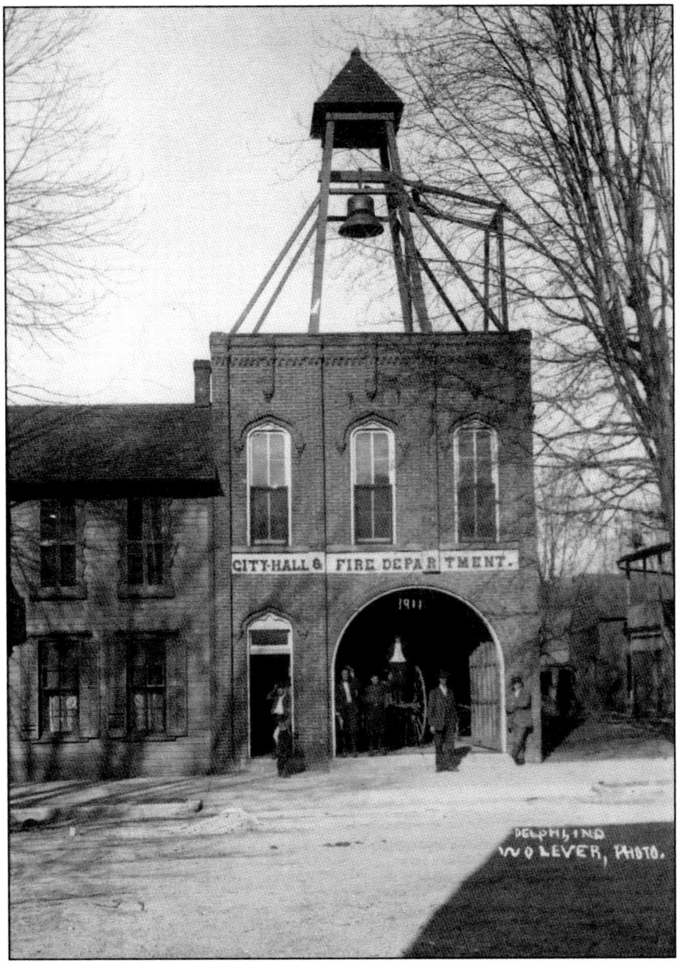

The City Hall and fire department (left) sat on the east side of South Union Street. It was replaced in 1928 by the armory, fire station, and community building (below) built on the southeast corner of Union and East Main Streets at a cost of $75,000. Prior to this time, the National Guard had been sharing space with a car dealership and garage at the northwest corner of West Main and Market Streets.

A major use for the facility was high school basketball games. This was the zenith of high school basketball in Delphi, as the Oracles sent four teams to the state finals in 1928–1938. The armory was used not only by the National Guard and school, but also for many community events, including the annual children's Christmas party, sponsored by the American Legion, Moose Lodge, and Globe Valve.

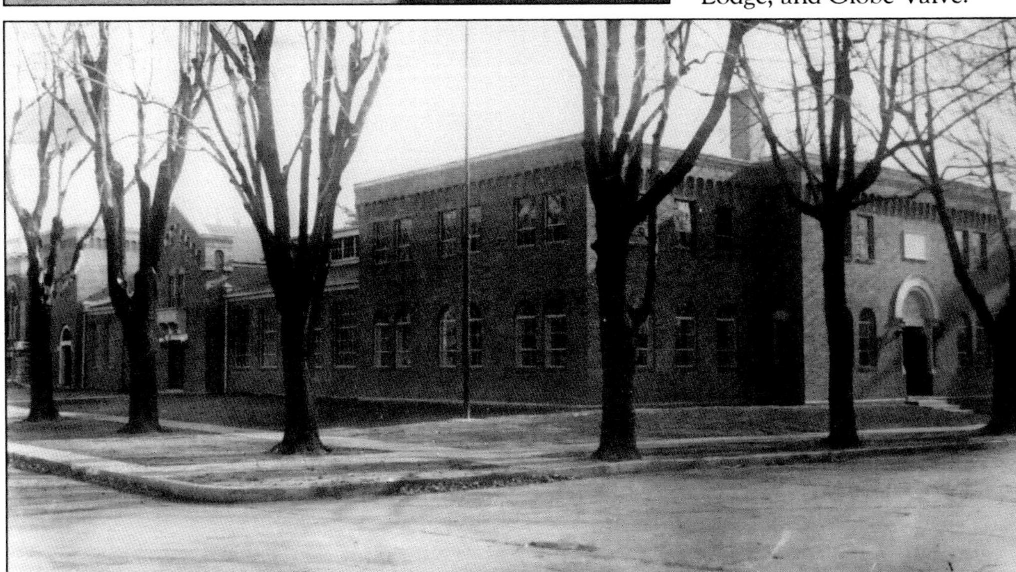

Four

SOUTH OF THE SQUARE

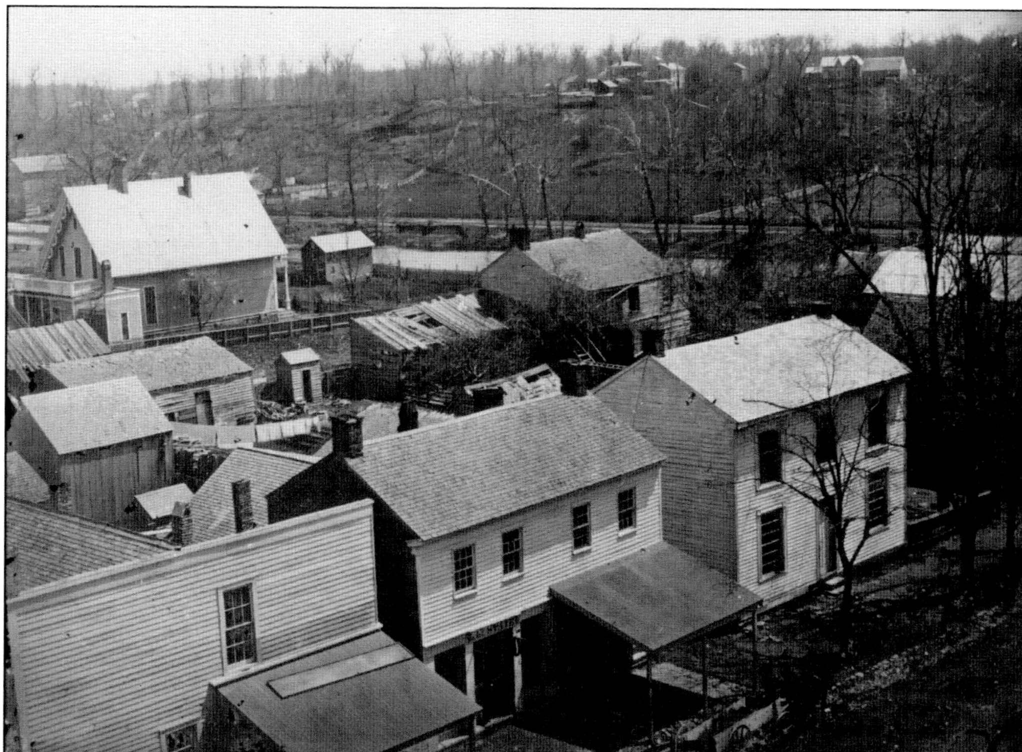

Washington Street, known first as Bridge Street for the covered bridge crossing Deer Creek, was the main road into Delphi from the south. In the 1860s, Washington Street south of Main Street contained frame buildings past the Pigman building. Hogan Boots and Shoes and Gustavel Harness occupied two of these. The white roof seen behind is the John Lathrope residence, later known to older Delphians as Dr. George Wagoner's office. On the other side of Deer Creek, is the Red Mill (top left).

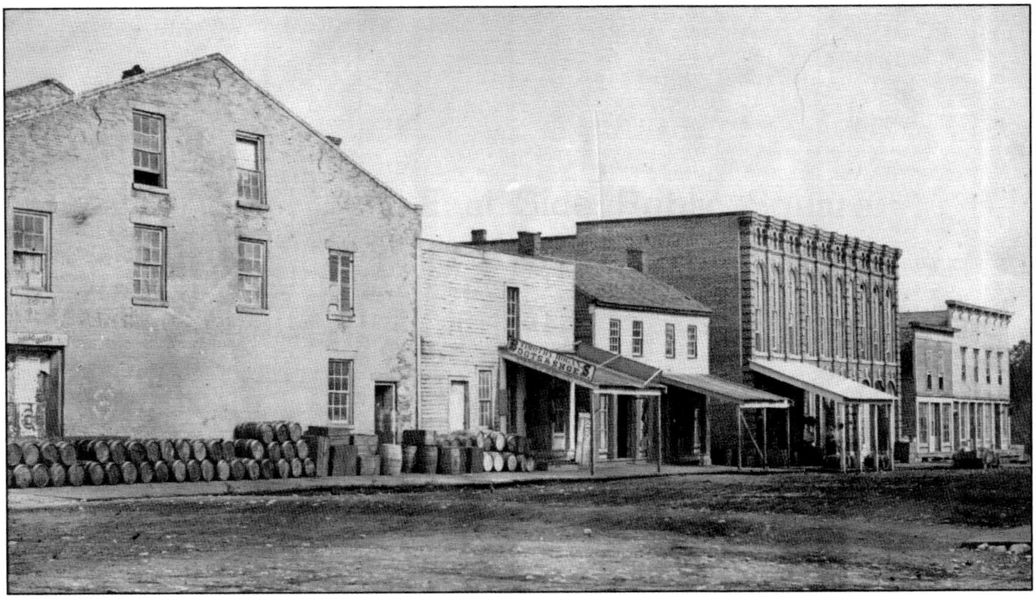

The two-story brick past the alley in this 1875 photograph of the east side of South Washington Street was built in the mid-1860s. The arched windows and brickwork match the façade on the Moore block across the street. This building was a saloon and hotel in the mid-1870s. The frame buildings farther south were built by Robert Martin by the 1860s and remain today as apartments.

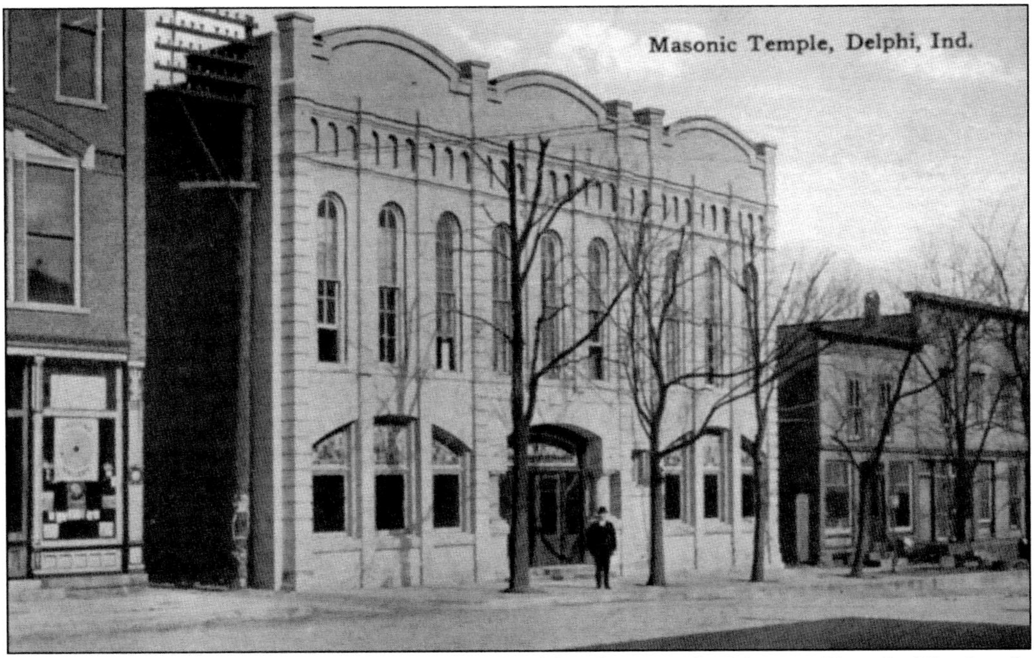

This postcard dates after 1913, when the center building became the Masonic Temple. The façade was completely remodeled, hotel rooms were removed, and the lodge placed on the second floor. In 1892, during the mineral bath craze, the hotel was fitted with twelve baths, and mineral water was pumped in from artesian springs in the area. The building now houses Times Past Antiques and Artisans Gallery.

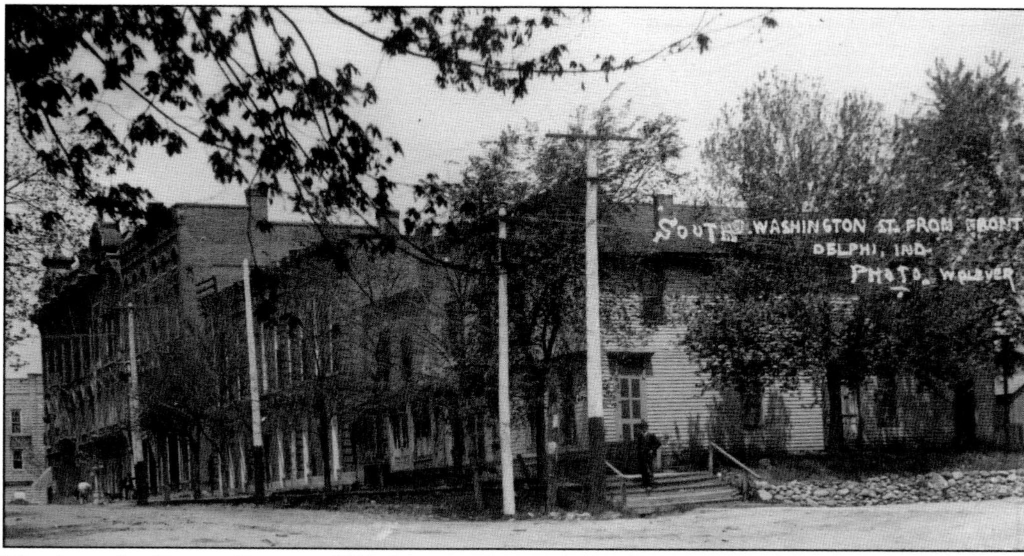

The frame building at Front and Washington Streets housed Steve Beja's shoe repair shop. Past the hotel and alley, the 1888 Swegman building was home to many different stores, including Clawson Appliances, located here from the 1940s into the 1960s, when it moved north. They are on the square today, operated by the third generation of the Clawson family. The Swegman building had a skating rink and movie house on the upper floors. On the corner is the Odd Fellows building.

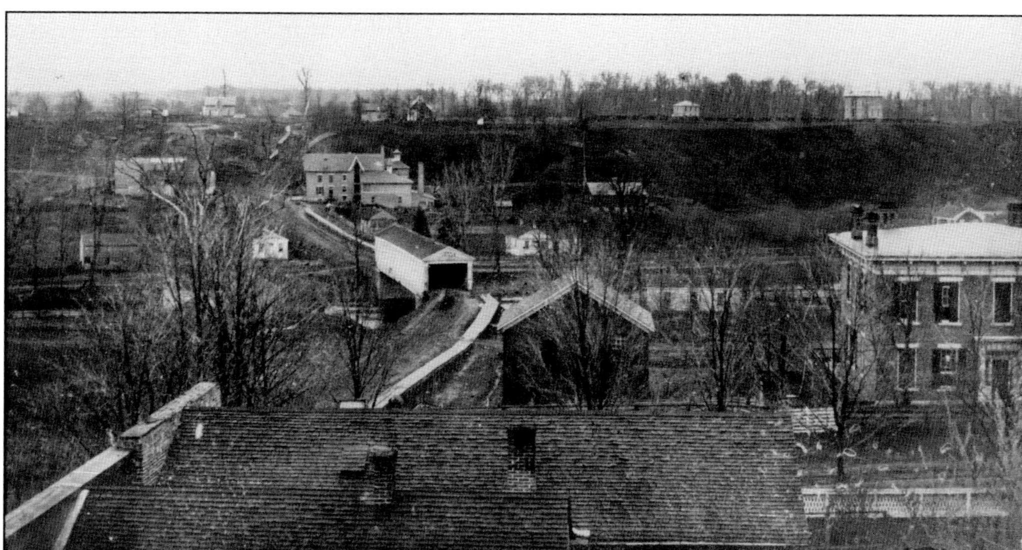

This 1860s photograph shows the covered bridge over Deer Creek and the South Delphi hill in the distance. The brick home (right) is the Enoch Rinehart residence. Past the bridge is the Delphi Brewery. The zigzag lines beyond the brewery are boardwalk steps from the hill into town. A boardwalk for foot traffic also edges the dirt road.

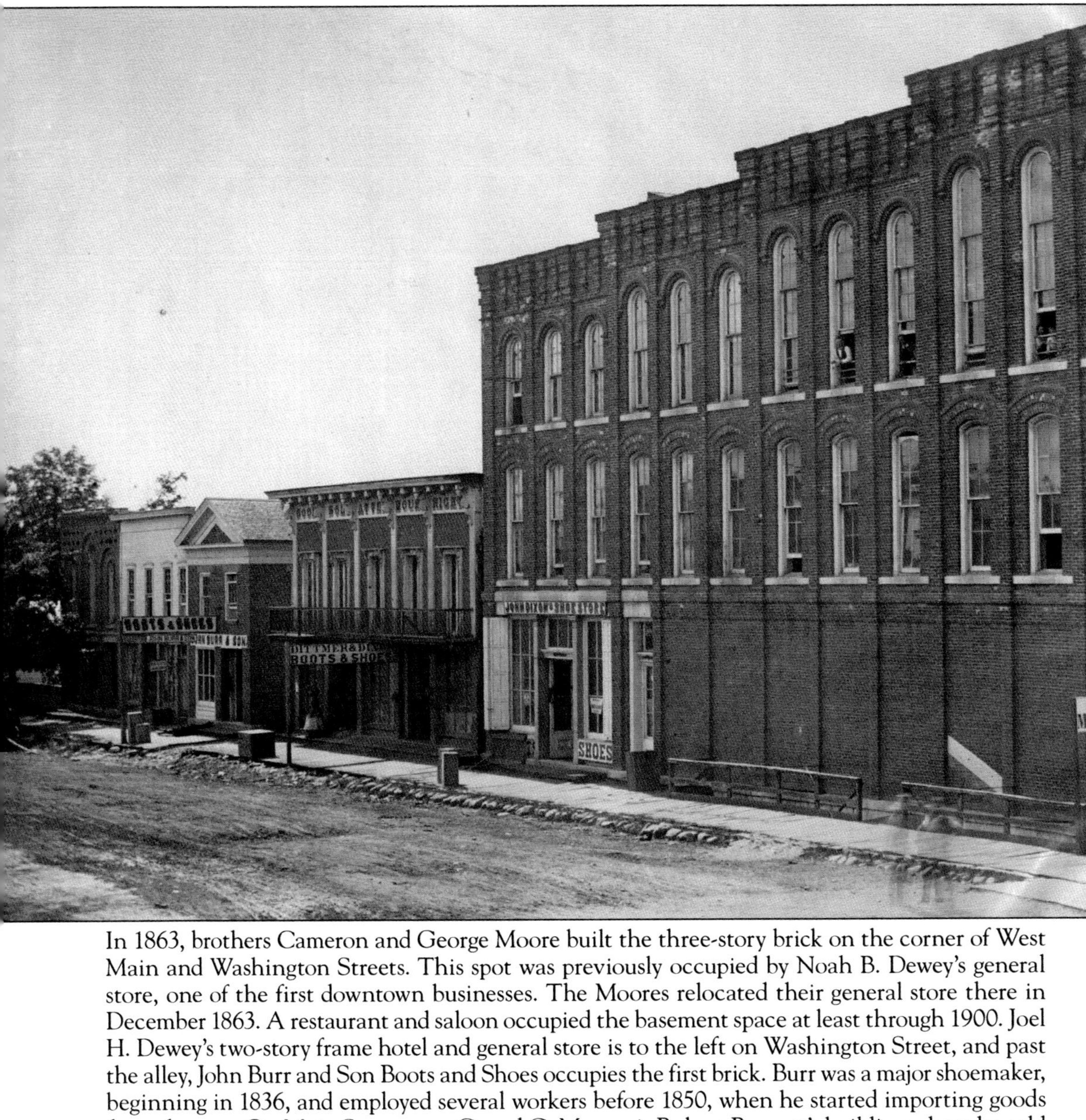

In 1863, brothers Cameron and George Moore built the three-story brick on the corner of West Main and Washington Streets. This spot was previously occupied by Noah B. Dewey's general store, one of the first downtown businesses. The Moores relocated their general store there in December 1863. A restaurant and saloon occupied the basement space at least through 1900. Joel H. Dewey's two-story frame hotel and general store is to the left on Washington Street, and past the alley, John Burr and Son Boots and Shoes occupies the first brick. Burr was a major shoemaker, beginning in 1836, and employed several workers before 1850, when he started importing goods from the east. On Main Street, past C. and G. Moore, is Robert Barnett's building where he sold stoves and tinware.

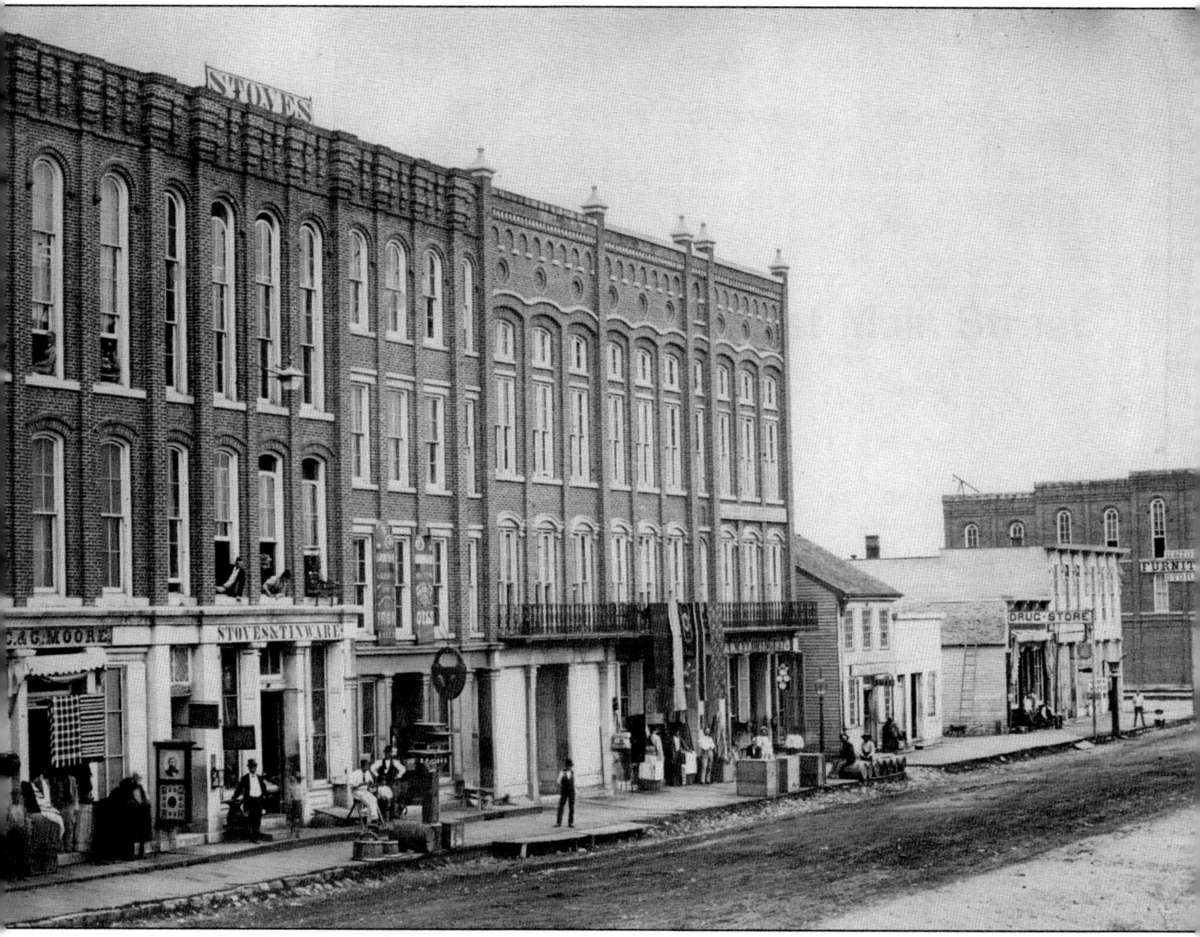

The four-story brick was built by Lewis Martin and was occupied by a hardware store. Holt and Rinehart's three-story, three-bay building on the alley was the first brick in this block, built in 1858. Holt and Strawbridge and A. M. Eldridge and Company are in the far bays. Past the alley are Dunkle and Kilgore Hardware, Coyner and Garrett Druggists, and R. L. Higgenbotham Jewelry in the two-story frame building on the corner. The three-story Union Furniture Store was built by Michael Lehnert in 1869. These and other 1875 photographs from around the square are from an underwriter's album owned by Bradshaw Insurance and used here courtesy of William Bradshaw, great-great-grandson of William H. Bradshaw, who began the business in 1851.

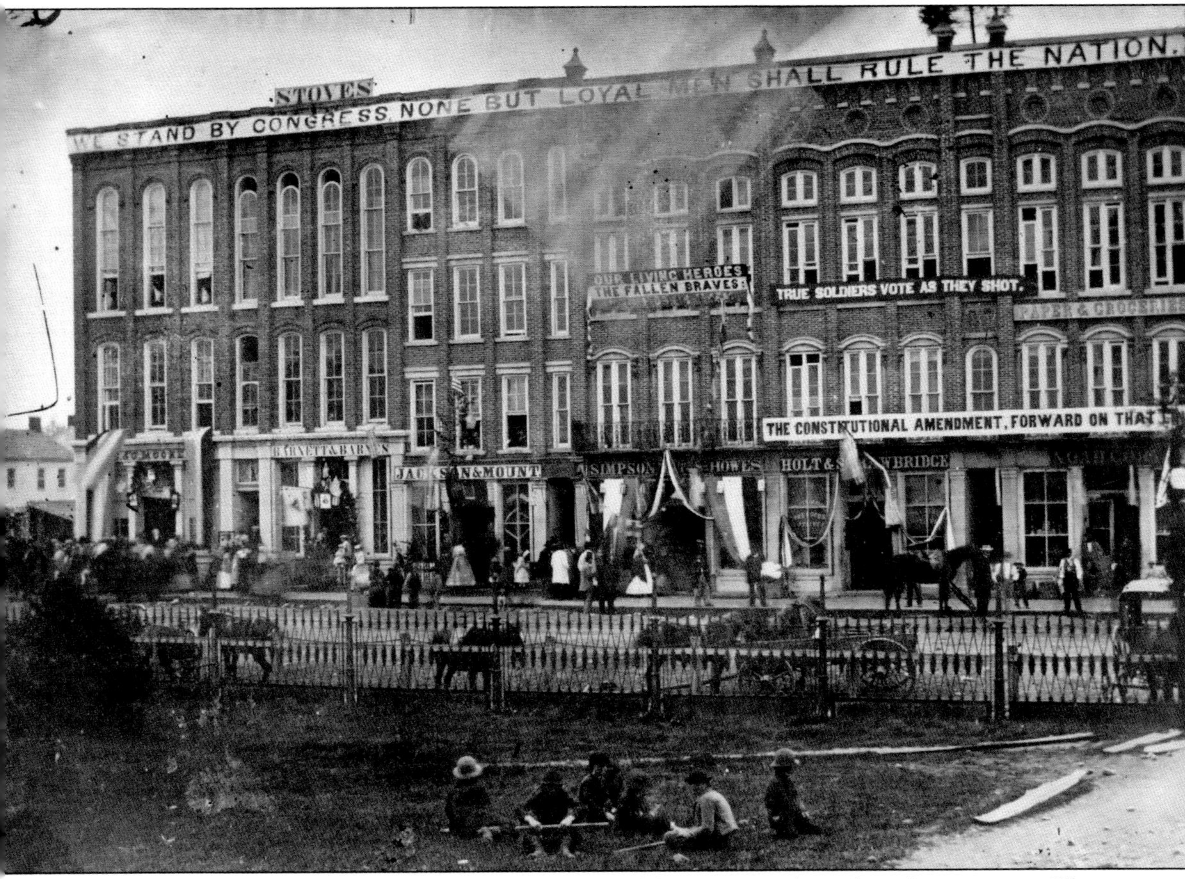

As this 1868 photograph demonstrates, large buildings can make political statements. The top banner, "We Stand by Congress. None But Loyal Men Shall Rule the Nation," likely refers to the impeachment proceedings of President Johnson. The people in their finery are perhaps attending an event in the third-floor Holt and Rinehart Hall (right). Merchants operating in this half block of West Main Street included C. and G. Moore; Barnett and Barnes; Jackson and Mount Hardware; Simpson, Watts, and Howe Dry Goods; and Noah Cory Paper and Groceries. Another notable merchant in this block was Benjamin Z. Strawbridge, originally from Pennsylvania, who left this dry goods partnership with his father-in-law, Vine Holt, to go to Philadelphia to found Strawbridge and Clothier Dry Goods. The frame building pictured right has faint letters "Philadelphia Store" above Dunkle and Kilgore's sign.

After moving to Carroll County in 1846, James W. Kilgore (1822–1886) joined Dunkle and Witherow Wagon Makers. In addition to his pioneering efforts in manufacturing (described elsewhere), he was county commissioner, city councilman, and school trustee. Kilgore built the first complete wagon made in Carroll County as well as the first engine.

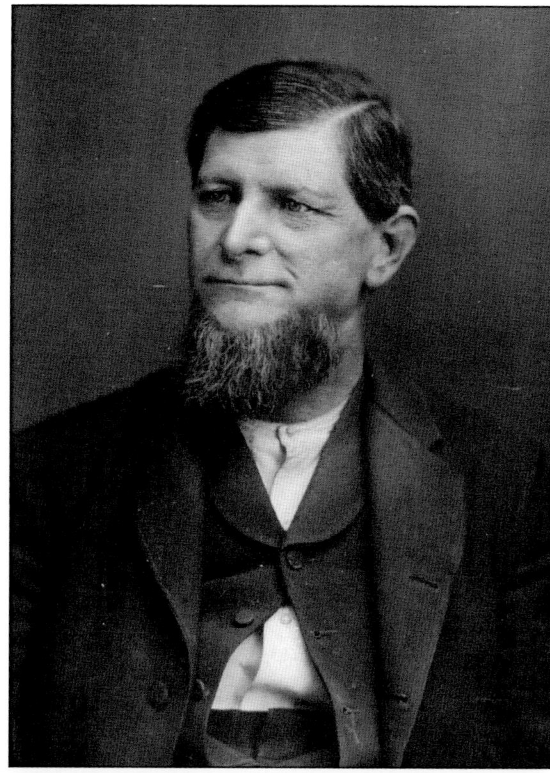

Dunkle and Kilgore Hardware and Implements (left) operated on the south side of the square from about 1855 to 1882. Begun in 1848, its wagon, implement, and machining business continues today as Delphi Body Works. To the west are Coyner and Garrett Druggists. The brick building seen behind was the Rinehart Paper Mill office. The ornate brick residence behind was built by Enoch Rinehart on Front Street in 1858.

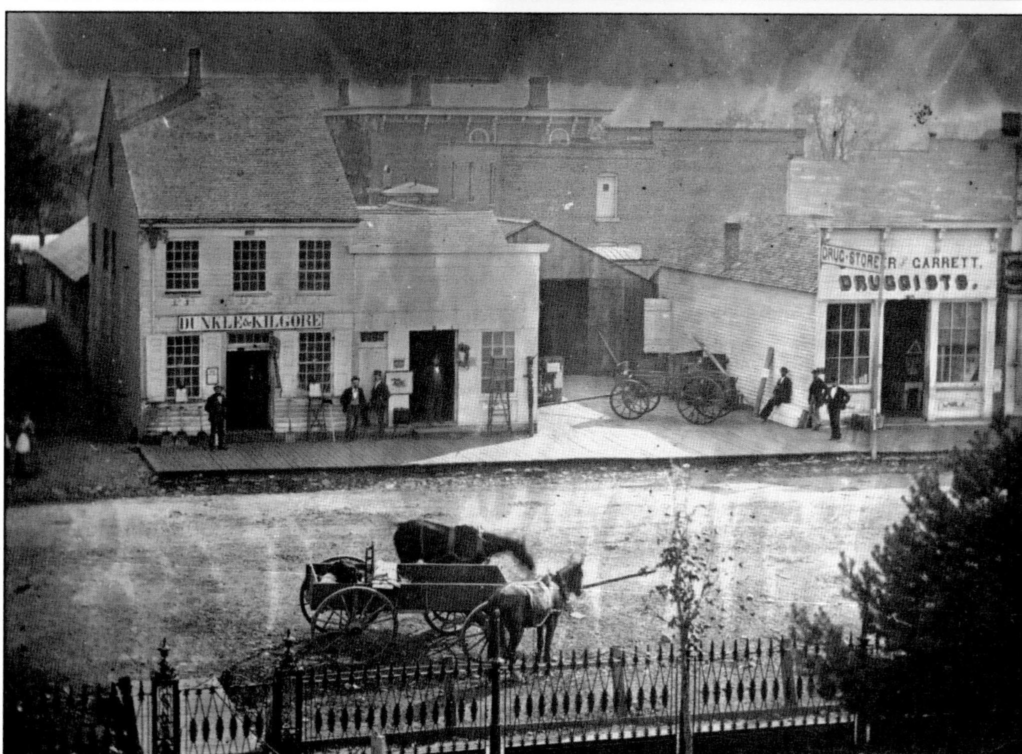

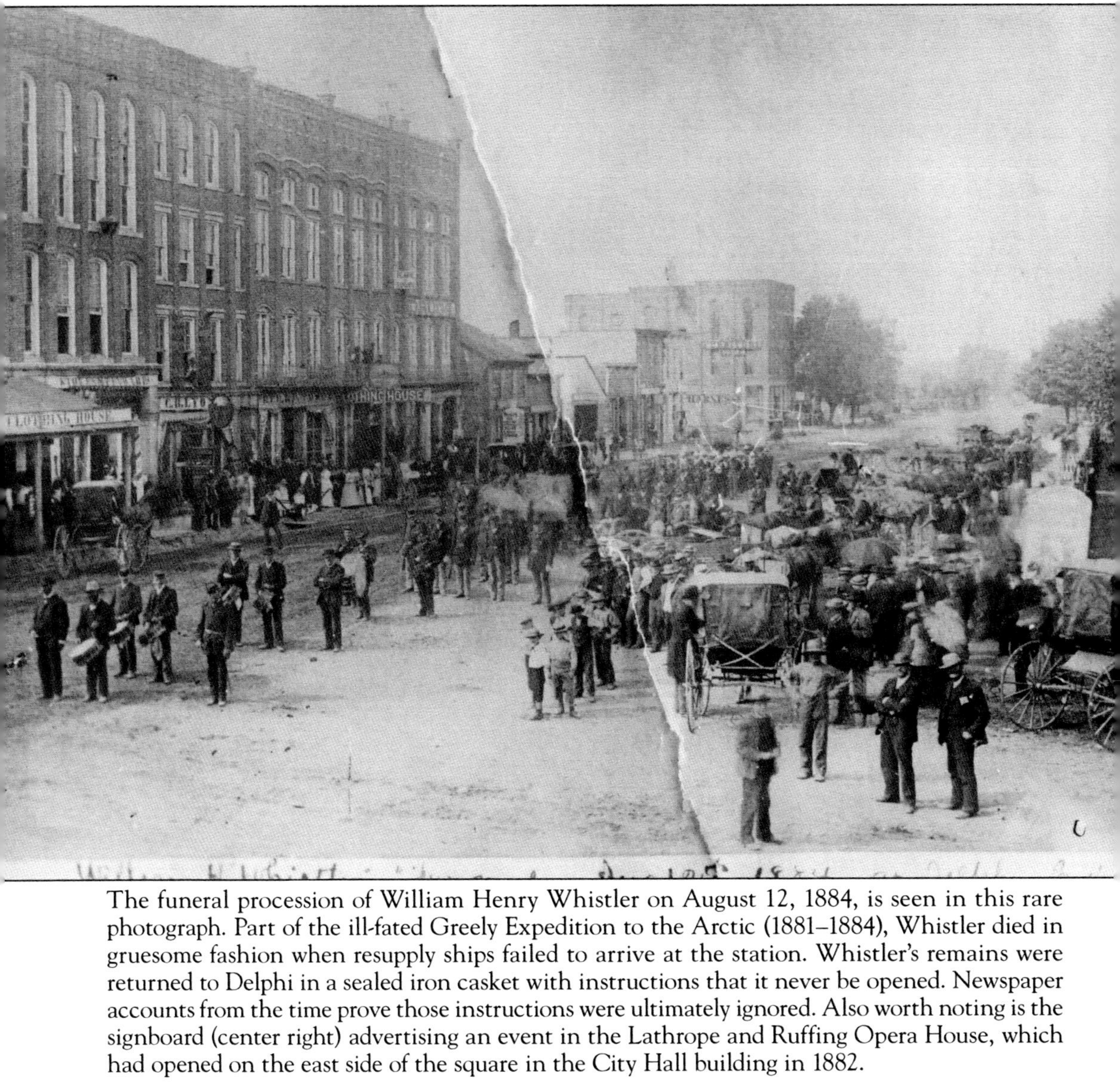

The funeral procession of William Henry Whistler on August 12, 1884, is seen in this rare photograph. Part of the ill-fated Greely Expedition to the Arctic (1881–1884), Whistler died in gruesome fashion when resupply ships failed to arrive at the station. Whistler's remains were returned to Delphi in a sealed iron casket with instructions that it never be opened. Newspaper accounts from the time prove those instructions were ultimately ignored. Also worth noting is the signboard (center right) advertising an event in the Lathrope and Ruffing Opera House, which had opened on the east side of the square in the City Hall building in 1882.

A street fair is underway in this 1890s view of the west side of South Washington Street. Next to the Moore block (right) is a two-story brick with oriel windows. It was built in 1888 by Charles Brough following a fire that destroyed the Dewey and Burr buildings. Merchants shown are Barnett and Mohr's Hardware and Gregg's Novelty Store. From 1912 until its destruction by fire on November 25, 2009, it housed a tavern and, for many years, Kerlin law office.

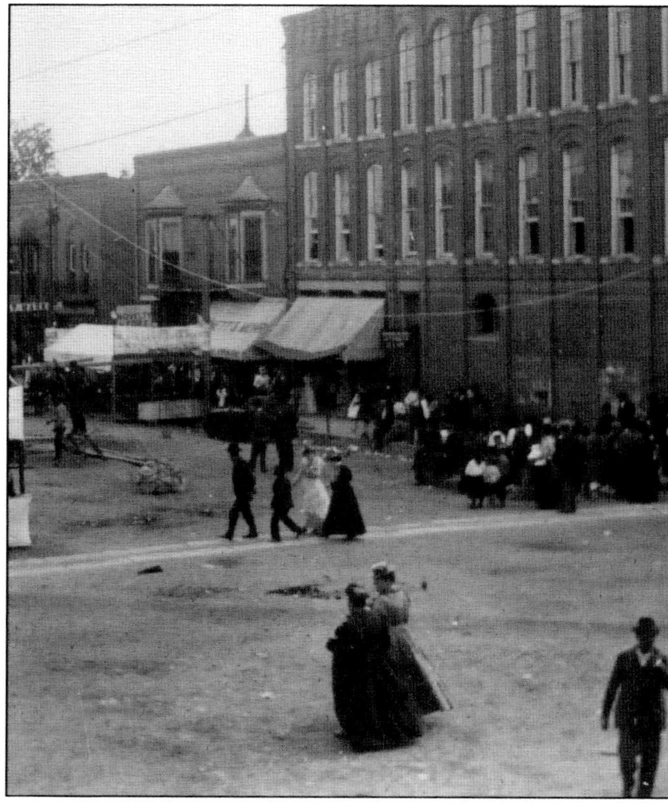

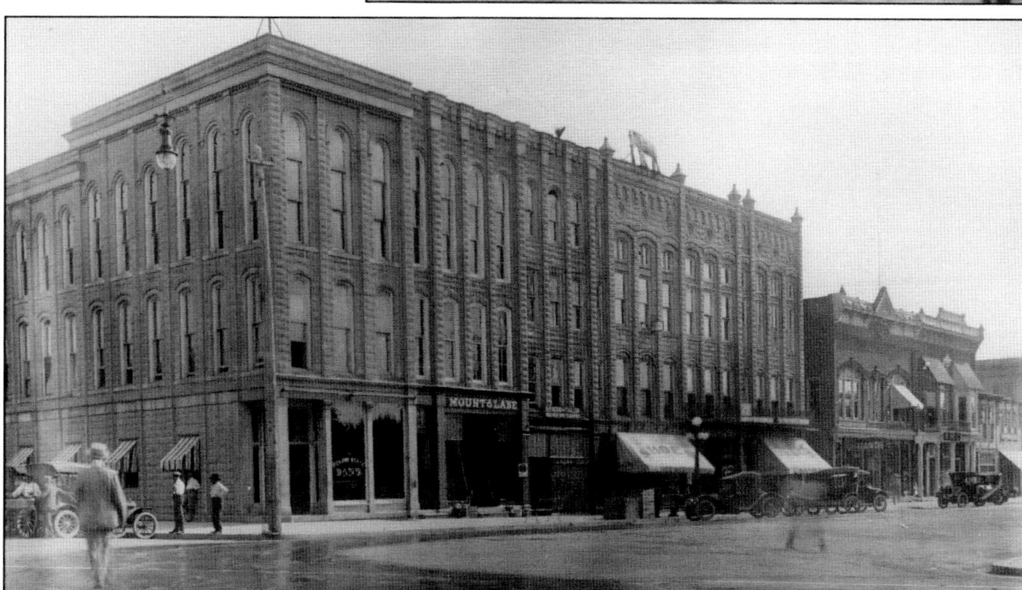

The façades in the foreground were resurfaced by 1910 to resemble cut stone. Delphi State Bank (left), later Union Bank and Trust, Mount and Lane Hardware, Jordan and Edson Clothing, Brewer Shoes, and Murphy Drugs follow. The elephant at the roofline was Brewer's trademark. West of the alley were Pletcher Hardware and the Arc Movie Theater. Gustavel Harness anchors the west end; Gustavel became a tire business by 1919.

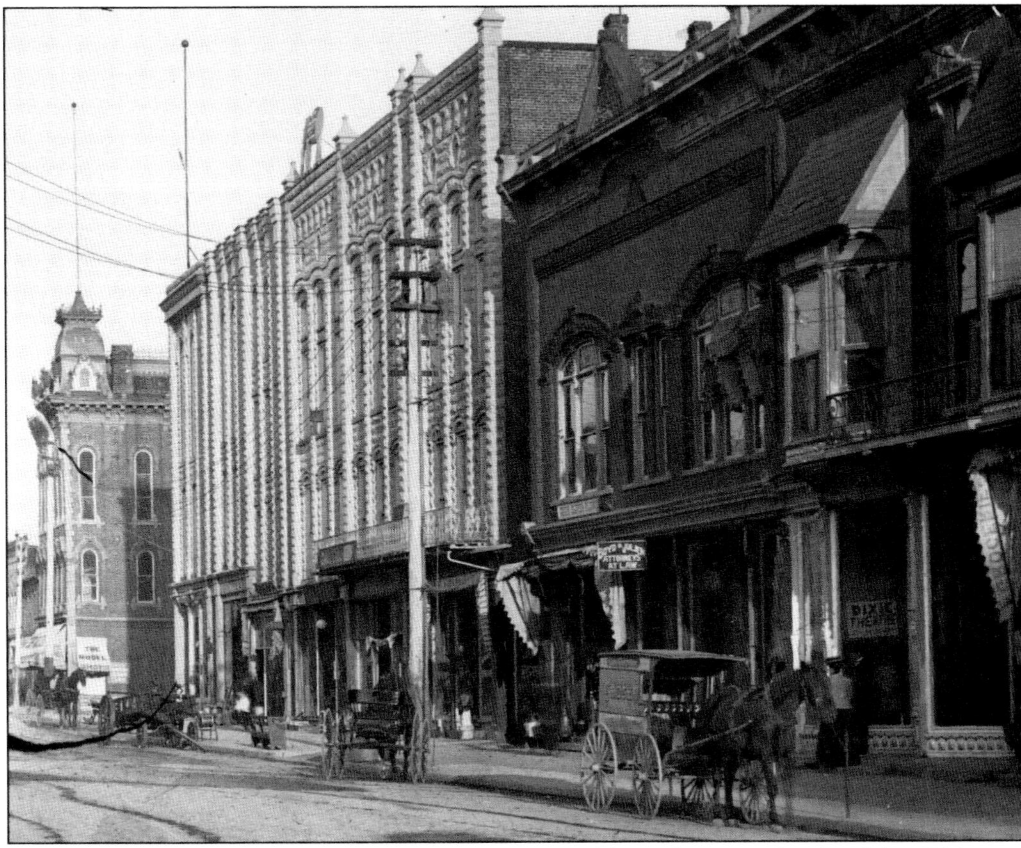

Viewed from the west, details of the 1891 Christian Gros building come into focus with its arched windows and terra-cotta medallions. Pletcher Hardware later occupied this building from 1914 to 1969. The huckster wagon is in front of George Gifford's Grocery (right). In between is the Dixie Theater: "Admission 10¢." Just past the alley is M. M. Murphy's Drugstore, in this location from the early 1870s until 1911.

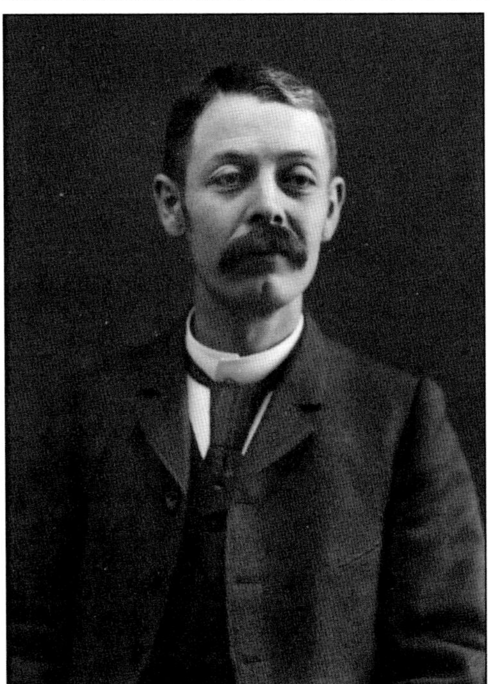

A town druggist for many decades, Mitchell M. Murphy (1842–1912) partnered for some time with James Watts, who was also the postmaster. The store's location was shared for many years with the post office. As was the custom, the drugstore also sold schoolbooks. Murphy was active in the Masons and was a member of the school board. In 1911, after 37 years in the drug business, Murphy retired. He and his wife, Clara, donated the funds to the city for the Water Maiden statue and fountain on the southwest corner of the courthouse square.

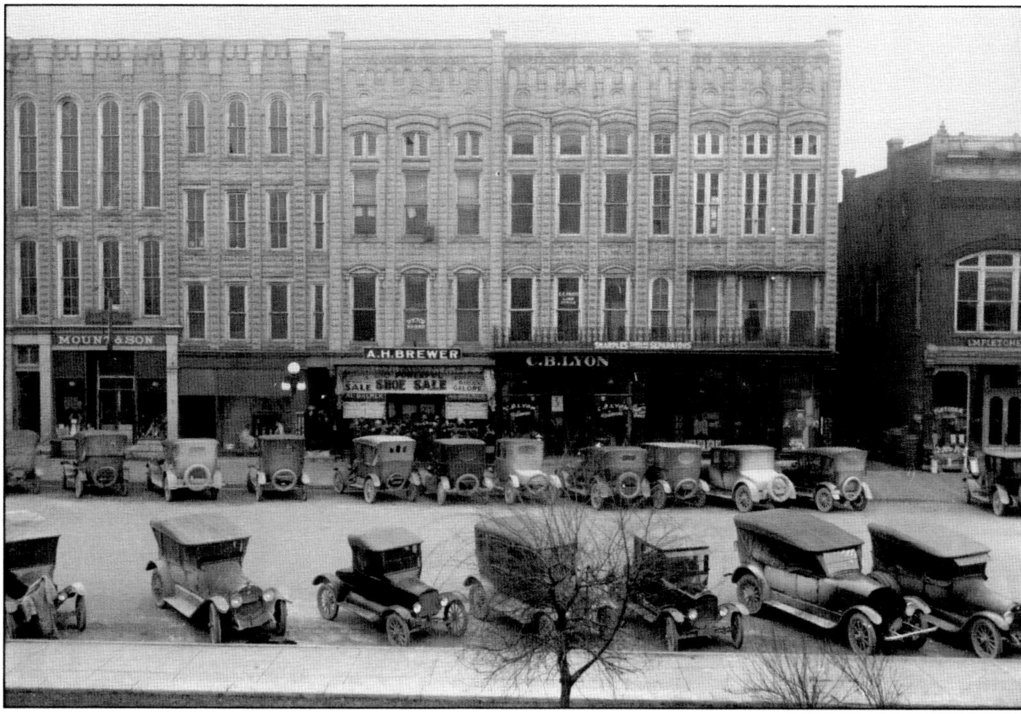

As East Main Street was a traditional home to butchers, grocers, barbers, saloons, and clothing stores, West Main Street was for many decades home to hardware, implement, stove, shoe, and drug businesses. Murphy Drugs was followed by Elless and Orr and then Orr from 1911 to 1989. Besides Dunkle and Kilgore, followed by Christian Gros, then Pletcher Hardware, Charles B. Lyon and son George were located there in 1874–1927. The Mount family hardware store began there as Jackson and Mount in 1865, followed by Mount and Lane in 1909, then Mount and Son through the early 1980s. Burr Shoes, from the 1880s, was followed by Burr and Brewer, Brewer, Denk's, and later Darby's Shoes into the 1960s. Pictured above, a big sale at A. H. Brewer has drawn a large crowd waiting for the doors to open.

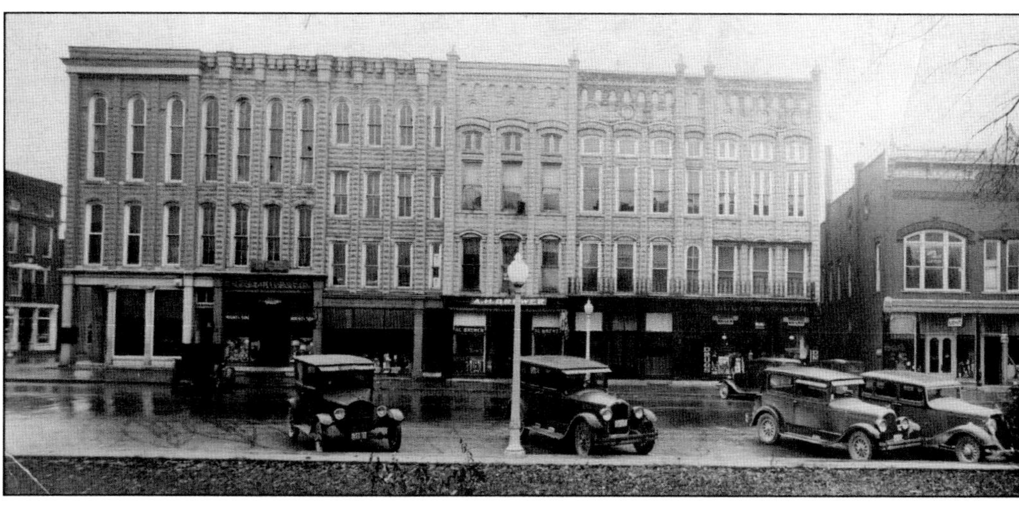

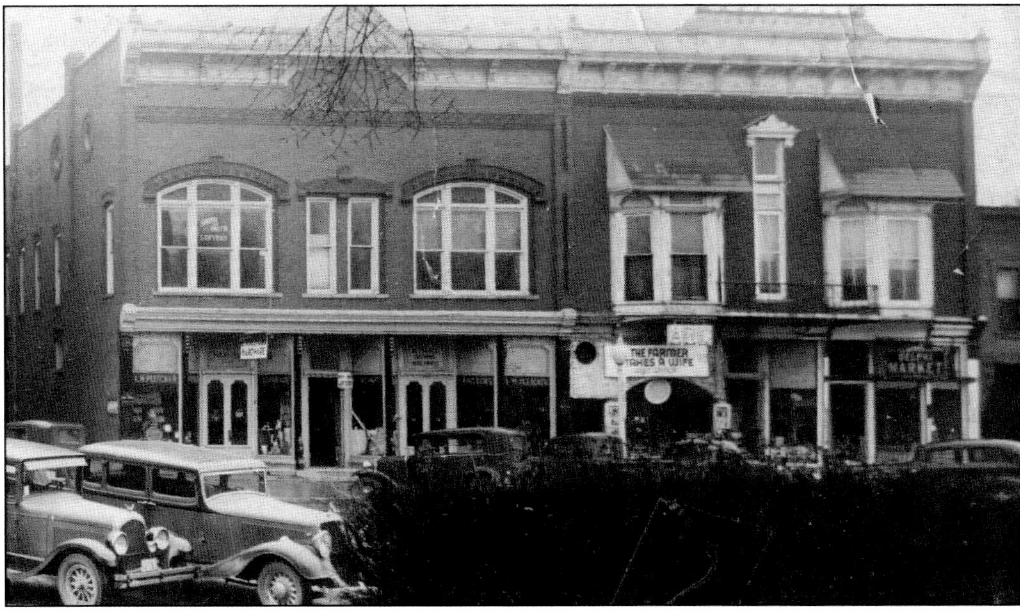

The 1891 building on the left was constructed for Christian Gros Hardware and George H. C. Best, tailor. Below is the interior of Pletcher's Hardware Store in 1954 with Lawrence M. Pletcher (left), Beulah James, and John Delaney. Pletcher had been a local teacher and principal. On the second floor were the offices of father and son William C. Smith and William B. Smith, attorneys. William C. Smith was also an agriculturalist, historian, and mayor of Delphi. His series "Up the River of Time," published in the *Delphi Citizen* in 1930–1931, is a fascinating read. William B. Smith served as county judge and civic leader. The Arc Movie Theater was replaced in the mid-1940s by the Welcome Inn, which served up meals on the square well into the 1970s. It had held sway on East Main Street for decades prior.

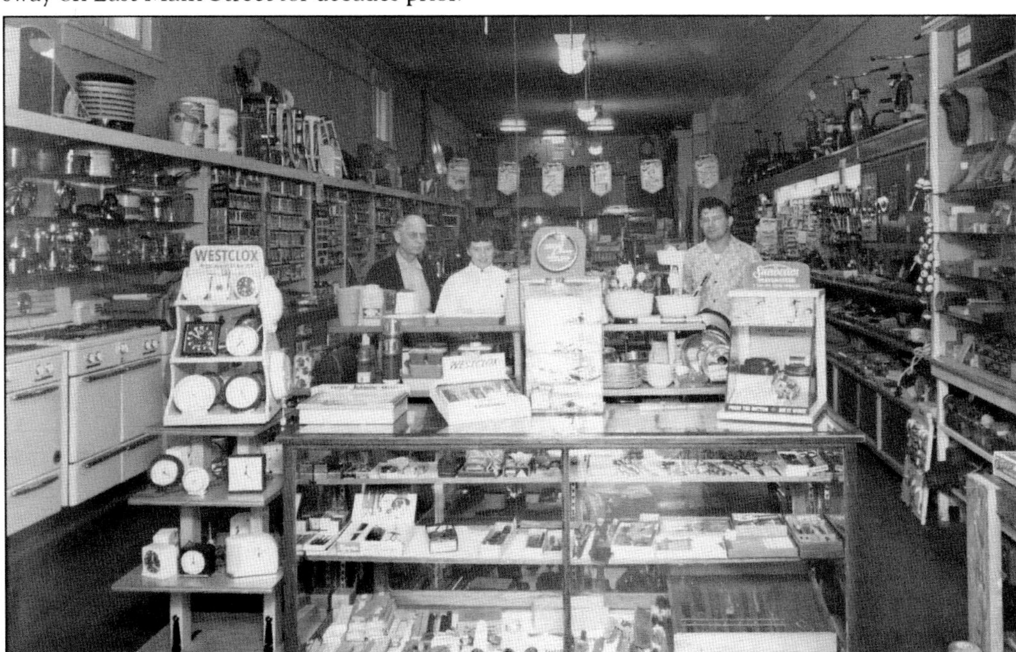

Five

West of the Square

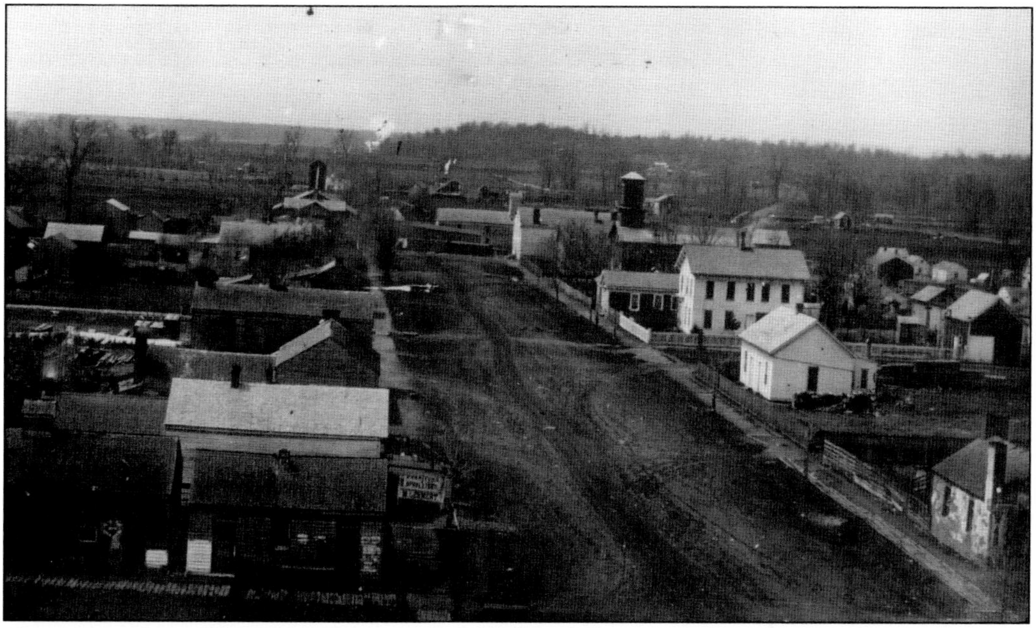

Continuing down West Main Street, only a few blocks separated the courthouse square from the side-slip to the Wabash and Erie Canal and the Wabash Railroad, as seen in this 1860s view. Canal boats load and unload on the other side of the Spears and Case grain elevator and warehouse. Beyond the canal is the Rinehart Paper Mill. The Delphi Hotel and St. Mary's Episcopal Chapel are visible (center right) and Delphi Lumberyard (left). Lehnert Furniture is front left.

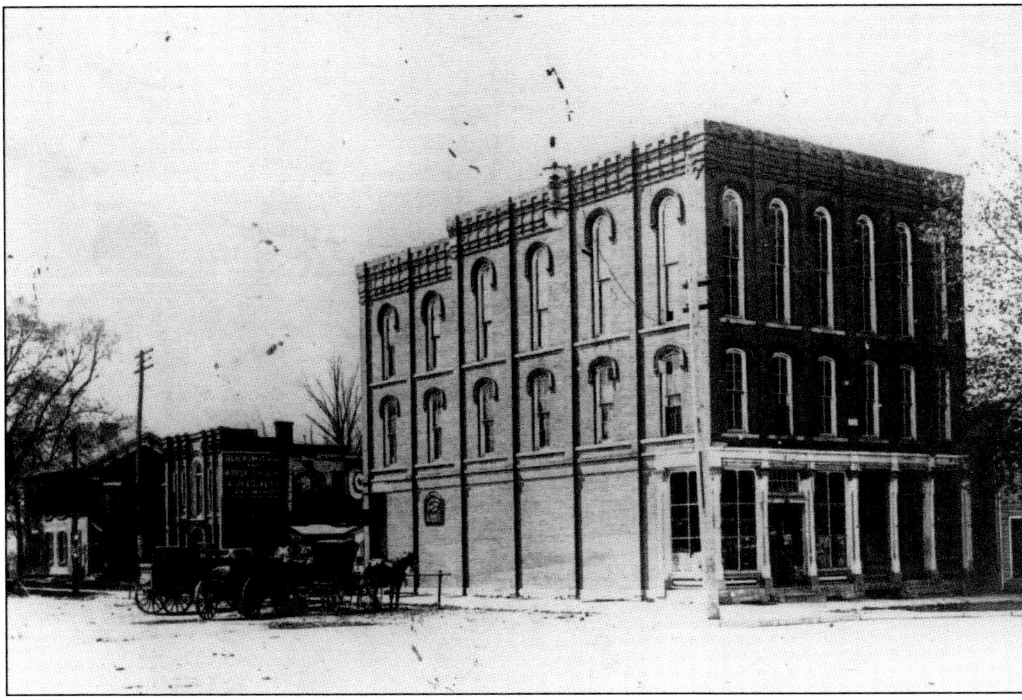

In 1869, Michael Lehnert built this Italianate brick at the corner of Market and West Main Streets. He operated his furniture and upholstery business there until 1900, when he sold out to Delphi Furniture Company. This photograph from the early 1900s has T. D. Thayer's Furniture at the Market Street entrance. A pool hall and lunchroom occupy the east bay on Main Street. James Mabbitt's Blacksmith Shop is located midblock on Market Street. In 1911, the Knights of Pythias bought the building and doubled its size, taking Mabbitt's with it. The enlarged structure received a concrete parging coat to resemble cut stone. A. Grimm and Son Furniture and Undertaking occupied the ground floor from 1911 to 1930. Grimm moved the funeral home to East Main at High Street in 1930. Melvin Jackson bought the business in 1945, and it continues now as Abbott's Funeral Home.

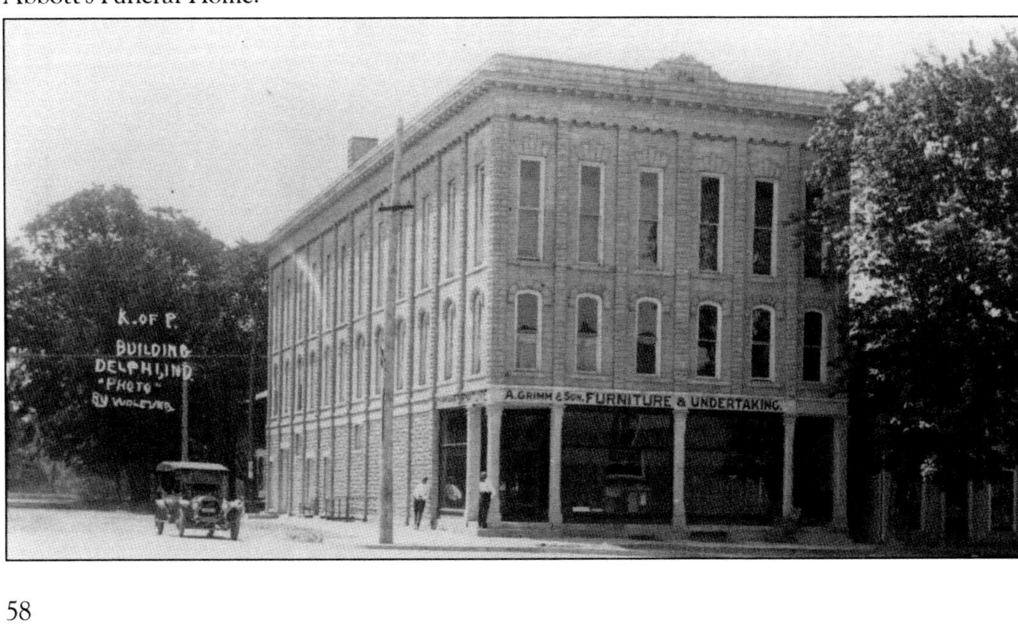

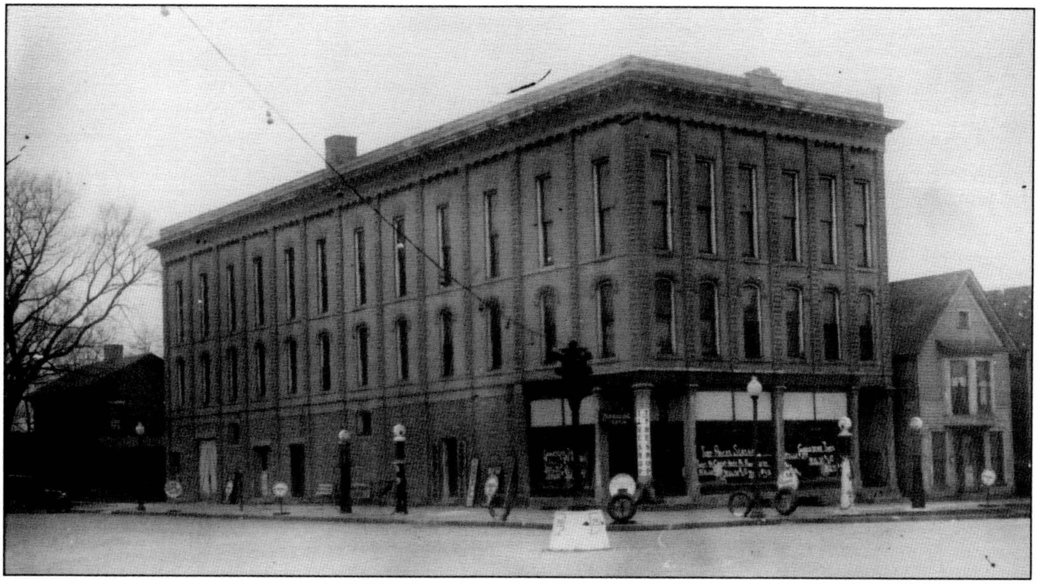

By the 1930s the ground floor of the Knights of Pythias building is a tire shop and gasoline station. Note the traffic signal on a concrete cone in the middle of the intersection marking Indiana State Road 25. Kroger Grocery later occupied the ground floor at this location until 1962.

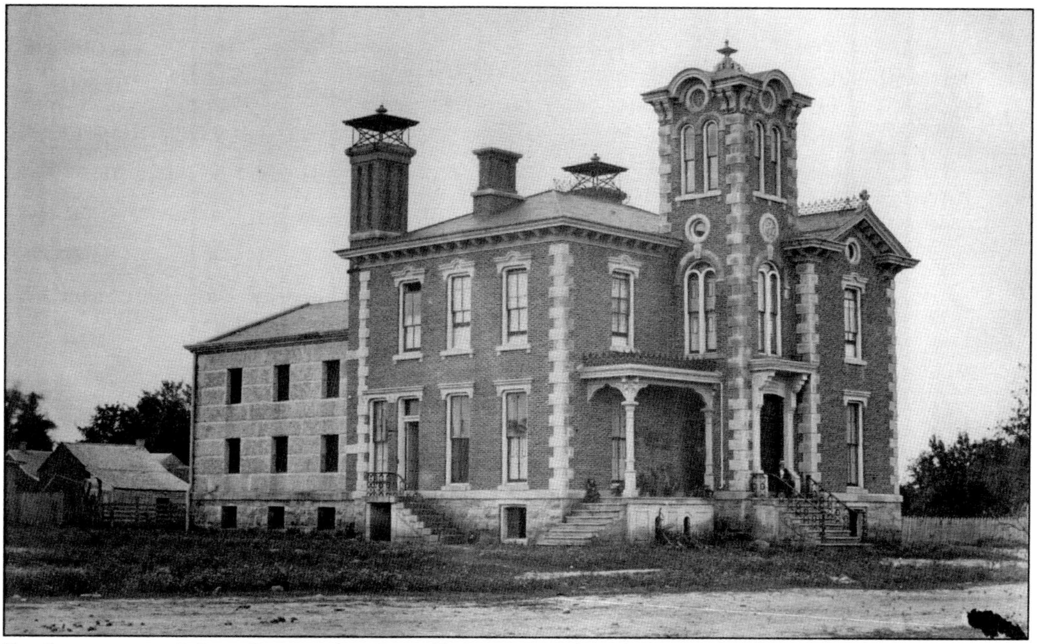

Farther west on Main Street, the Carroll County Jail and sheriff's residence were completed in 1873, constructed by Francis Farman under the supervision of local architect Colbert A. McClure at a cost of about $40,000. This main part of this magnificent structure was torn down in 1955 to make way for the new county jail at West Main Street between South Wabash and South Illinois Streets. The rear cellblock was retained until 1977, when a completely new jail was built.

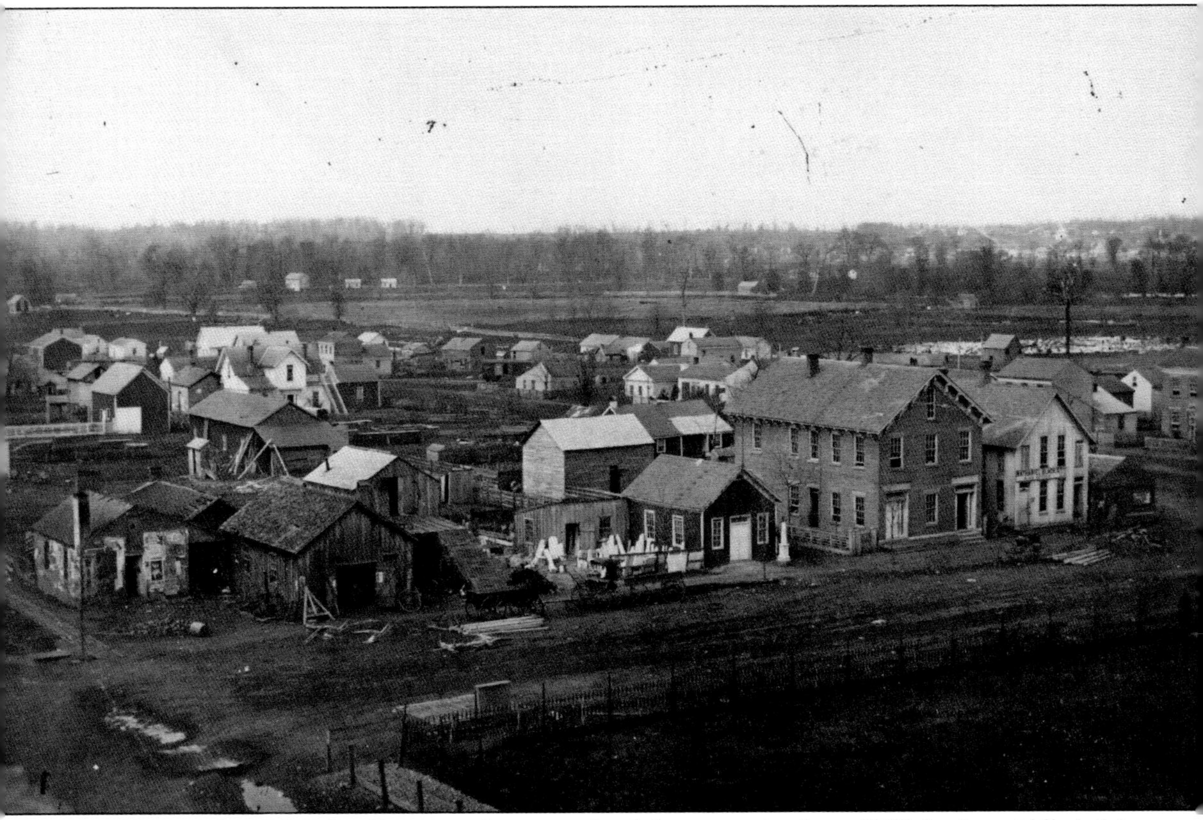

Above is South Market Street on the west side of the square in about 1865. In the middle is J. L. and C. M. Knight's Marble Works. The white frame building at right is Nathaniel Black's Law Office, later the Lone Star Grocery. The three-story brick, known as the "House on the Square," is the only old building surviving today. Likely built in the mid-1850s by Dr. George McFarlane, this brick has endured while many buildings have come and gone around it. It first had two front doors, perhaps one for business and the other for a residence. Dillinger Grocery was on the left side in early years. John Clark, a dry goods merchant in the 1870s, lived there for many years. In the early 1900s, it was a boarding house. Among the residents who have owned the house is Charles Clay Pearson, county clerk in 1916–1924 and mayor of Delphi in the 1930s. He was preceded by his father-in-law, Thomas Colvin, who was a harness maker. Ann Doerr Brooks had her in-home hair salon there in 1962–1997.

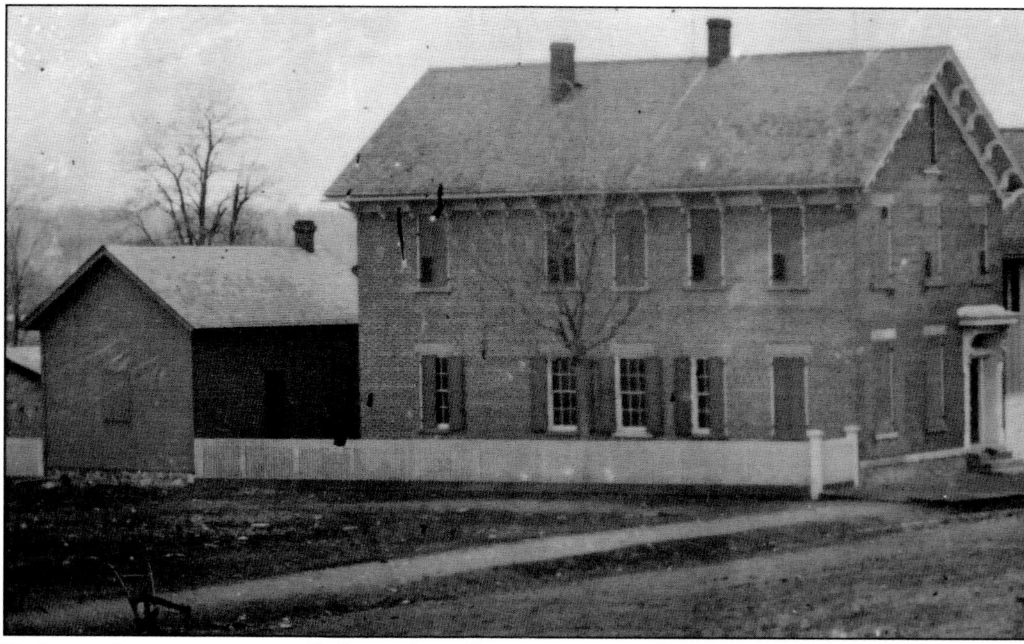

Early on, shutters were installed, one front door was removed, and a fence was installed.

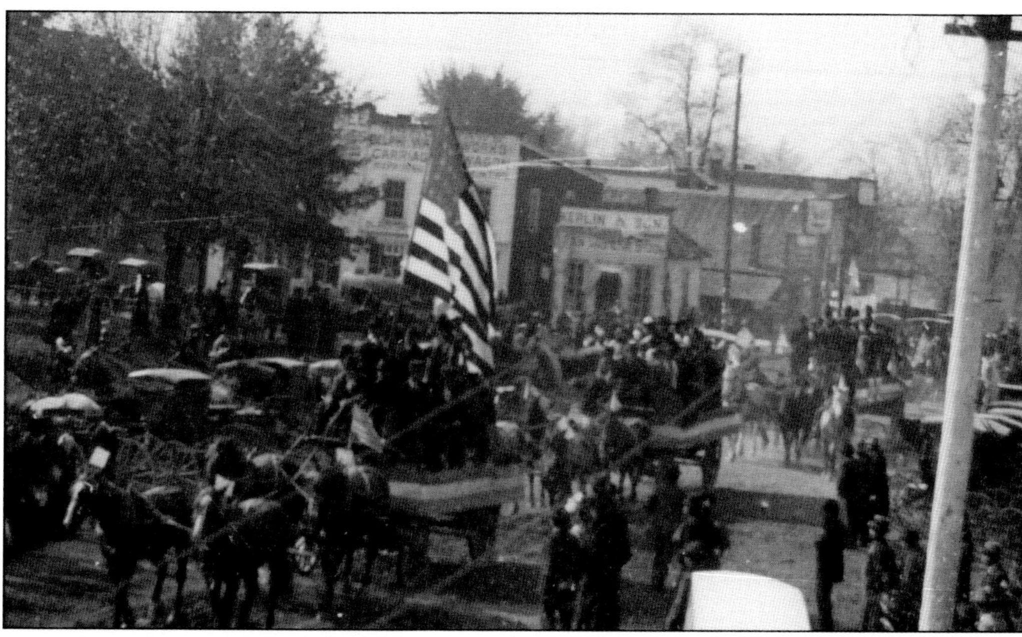

Behind the flag is the blacksmithing and carriage operation of Delphi Wagon Works, which continues today on South Washington Street as Delphi Body Works. In 1896, William Jennings Bryan made a campaign stop in Delphi during his first bid for president of the United States. The parade that day is shown arriving on the north side of the courthouse.

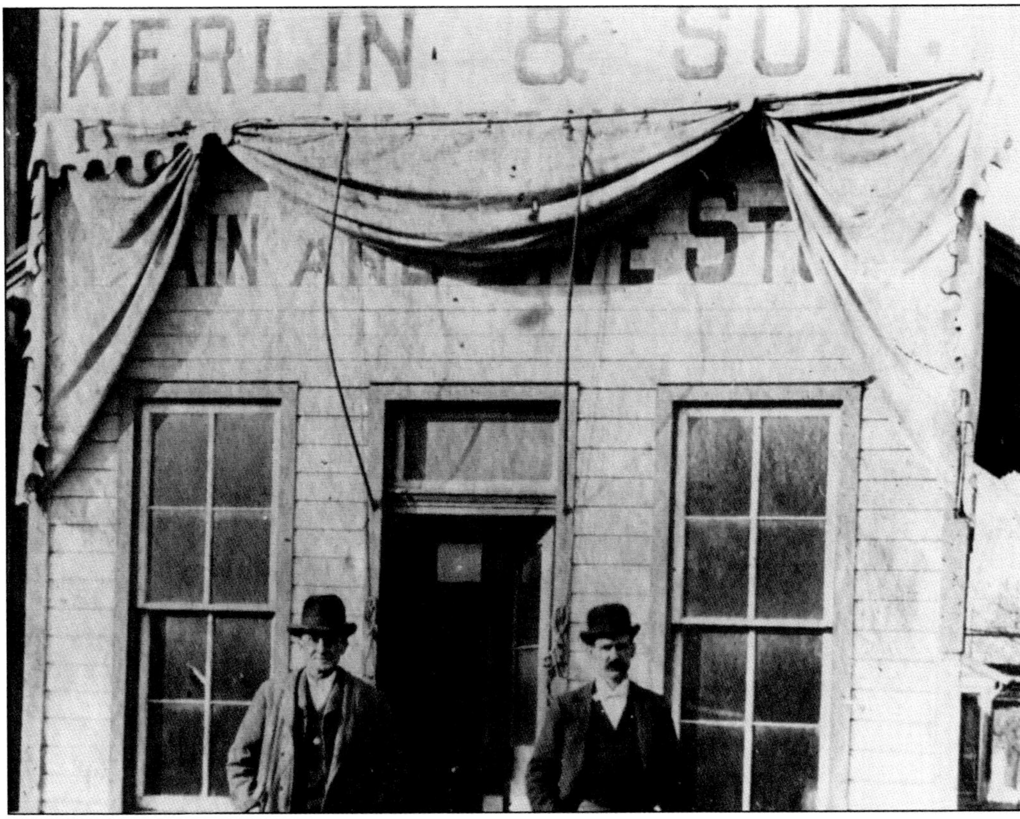

Located at the corner of Market and West Franklin Streets is the Kerlin and Son office. Hiram (left) and his son, Charles M., are pictured here. The Kerlin grain elevator and stockyard were a few blocks away on Hamilton and West Main Streets. The frame building was moved to this location in 1892 from the corner of Main and Market Streets and later moved to the elevator yard.

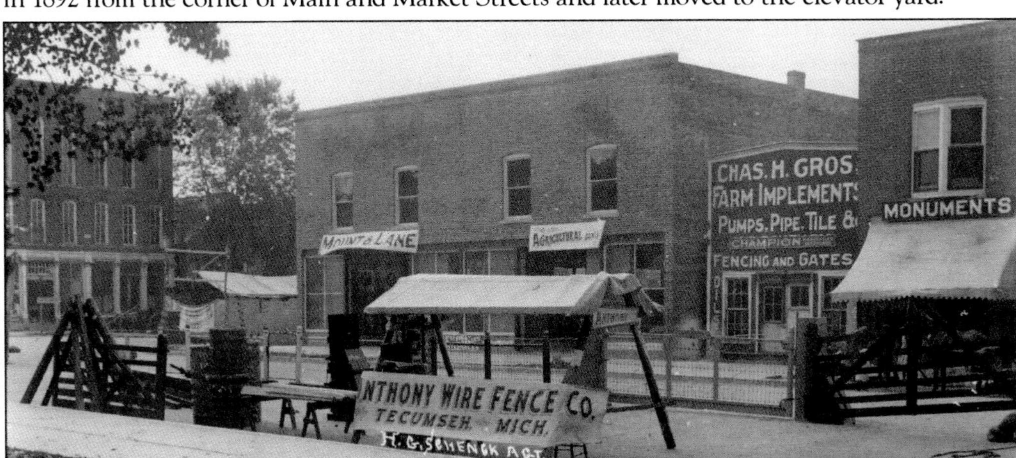

Mount and Lane Furniture and Hardware is located in their new building on the corner of West Main and Market Streets. The frame building is Charles H. Gros Implements. Boothroyd's Monuments is in the brick building (right), constructed by Alfred Boothroyd in the early 1880s. A street fair is underway, and Anthony Wire Fence Company's display can be seen in the foreground. On the south side of Main Street is the Lehnert building.

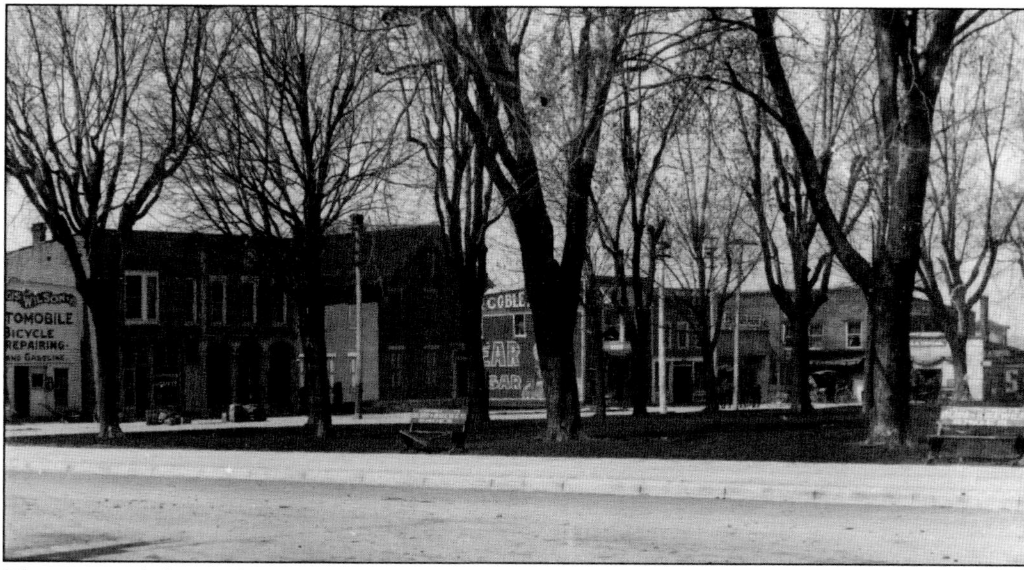

The automobile quickly changed the makeup of businesses on the square. Francis Wilson's Automobile and Bicycle Repair (left) is next to Boothroyd's Monuments. Gustavel and Brewer Harness was in the next building, which soon housed a Hudson dealership. Colvin and Coble Harness is past the alley. J. W. Colvin owned the House on the Square at this time. On the corner is the Automobile Garage.

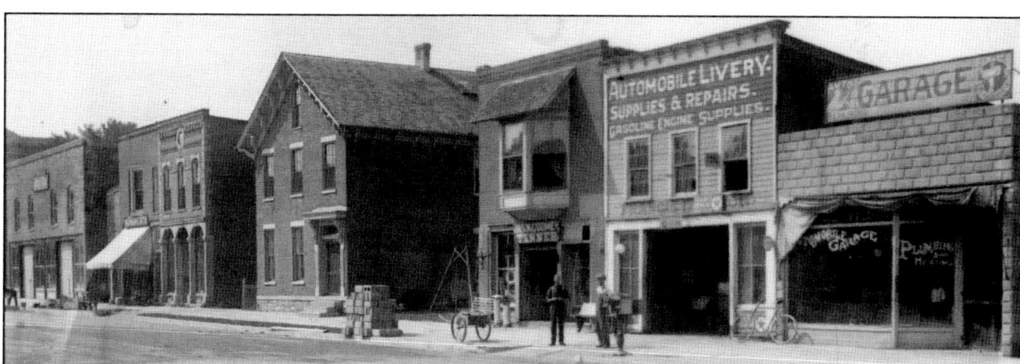

Francis Wilson soon moved his business to the north end of the block in the automobile "livery" next to the "garage," showing how the terminology was evolving. James Coomey started his tinsmith business next door, having worked for Barnett and Mohr on West Main Street. The small frame building next to Boothroyd is now W. H. Bragunier's Steam Heat and Plumbing Shop, which remained there for many years.

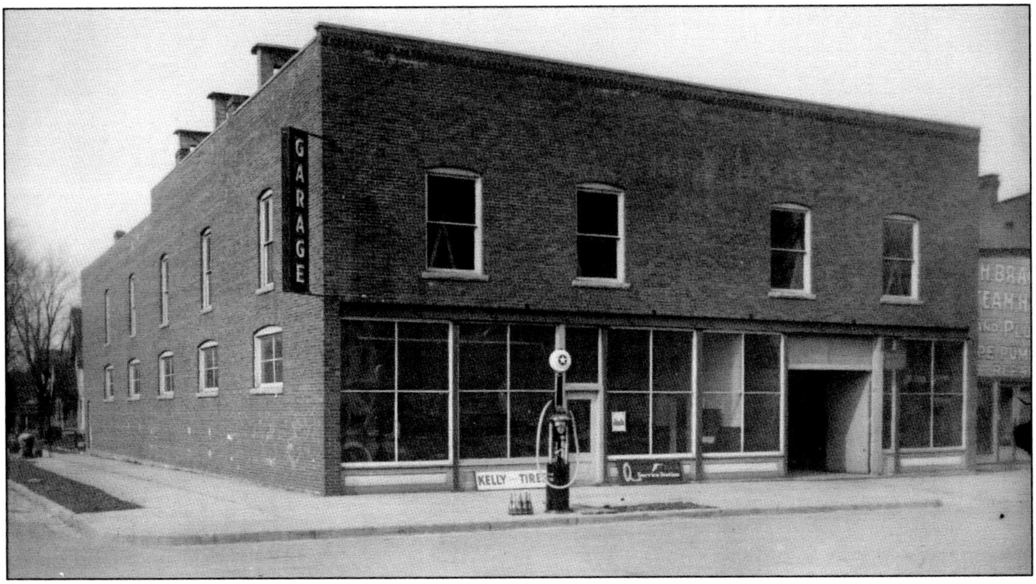

The corner of West Main and Market Streets is a garage in this c. 1920 photograph. First used for furniture and agricultural implements when built in 1909, it was a service garage and Ford dealership during most of its term. Wheeler Delphi Motor Sales, R. G. Bradshaw Ford, and Weldon Motor Company were among its early occupants. In the 1930s, the front and side were opened for a drive-through filling station. Paul Johnson Ford was here in the 1930s to 1959, when the building was demolished. The National Guard Armory used the second floor for some time prior to 1928, when the armory and community building were completed on East Main Street at Union Street.

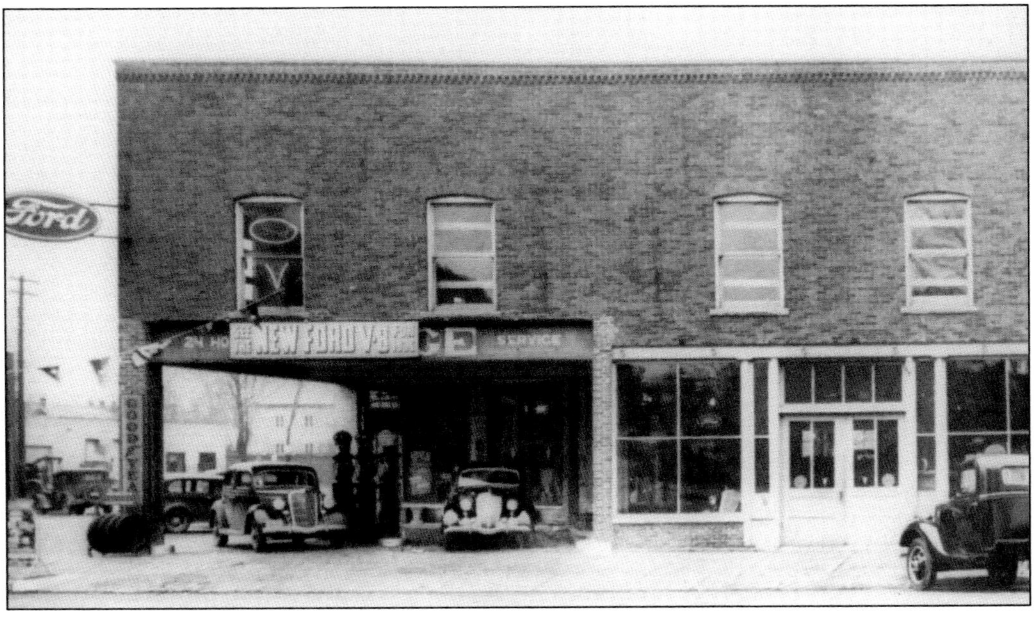

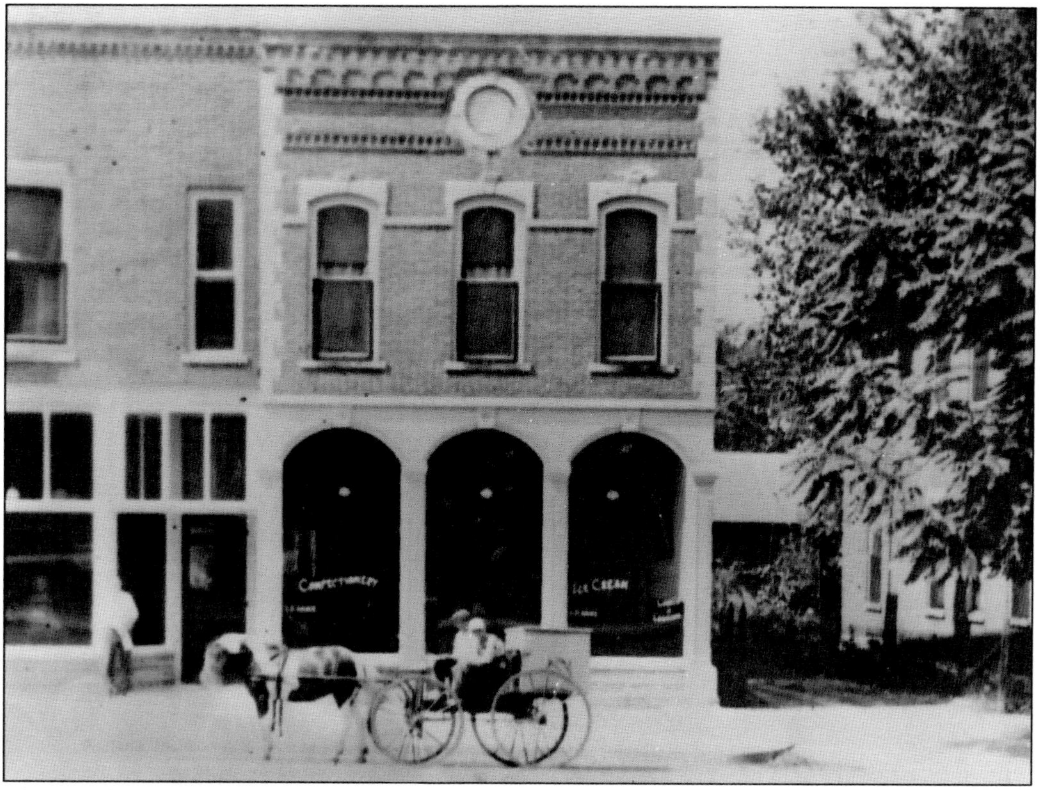

The two brick buildings south of the alley were built in the 1880s by Alfred Boothroyd and purchased by Edward "Cap" Dame in 1918 for Dame's Ice Cream and Confectionery (right). Dame's was famous for its 5¢ soda. Dame and his wife ran a hotel, restaurant, and ice cream parlor here through the mid-1930s. (They also operated a steam laundry and ice cream factory at their home on Water Street.) Afterward, Ratcliff Hotel and Lester's Hotel were at this location. The buildings were demolished in 1978 after a destructive fire in August 1977.

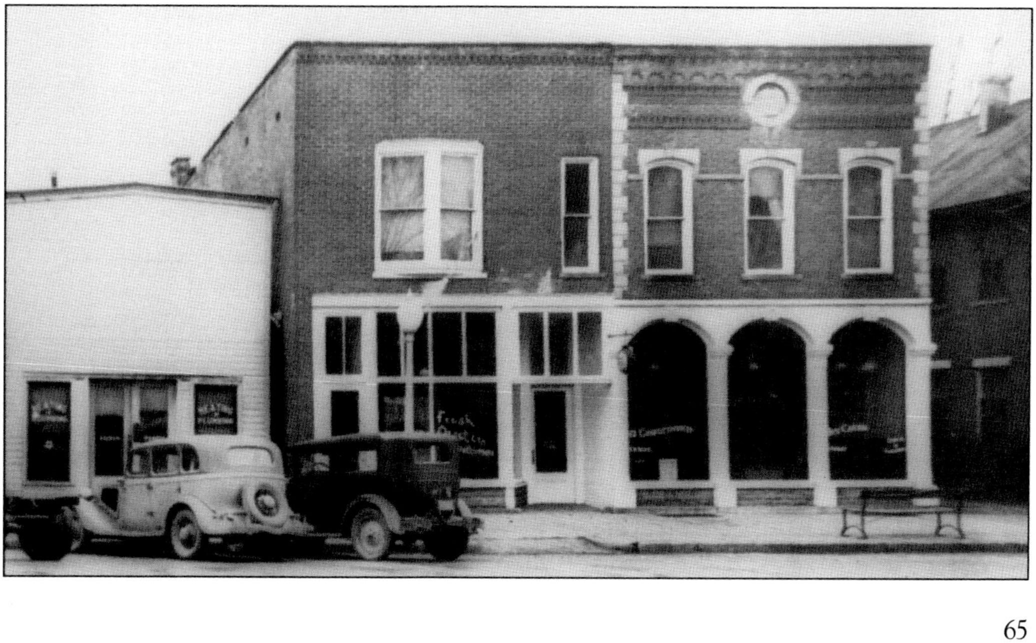

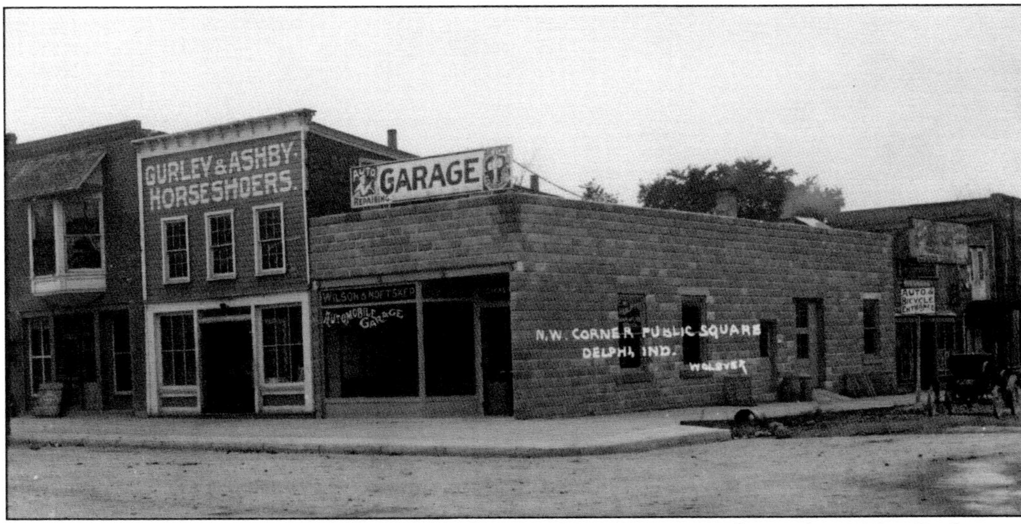

At the southwest corner of Market and West Franklin Streets in the early 1900s, Gurley and Ashby Horseshoers is next to Wilson and Noftsker's Garage with an automobile and bicycle entrance on West Franklin Street. Adjacent is C. M. Kerlin's Grain and Livestock office, which moved around the corner.

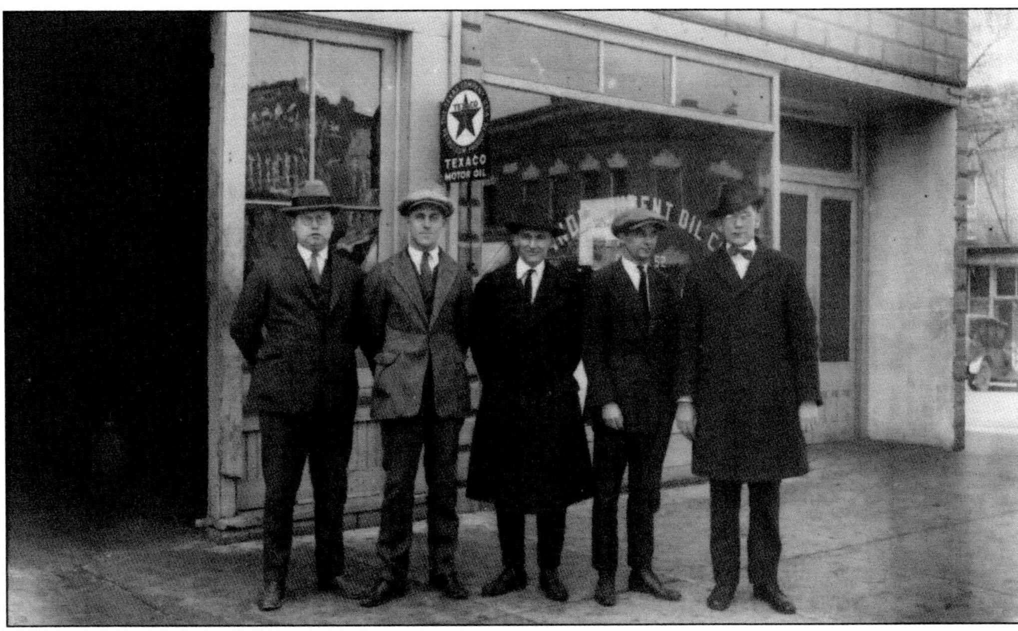

The Independent Oil Company was on the southwest corner in the mid-1920s. In front of the building stand the founders of the Harry Bohanon Post of the American Legion in Delphi. They are, from left to right, clothier Paul Quick, Charles Bowen, attorney Floyd Julien, Charles Wilson, and Dr. Charles Crampton with his trademark bow tie. "Doc" Crampton practiced here for 72 years, delivering over 3,000 babies from several generations and serving as the Monon Railroad surgeon. Son of newspaper editor A. B. Crampton and brother of Mindwell Crampton Wilson, Doc was a typesetter as a lad. He first practiced with Dr. Wycliffe Smith, friend of Hoosier poet James Whitcomb Riley.

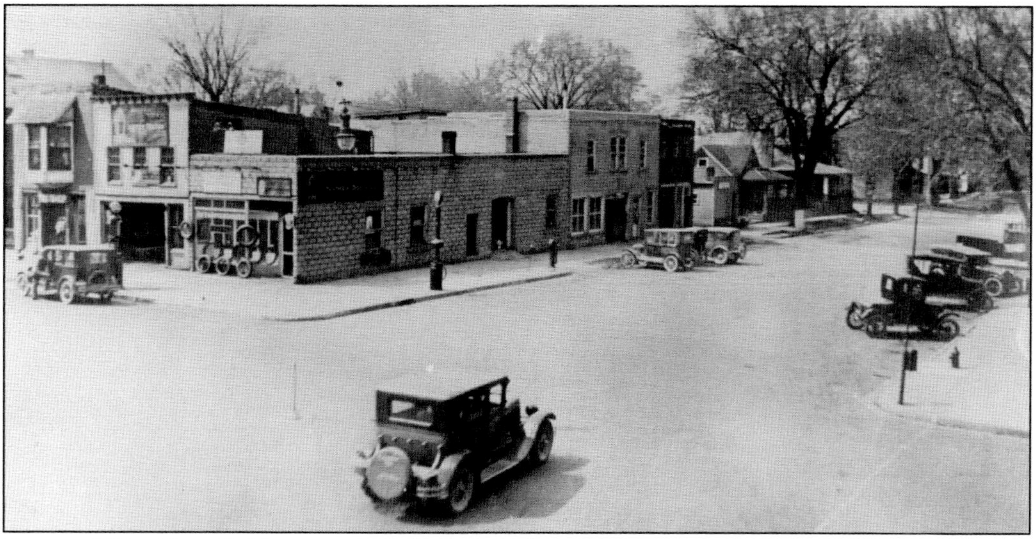

Coomey's Tin Shop (left) is next to a service station and automobile accessories store in this 1920s photograph of the corner of Market and West Franklin Streets. Salin Bank occupies this corner today. On West Franklin Street, a two-story block building is now in place. It was occupied by the Farm Bureau from 1928 to 1935. This corner was also home to many blacksmiths, including Finley and Sheriff, Landis, Roskuski, and Walker. Carriage makers were here as well, including Badorf and Embree.

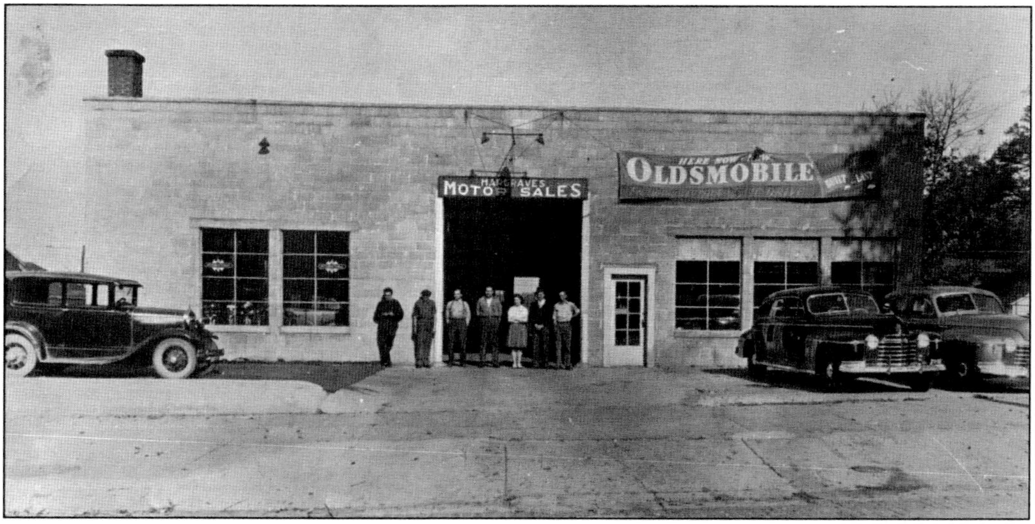

Hargraves Motor Sales was located on the north side of West Franklin Street, west of the post office, from 1939 until 1964, followed by Todd-Bowman. Today this is the location of the Delphi Hardware and Paint store. The only new car dealership remaining in Delphi today is Dick Krieg Motors on Delphi's west side.

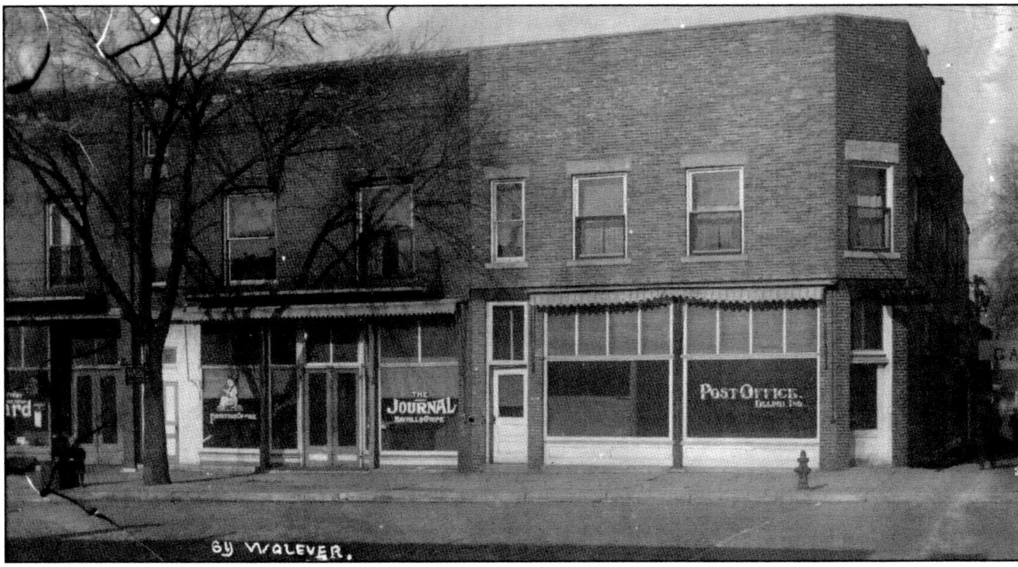

The post office moved from East Main Street into the 1911 Landis building on the northwest corner of West Franklin and Market Streets about 1914. The two buildings to the west were built by J. H. Barnes in 1897. The *Delphi Journal* printing office, owned by the Mayhill family, occupied the east side with Willard's Battery Station to the west. Around the corner on North Market Street was the D and D Garage. The buildings were destroyed by fire in January 1935.

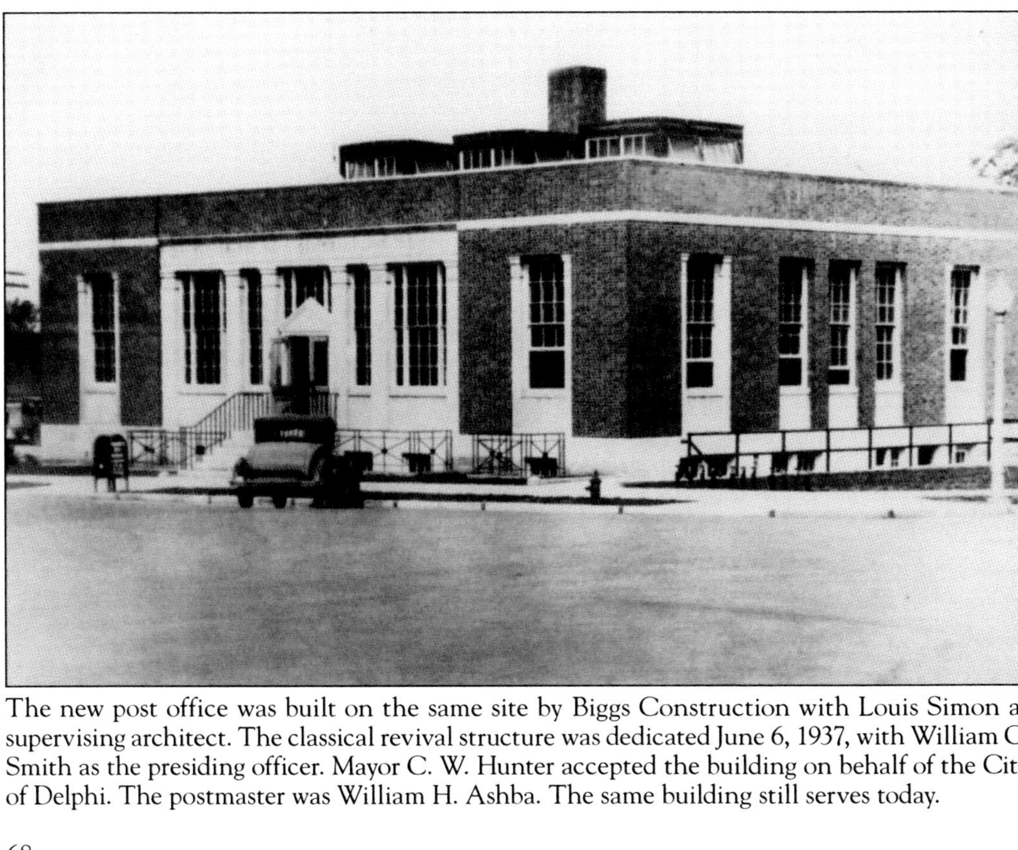
The new post office was built on the same site by Biggs Construction with Louis Simon as supervising architect. The classical revival structure was dedicated June 6, 1937, with William C. Smith as the presiding officer. Mayor C. W. Hunter accepted the building on behalf of the City of Delphi. The postmaster was William H. Ashba. The same building still serves today.

Six

INTO THE NEIGHBORHOODS

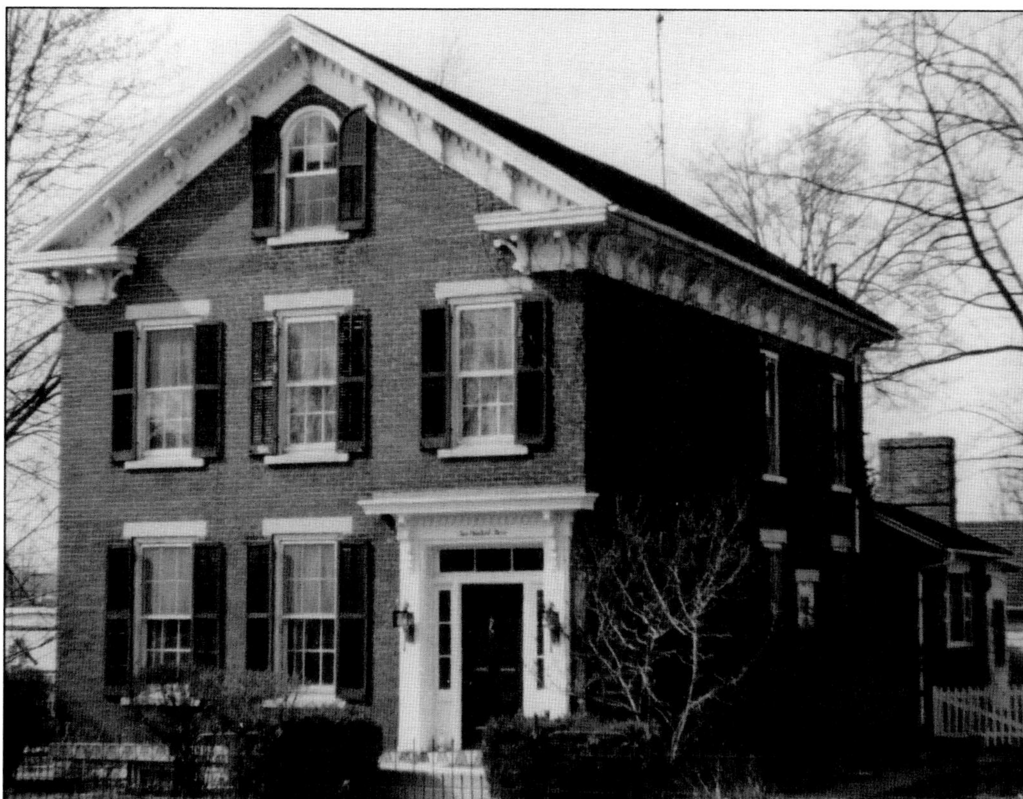

Canal-era merchants built many fine homes in the neighborhoods surrounding the square. Above is the 1857 home built on East Monroe Street by William Barnett, a furniture maker and mayor of Delphi. Franklin D. Roosevelt had tea here during a campaign stop while the home was owned by Henry B. Wilson, Delphi newspaper editor and influential Democrat. Known locally as "the Brick," this Greek Revival structure with Italianate features was listed on the National Register of Historic Places in 1980.

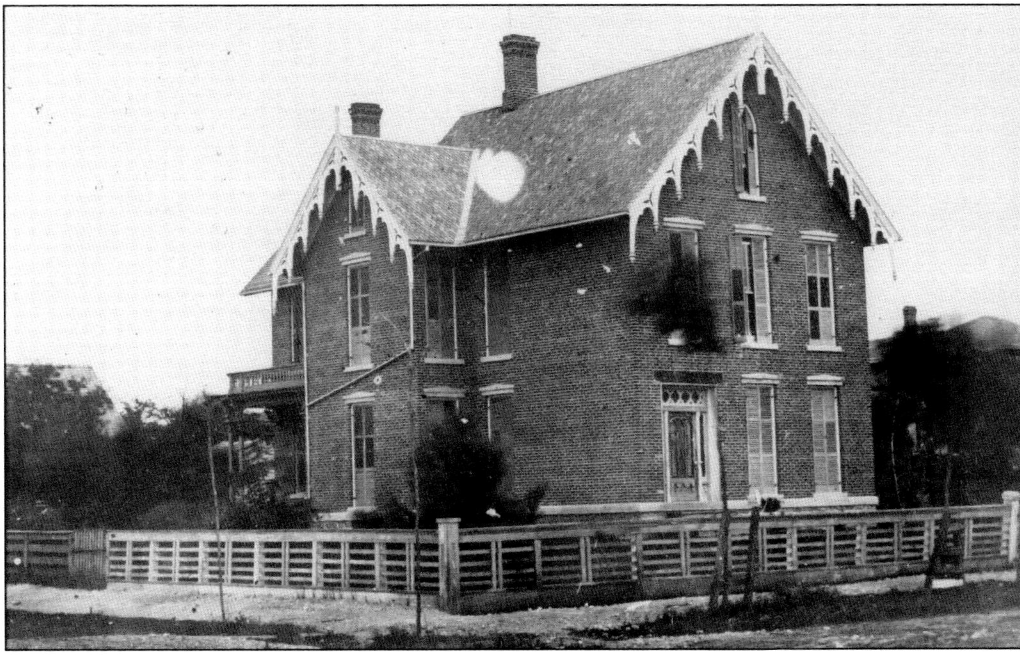

At the corner of Monroe and Indiana Streets sits the Gothic Revival home of Jacob C. Bridge. Bridge worked in numerous retail establishments and then entered the grain trade with John Lenon in 1871. Fences, like the one seen here, were common around homes, churches, and schools in Delphi's early years, as cattle and pigs were driven through the streets to market and slaughterhouses.

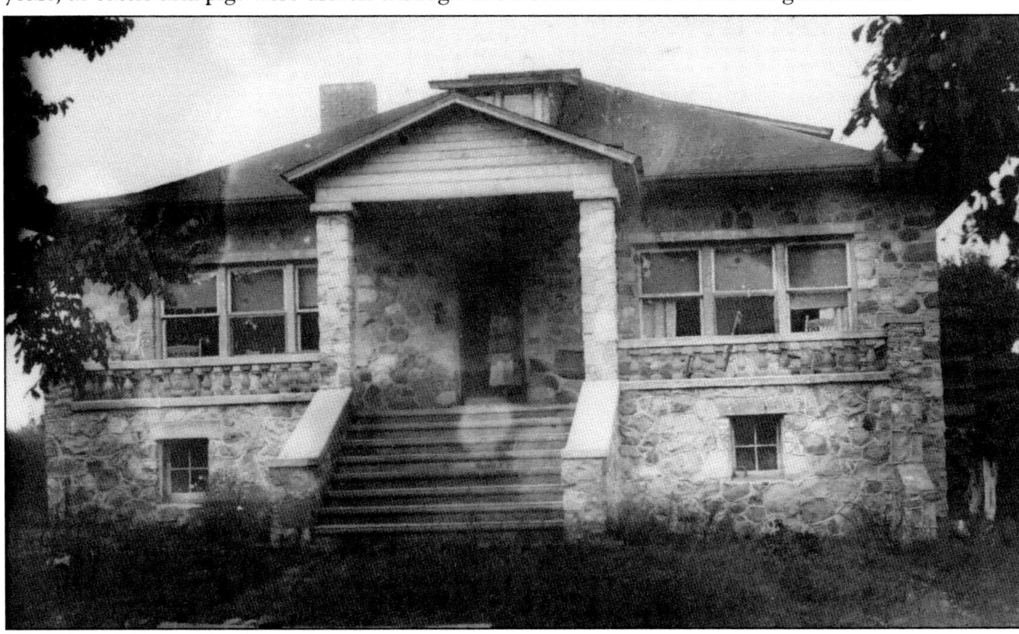

Built in the 1910s, this unusual stone bungalow was owned by Elizabeth Fisher Murphy who was reputed to have been the woman for whom James Whitcomb Riley wrote the poem "An Old Sweetheart of Mine." The home was later owned by the Laverne Goff family. James Goff and son, Laverne, operated a variety store, first on East Main Street and then for many years on South Washington Street.

This Queen Anne–style home on the northeast corner of Union and Franklin Streets was built in 1896 by Joseph Ruffing for about $3,000. Ruffing was proprietor of a jewelry store on South Washington Street. His father John Ruffing built the Ruffing block and partnered with Joseph Assion to build the City Hall block on the east side of the square.

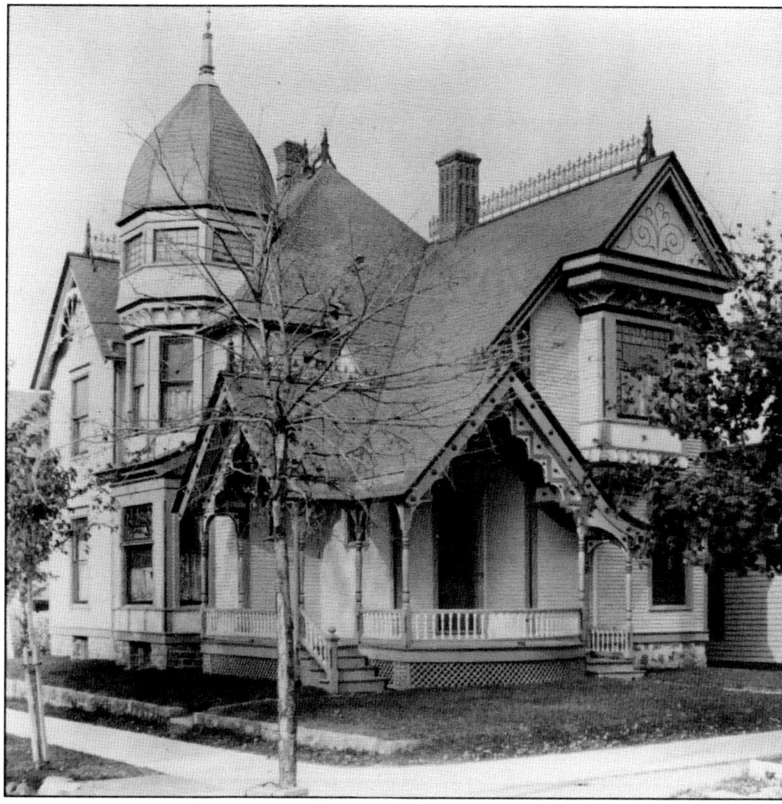

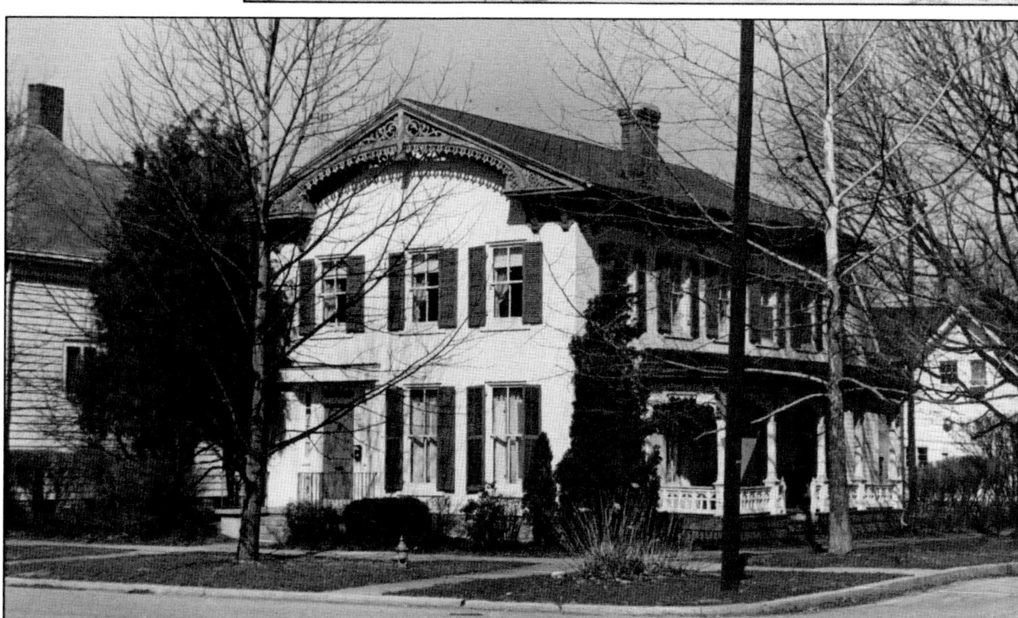

At Franklin and Indiana Streets is this Italianate home built about 1850. It was the residence and office of John H. Gould, elected Carroll County Circuit Court judge in 1876. His grandson was Vice Adm. John Gould Moyer, who commanded a flotilla in the South Pacific in World War II. The home was later owned by attorney Joseph T. Ives.

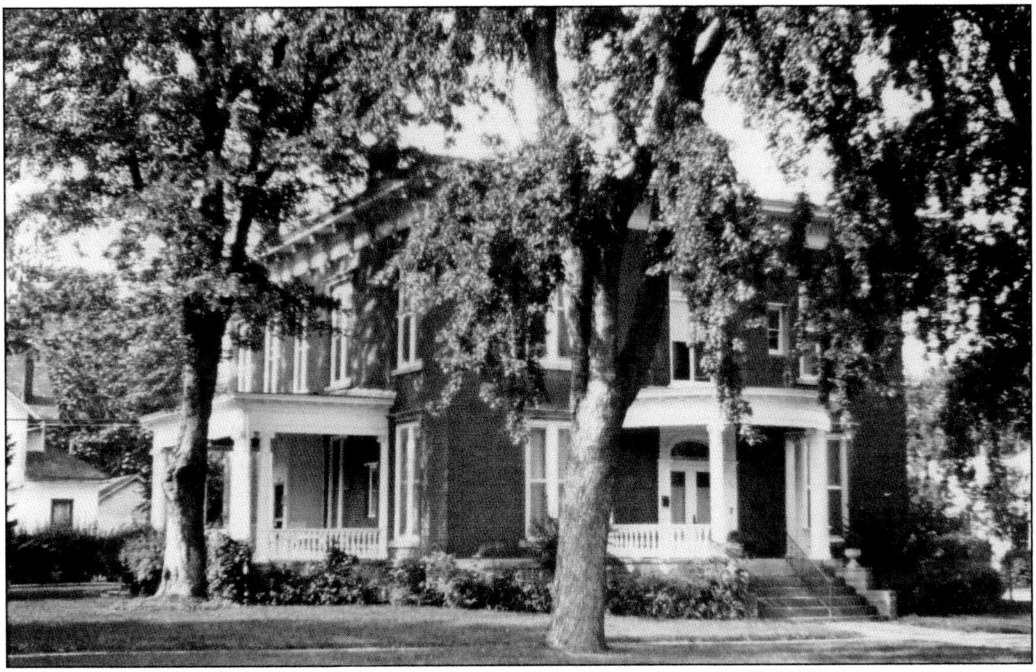

Vine Holt built this Italianate residence on East Main Street in 1861. In 1857, he partnered with Enoch Rinehart to build the four-story brick business block on the south side of the square, and he operated a dry goods store with Benjamin Z. Strawbridge in one of the retail bays. He held office in the Odd Fellows Lodge No. 28 and the Old Settlers Society. A major landowner, he was active in the Carroll County Agricultural Society, establishing the first fairgrounds at Bowen's Woods south of Delphi. The next house to the east is the Victorian home built by Matthew Sterling, an owner of the Delphi Lumber Company in the late 1800s and the early 1900s.

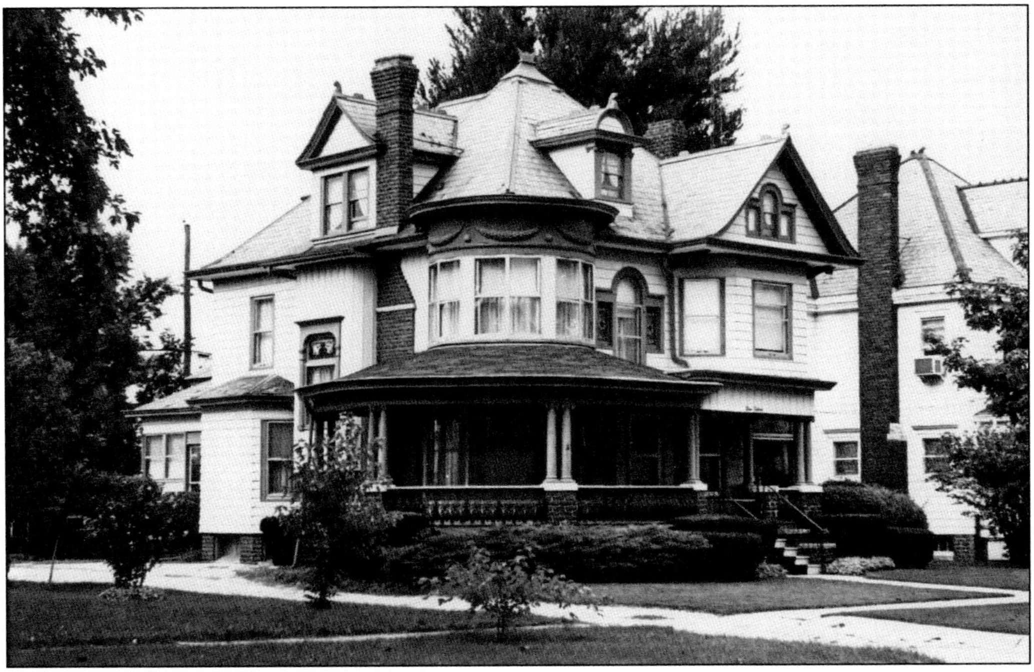

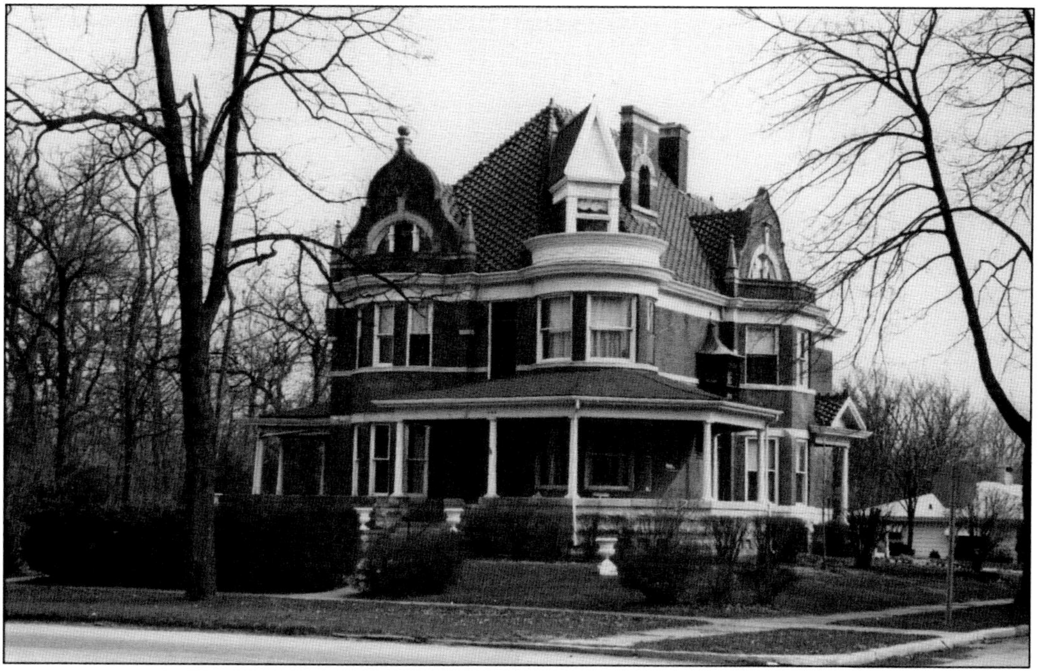

Built originally for Nathaniel W. Bowen in 1896, this magnificent tile-roof home with third-floor ballroom was part of the Bowen complex on the south side of East Main Street. The interior features Italian frescoes, fine woodwork, goatskin wall coverings, and parquet floors. The structure below is the carriage house located southeast of the main residence off Wilson Street. It is also a handsome structure made of cut stone with a tile roof. It reflects the owner's passion for horses.

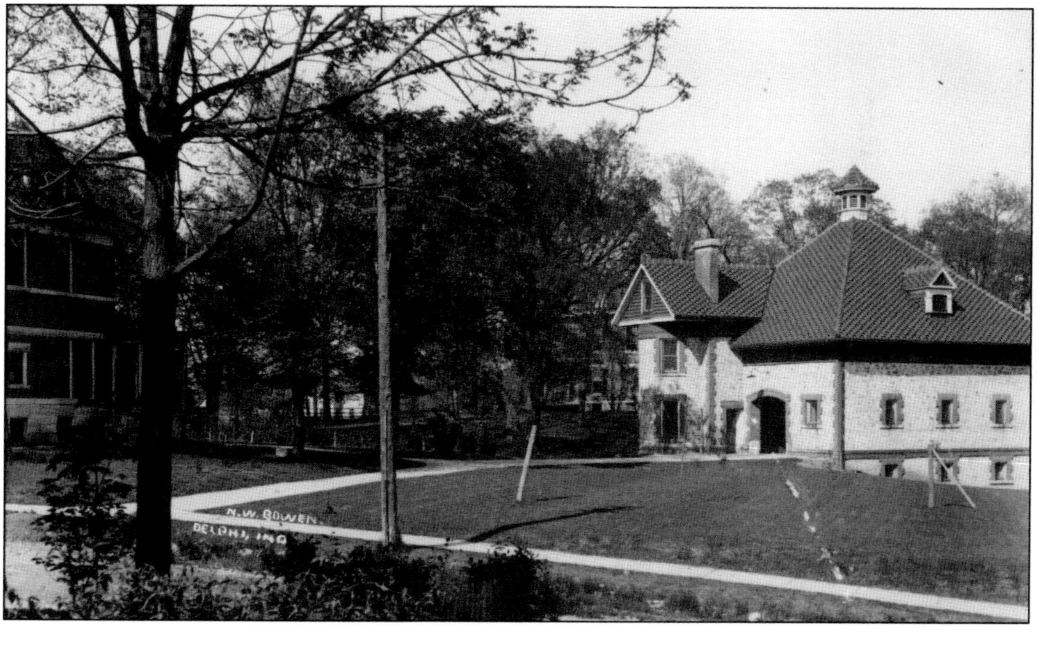

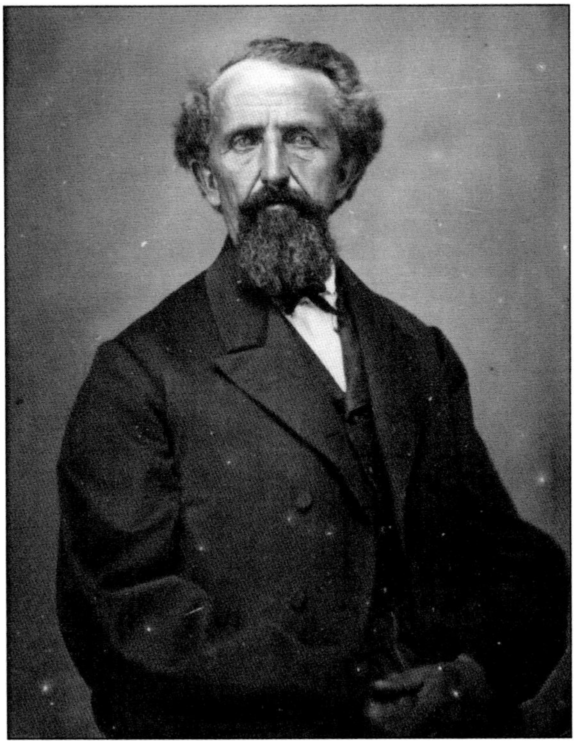

Enoch Rinehart (1815–1895) was one of the most prominent men in Delphi during the canal era. He moved here in 1839 and served as sheriff in 1844–1848. He entered the paper-manufacturing business in 1848 with George Robertson and later with Charles Wood and Abner Bowen. He was the sole proprietor from 1873 until 1882, when the destruction of the canal dam at Pittsburg caused all the mills to cease operation. Area farmers, irate over flooding, had taken matters into their own hands.

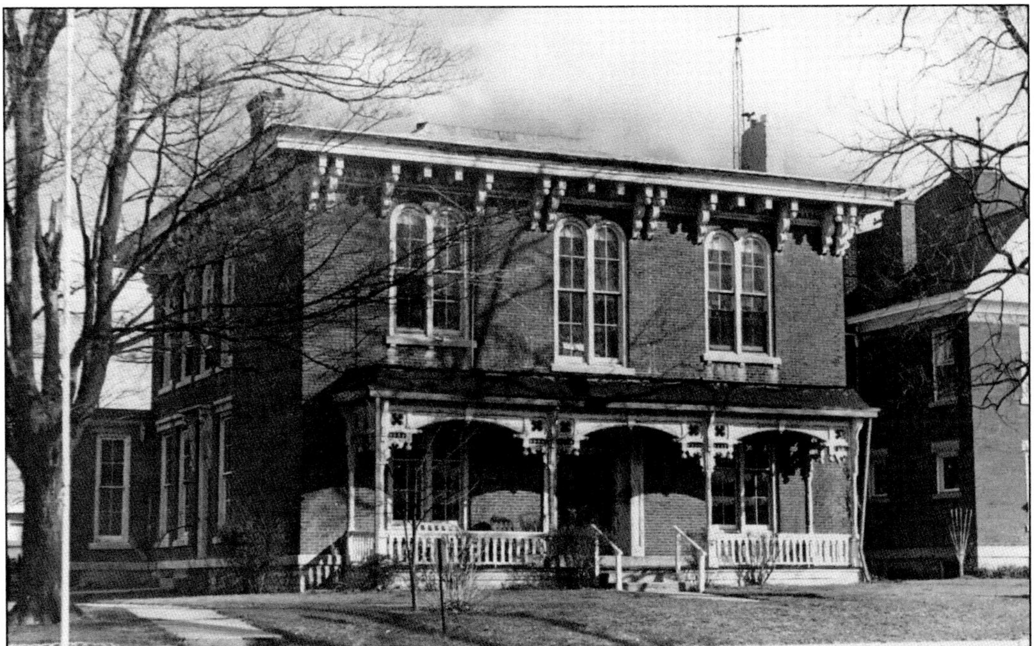

One of many beautiful homes on Front Street is the Italianate-style home of Enoch Rinehart, built in 1858 on the northeast corner of Front and Market Streets. The Rinehart Paper office was located in a brick building behind the house facing Market Street. The porch was likely added in the 1890s.

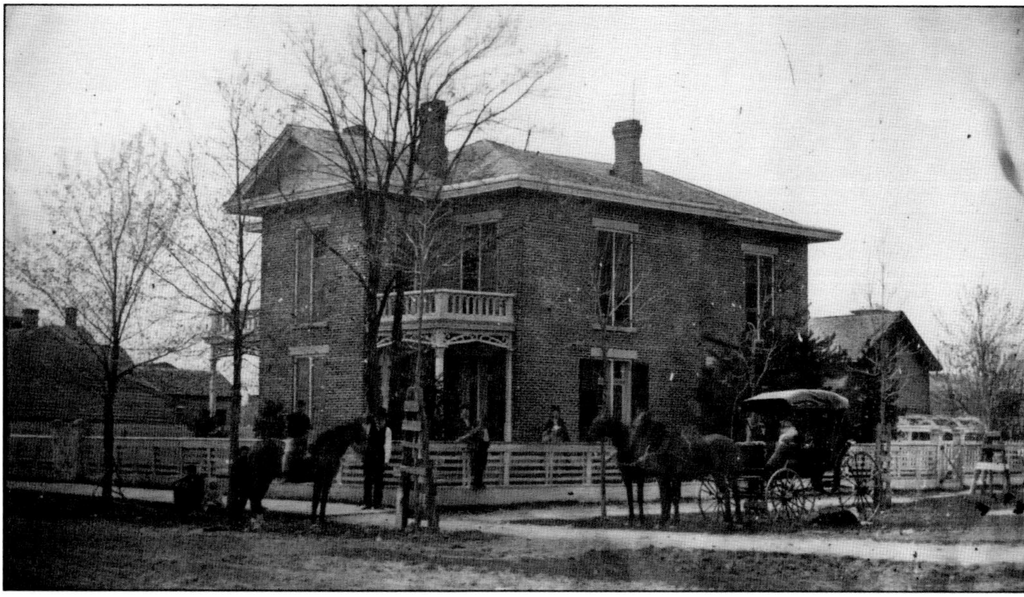

On the northwest corner of Front and Wabash Streets is this Italianate home built in 1863 by Charles Wood, who was in the paper-manufacturing business, first with Enoch Rinehart in the early 1850s and later with George Robertson. A brick carriage house is located at the rear.

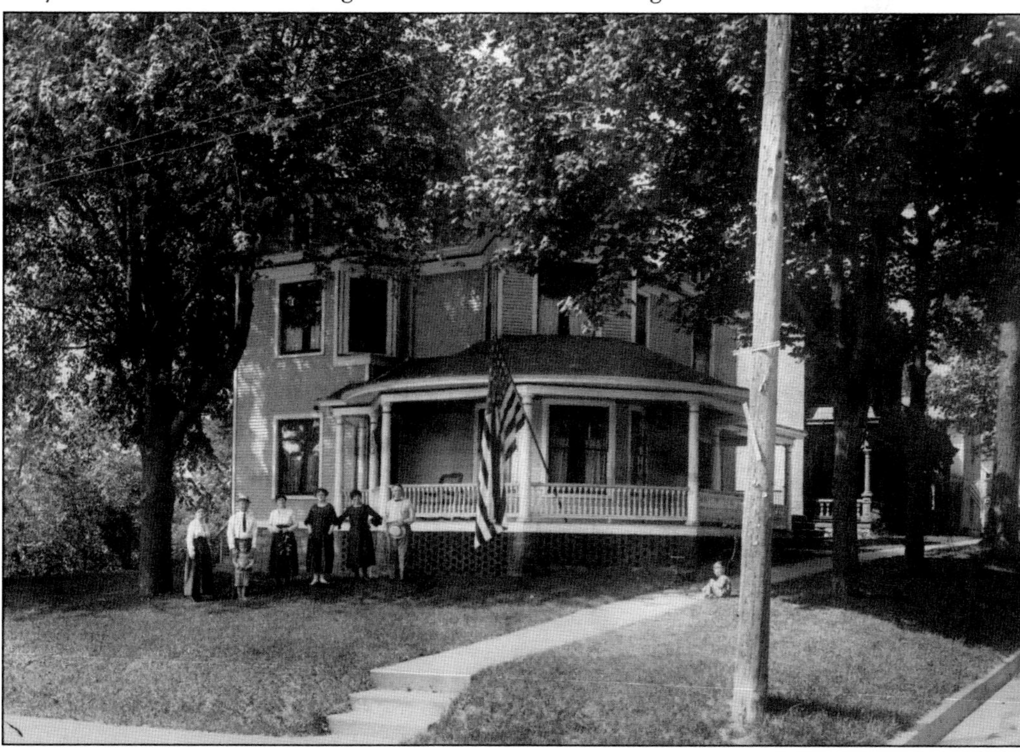

At the southeast corner of Front and Washington Streets is this Queen Anne–style frame house built in the 1890s by C. W. Thompson. The John Hamling family bought the house soon after and are seen in front of its inviting porch. This was one of the first homes built in the area in which the porch was part of the initial design.

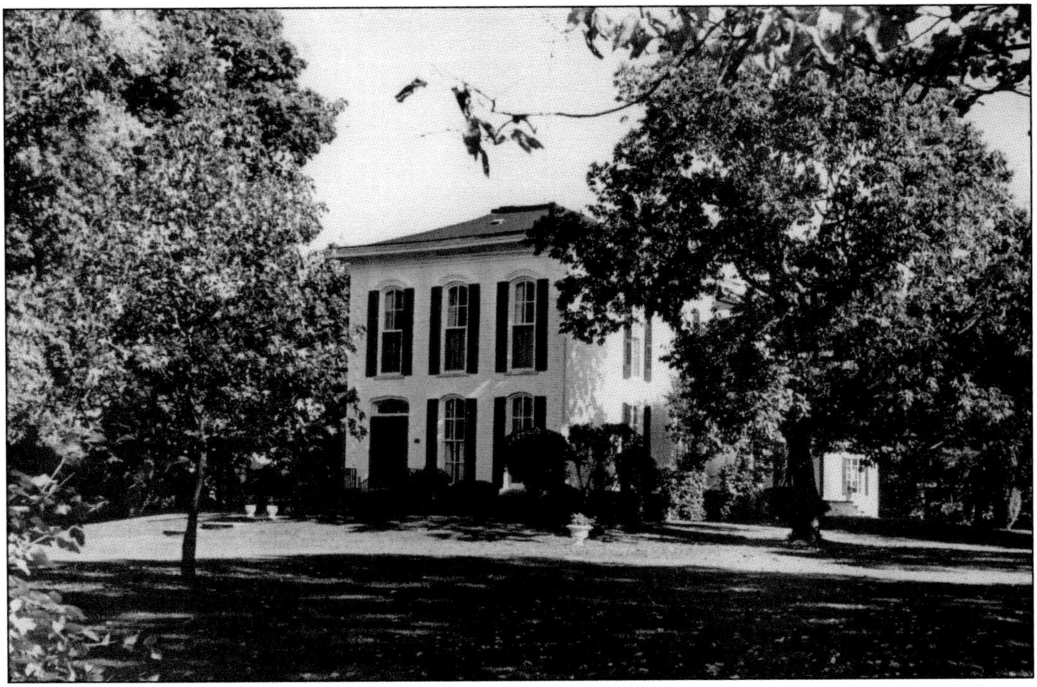

The hill south of town was another area favored by prominent early mercantile-class residents. Both of these houses are on North Street in what was South Delphi. Pictured above, sitting well back from the street, is the two-story home built around 1865 by Joseph A. Sims, a Delphi attorney who served one term in the Indiana House of Representatives. His brother, Lewis B. Sims, also an attorney, built the house seen below. Both homes are currently occupied by attorneys as well. (Photographs by C. E. Gerard.)

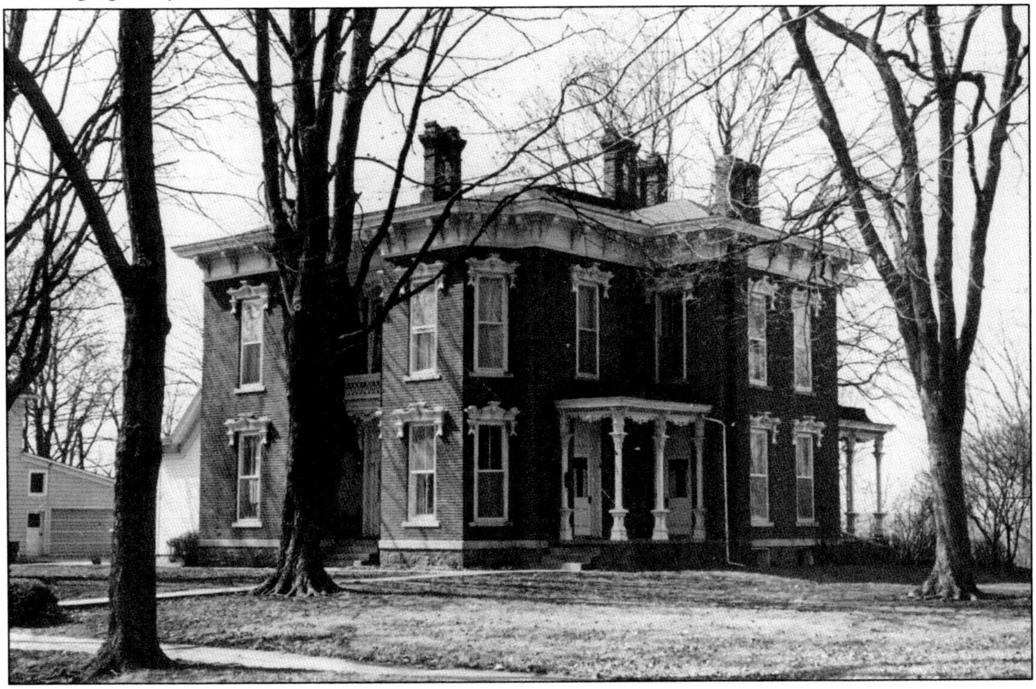

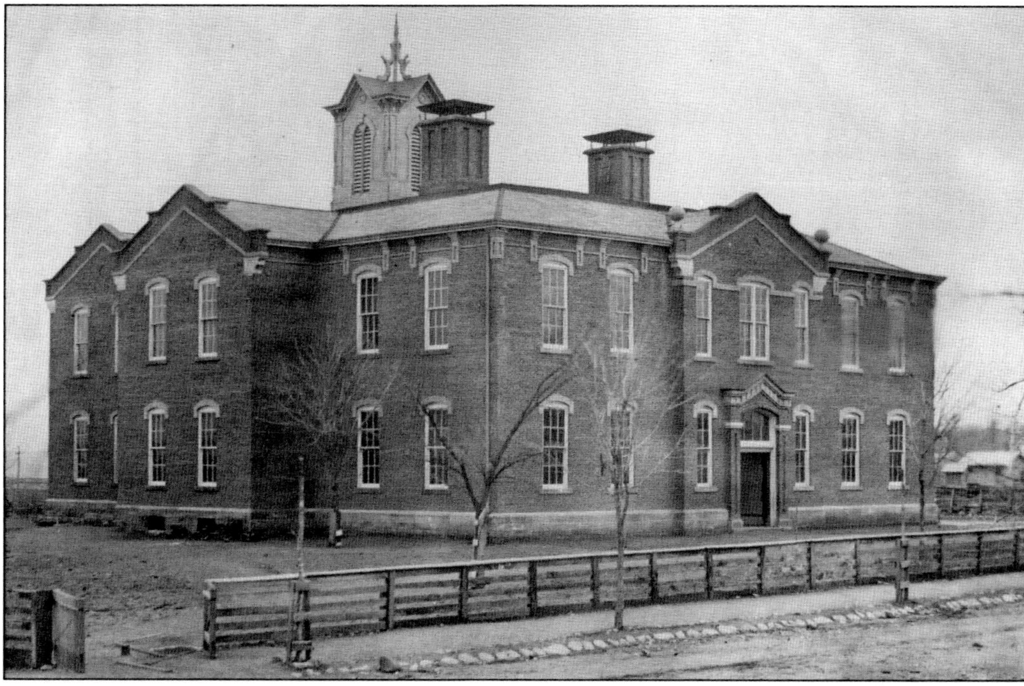

Built in 1872 at a cost of $30,000, the Delphi Public School on the northeast corner of Monroe and Wilson Streets was acclaimed as a model of school architecture. It housed all grades, including high school when that was added in 1874. It replaced a two-story oblong brick structure built in the mid-1850s. Other schools had preceded these in various locations in Delphi, including one used as a school and church for many denominations at the corner of Union and Monroe Streets. The first school was a log cabin built by Henry Robinson in the vicinity of the Robinson-Baum Cemetery in South Delphi. The seventh-grade classroom with teacher Nannie Thomas is shown below in this 1896 photograph.

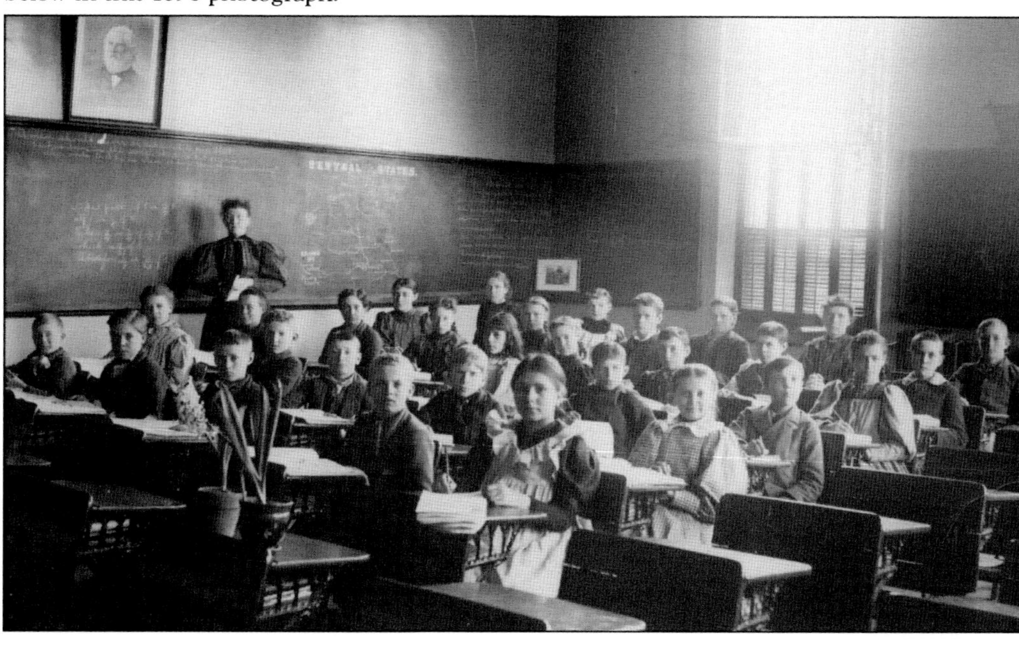

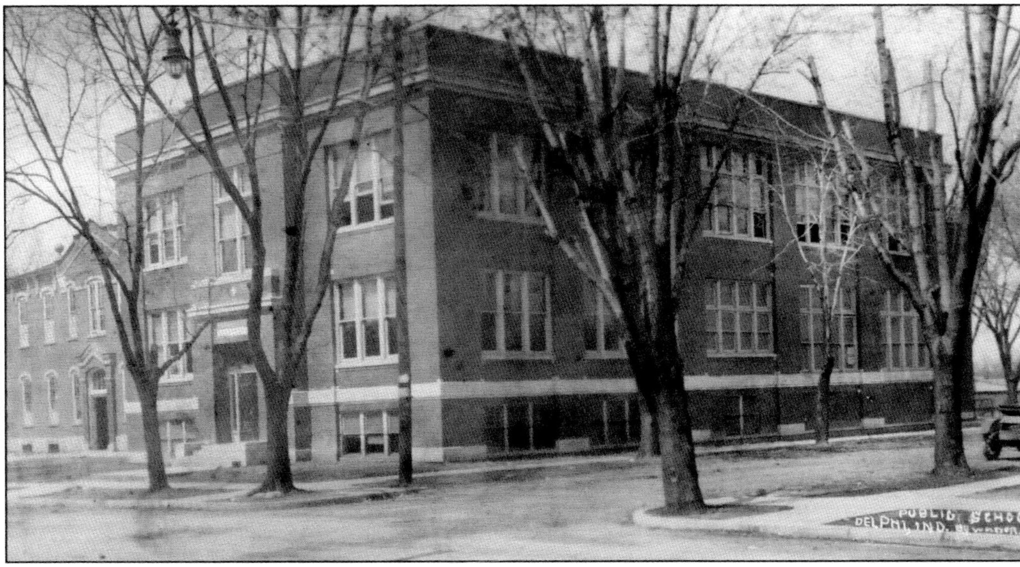

An addition was built to the east side of the school in 1915 to house the high school. The 1872 building was torn down in 1937 and replaced with new central and west wings in the same architectural style of the east wing. In 1958, a gymnasium (below, left) was built behind the school for high school sports and physical education. In the decades to follow, a new high school and middle school were built on Armory Road to the south of downtown near Hillcrest Elementary. The Monroe Street School was torn down in 1987 and was replaced with a parking lot for the gymnasium, which is still used by the middle school.

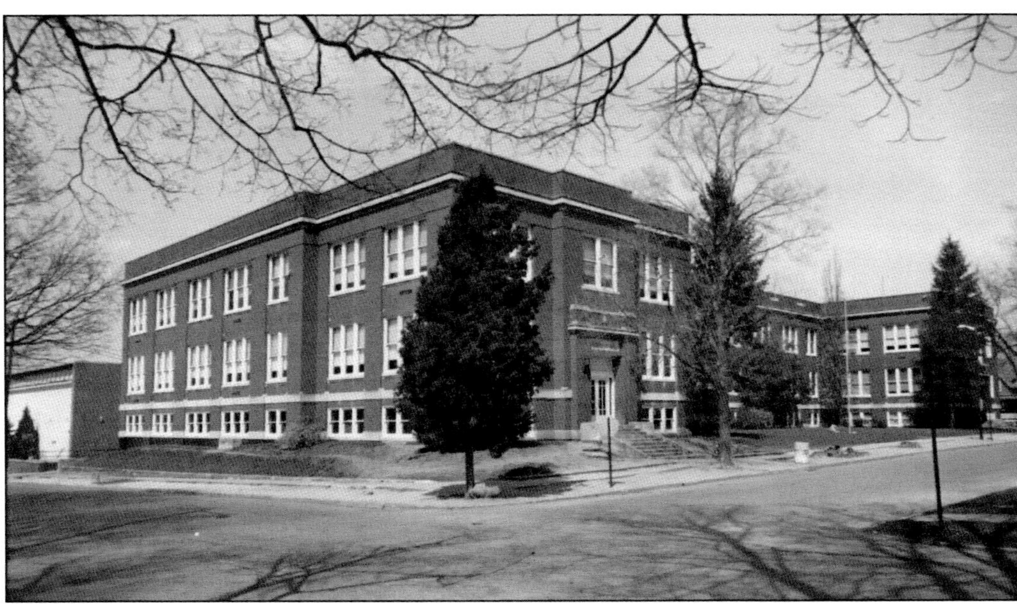

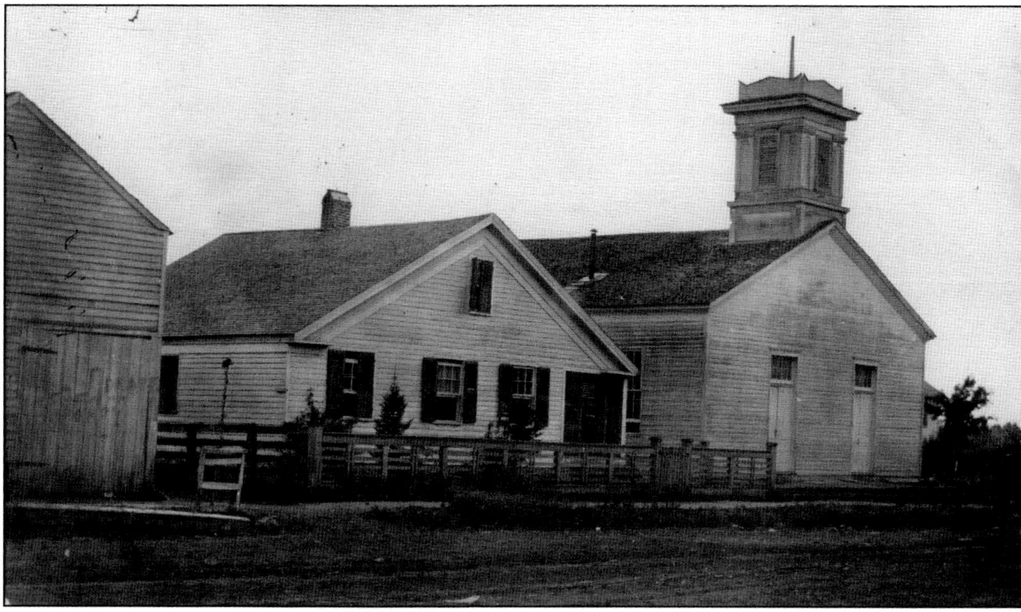

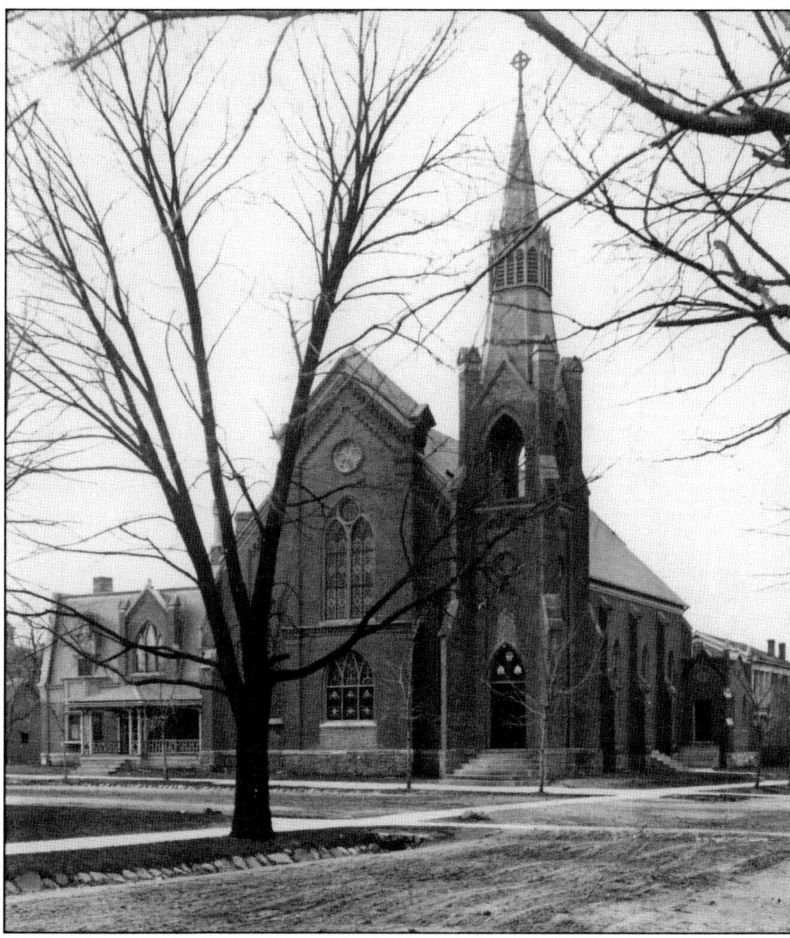

The Methodist Episcopal was the first church organized in Carroll County in 1826. Meeting first at the log schoolhouse, then at the Baptist church, a lot was acquired in 1837, and the frame structure was completed in 1840. At right is the Victorian Gothic brick building that was erected on the same site in about 1870. The parsonage building was added in 1898 during an extensive remodeling of the church and is now used for offices and classrooms.

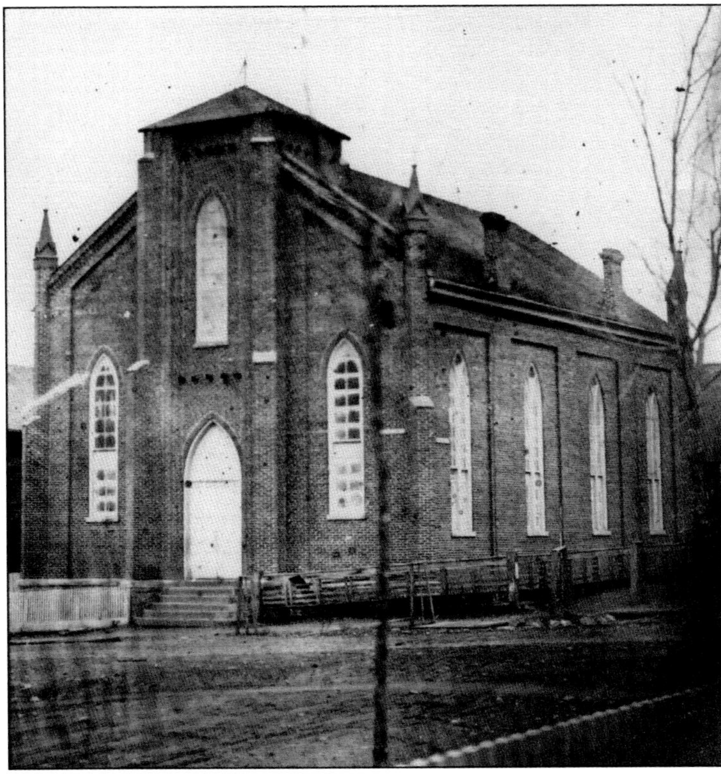

The Gothic-style St. Joseph's Catholic Church was built in 1860 at a cost of $9,000. It was constructed from brick fired at Donovan's Brick Kiln in nearby Pittsburg. The steeple was constructed in two more stages with the final spire added in 1899. The 1860s photograph at left was taken by J. M. Boltz and the one below by C. E. Gerard.

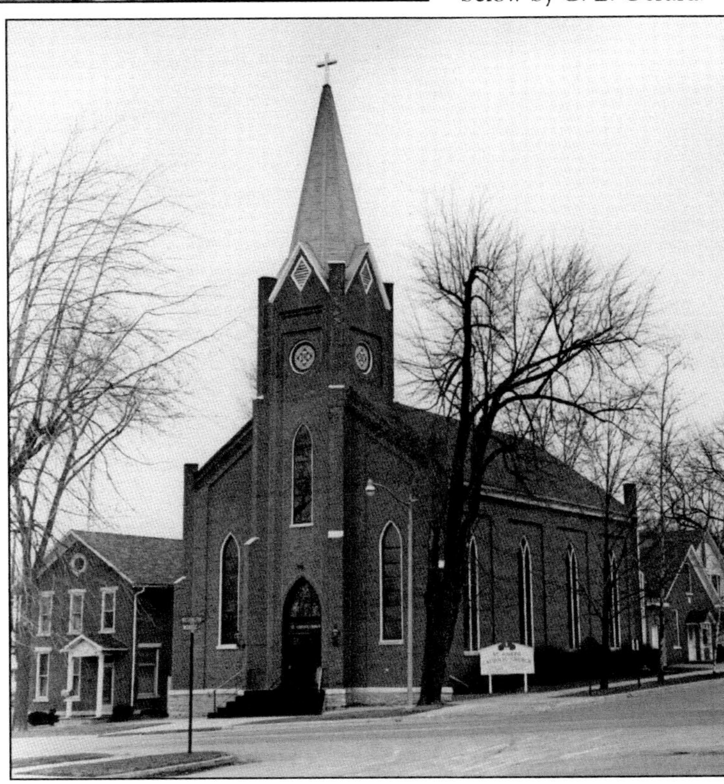

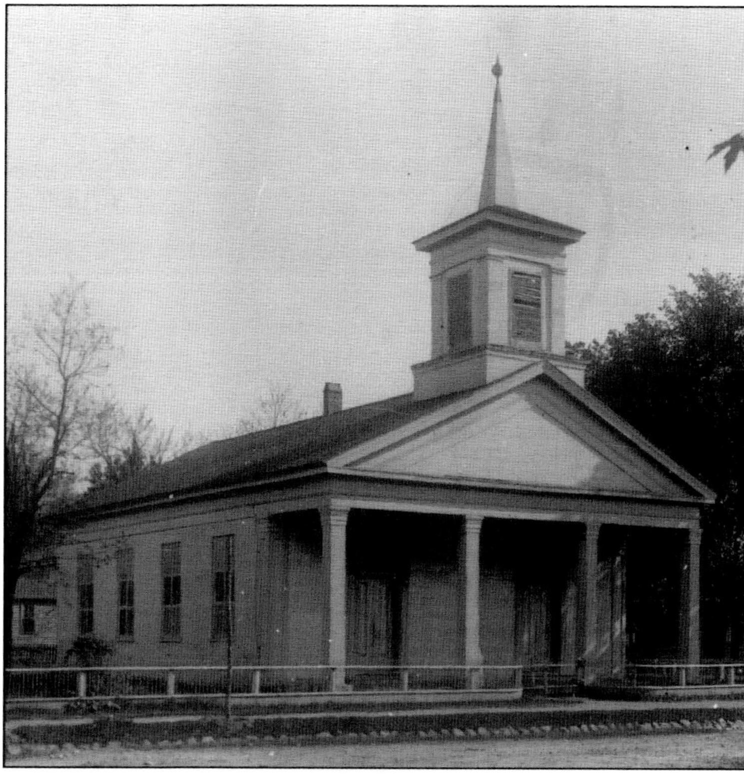

The Baptist church held its first meeting in 1829. For some years they met in the log school at Monroe and Union Streets. The first church was built in the mid-1830s at Indiana and Franklin Streets. The present building was constructed on the same site in 1892. The building escaped major damage in a 1995 fire and has benefited from extensive restoration.

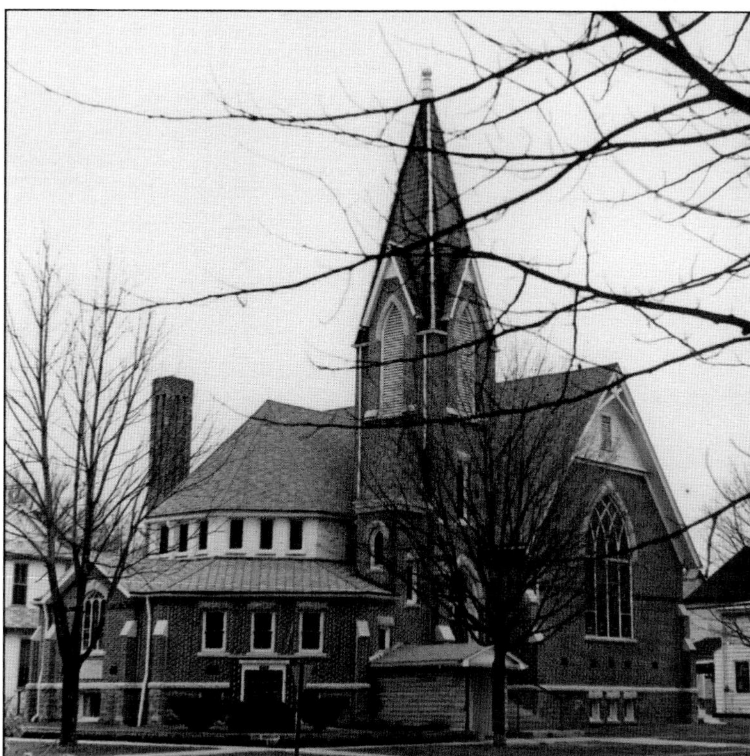

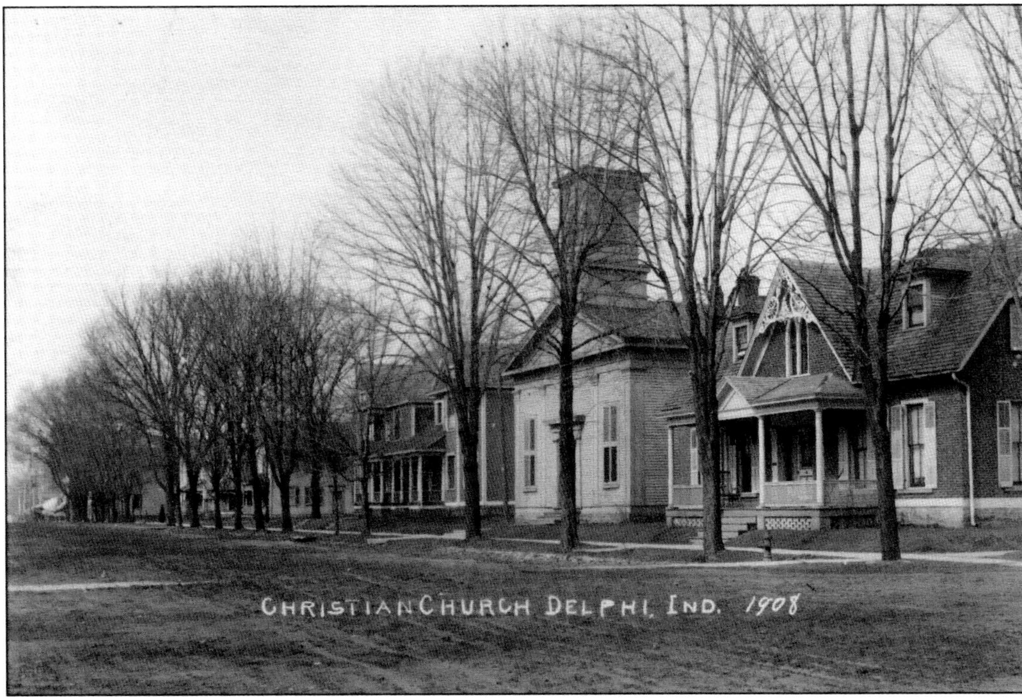

The first Christian Church, pictured above just before it was replaced, was originally an Old School Presbyterian Church that was transferred to the Christian Church in 1882. The present Christian Church is located on the same site between Indiana and Wilson Streets on the north side of East Main Street.

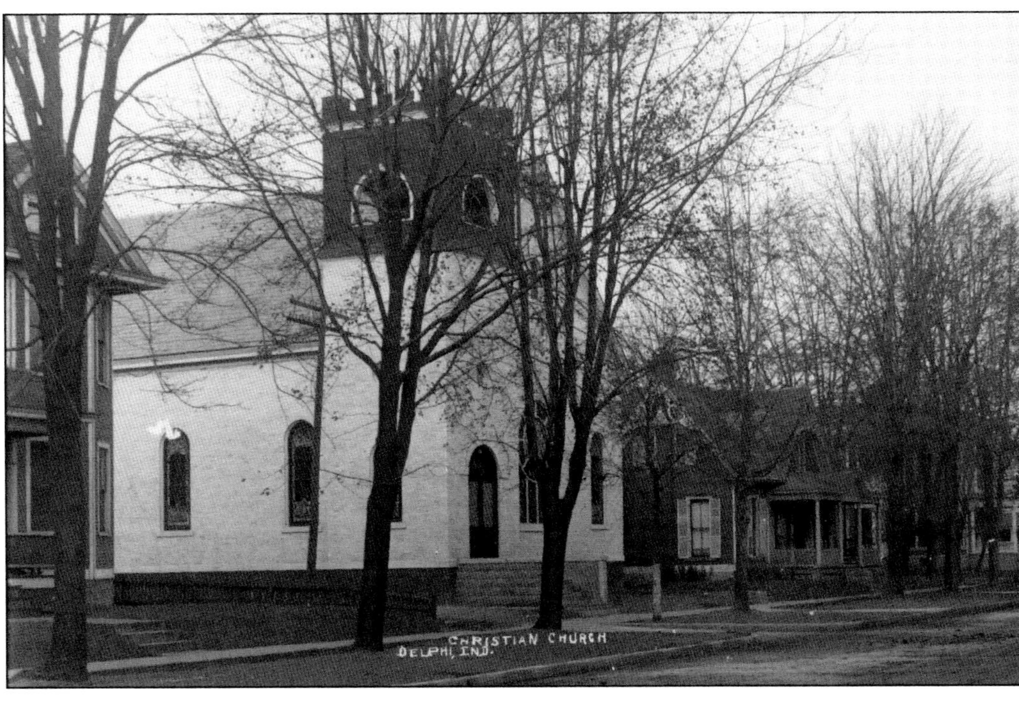

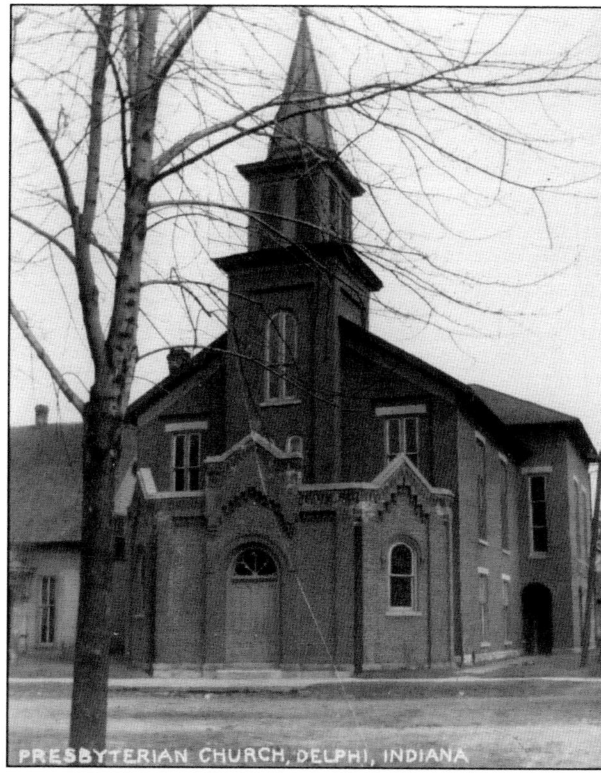

The New School Presbyterian Church constructed the brick church (right) in 1859 on North Union Street across from the Methodist Episcopal Church. This building was later used by the Church of the Brethren, the school, and Gray's Hatchery. It is now an apartment building. The present church with Tudor Gothic styling (below) was built in 1909 on the southeast corner of East Main and Indiana Streets on land deeded to the church by Catherine J. Bowen. The church celebrated its 175th anniversary in 2003.

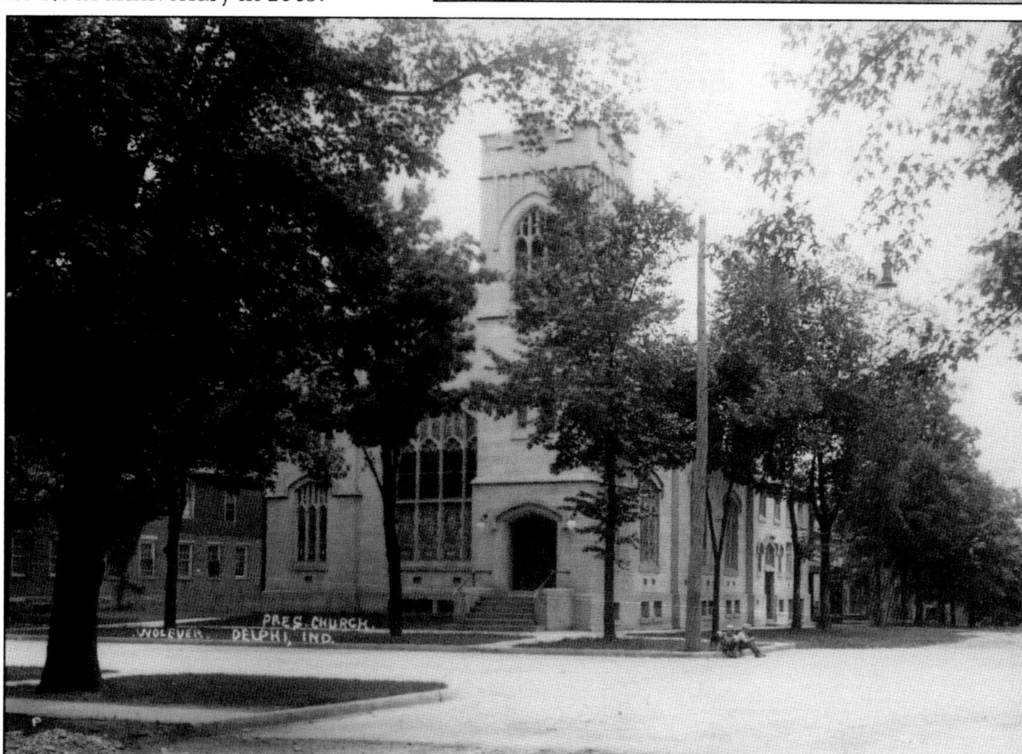

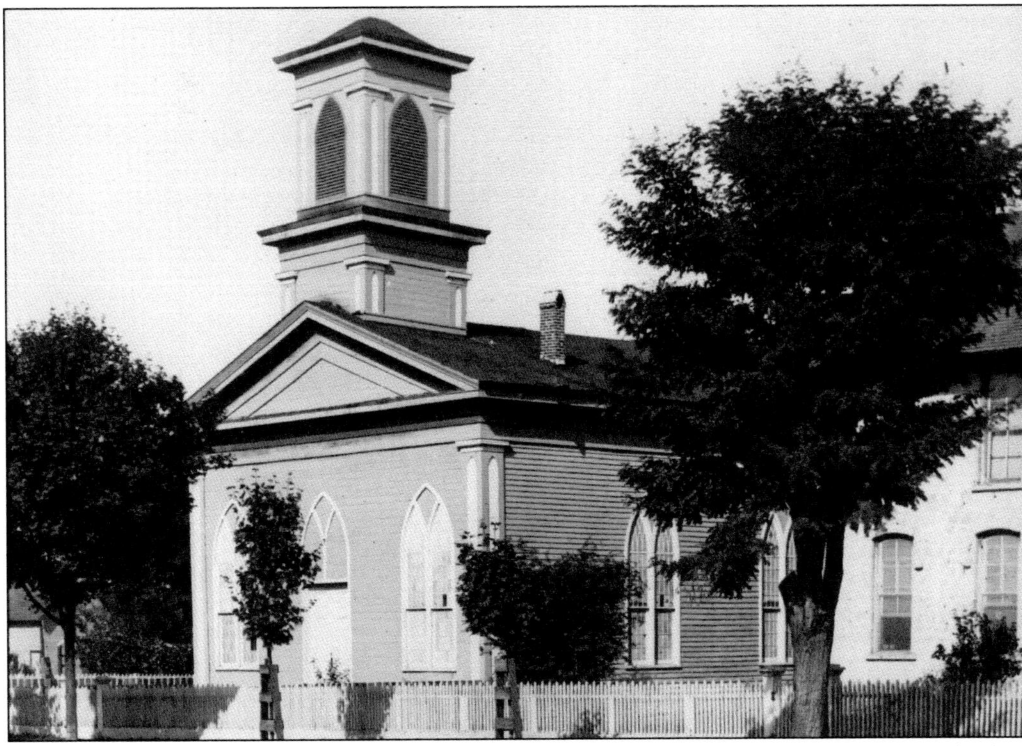

St. Mary's Protestant Episcopal Church was consecrated in Delphi in 1845. A chapel was built in 1846 on West Main Street. In that same year, the lot next door was purchased and a parsonage erected. The 1900 photograph above shows the church before it was replaced in 1901 by the chapel pictured below. The stone rectory, visible in both photographs, has been in commercial usage for some time and was the first location of the Stone House Restaurant, today found in the Niewerth building on East Main Street. Indy Spine and Rehab occupies the former rectory at this time. The chapel is presently home to the Delphi Community Church of God.

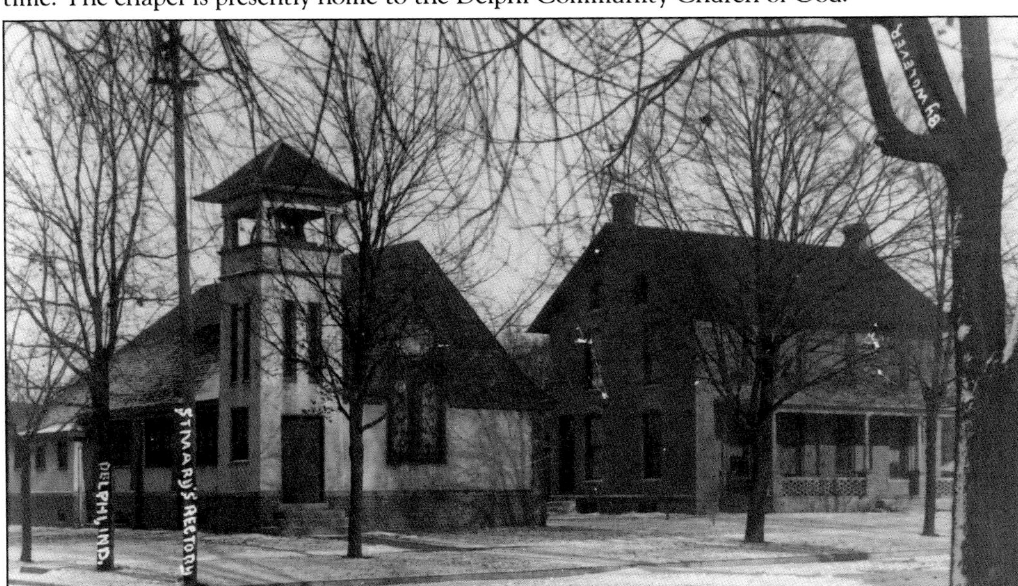

Seven

Entertainment and Culture

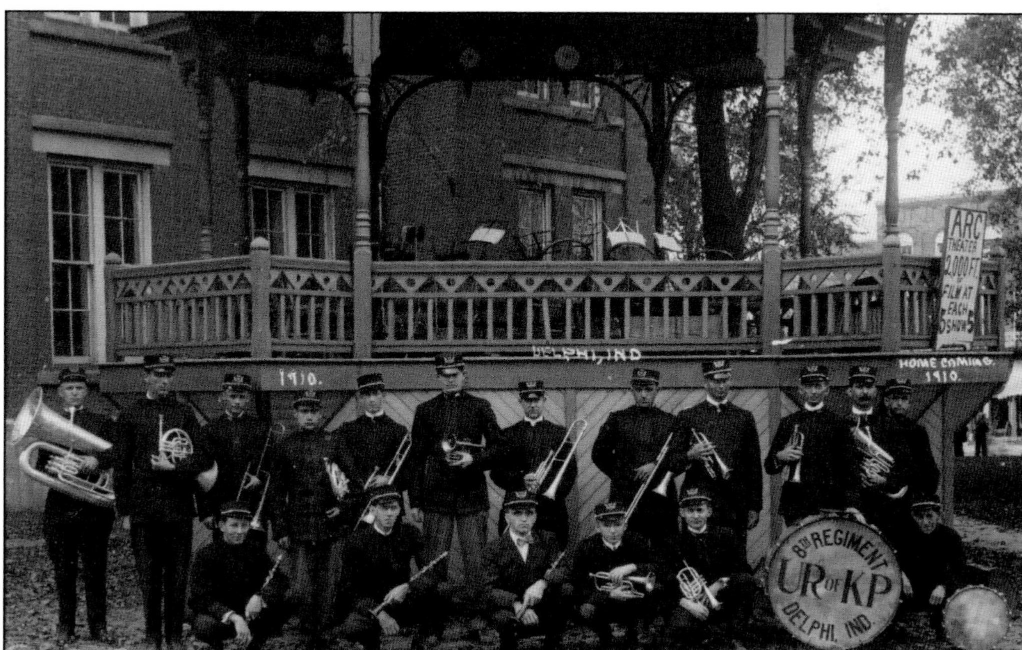

Strains from the brass bands were familiar sounds on the courthouse square during summer months. Lathrope's Cornet Band was a regular attraction. Most communities had bands in the late 1800s and early 1900s, as did some of the benevolent societies. Concerts were held in entertainment halls and lodges. Bands, or orchestras if they were playing indoors, provided the music for ballroom dances and the cadence for parades. The Knights of Pythias built this ornate bandstand on the east lawn of the courthouse in 1899. Their band is seen in this 1910 photograph.

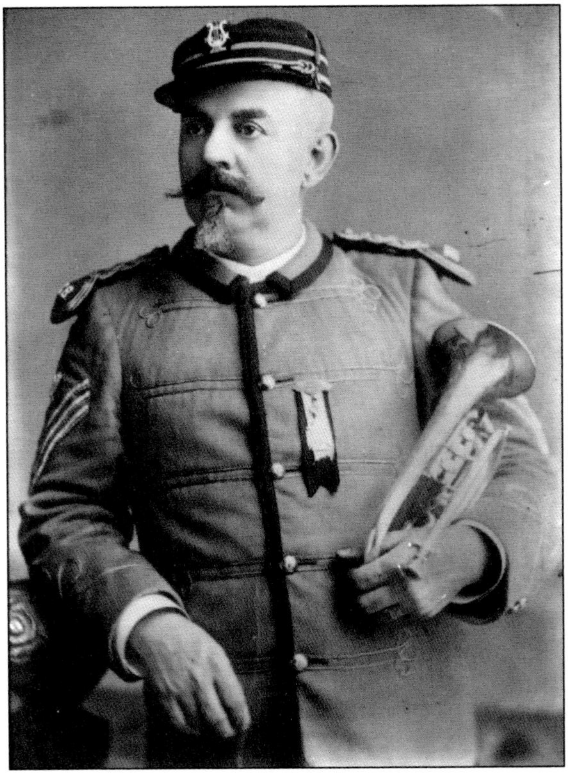

Born in Penzance, England, John Lathrope Jr. (1841–1917) immigrated to the United States in 1851. Already an accomplished musician at age 10, John and his father entertained passengers on the canal in return for passage from Toledo to Lafayette. They worked on several farms in the area before moving to Delphi in 1859. John served in the Civil War as a bugler and leader of the Ninth Regiment Band. He operated several retail establishments in Delphi, including a bakery and café. Lathrope was a renowned cornetist and bandleader, conducting the Lathrope Silver Cornet Band for many decades. In 1882, he opened the Lathrope and Ruffing Opera House and was its manager for many years. He died in 1917.

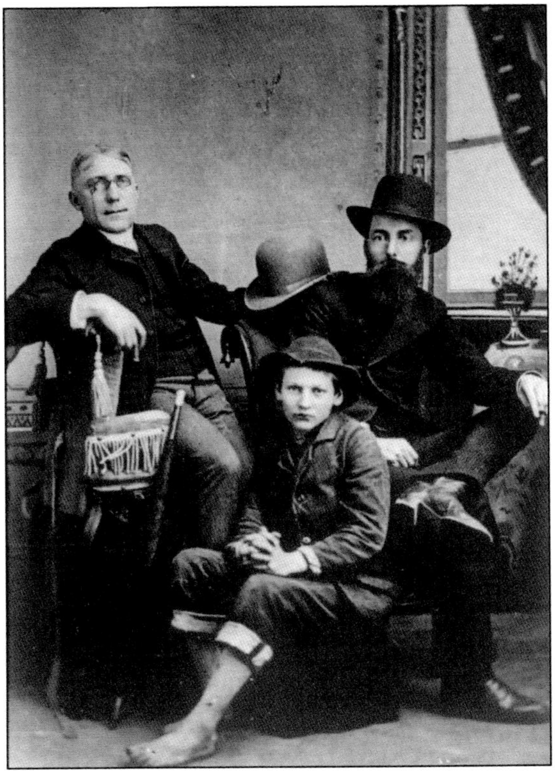

Hoosier poet James Whitcomb Riley (1849–1916) appeared in the opera house on December 21, 1882, and performed at least five other times during the next three decades. Riley frequented Delphi for relaxation, and found inspiration there for poems such as "From Delphi to Camden," "On the Banks O' Deer Crick," and "Little Orphant Annie." Riley (left) is shown with Dr. Wycliffe Smith and young Joe Sneathen.

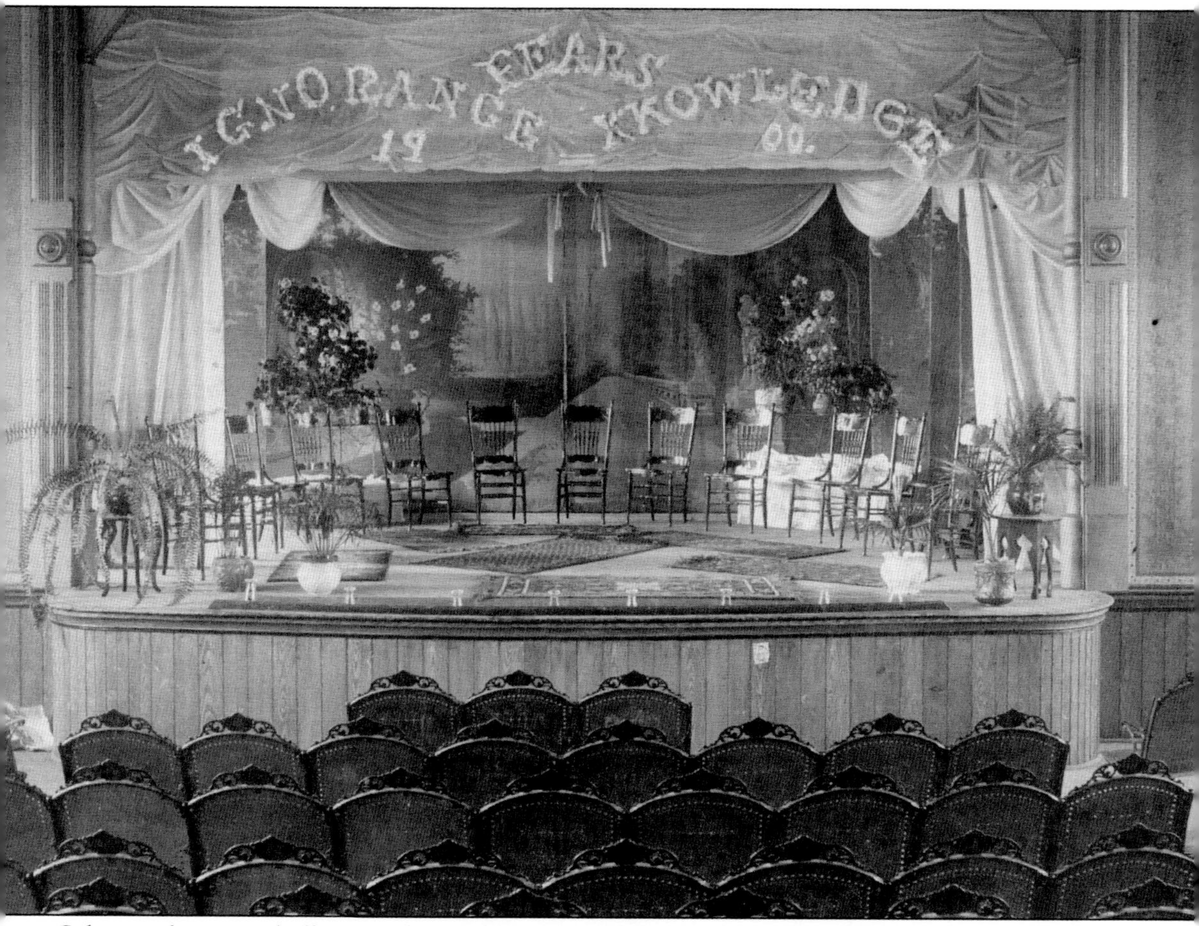

Other performance halls existed in Delphi before 1882—the Holt Rinehart Hall in the 1860s and the Carll Brothers Hall in the 1870s—but Lathrope and Ruffing's Opera House in the Assion-Ruffing City Hall building quickly became known as *the* Delphi Opera House. From 1865, City Hall was a third-floor ballroom and venue for dinners, concerts, and lectures. In 1882, John Lathrope Jr. partnered with Joseph Ruffing to convert the hall into an opera house. The stage was enlarged, a balcony added, tiered flooring and fine theater seats installed, and walls and ceiling richly adorned. More than 500 were in attendance at the grand opening in April 1882 as renowned soprano Marie Litta performed. Traveling theater troupes, minstrel shows, and musical performances were weekly events. The Delphi Dramatic Club used the opera house for monthly performances between 1903 and 1914, when the theater was closed by the fire marshal for having a single exit.

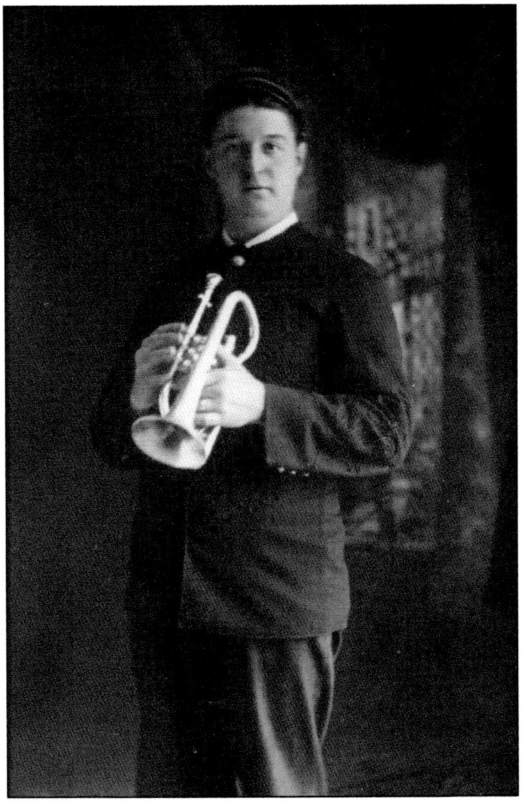

Delphi native Walter B. Rogers (1865–1939) received his early cornet instruction from John Lathrope Jr. Rogers studied theory and composition at the Cincinnati Conservatory of Music and was a soloist with the Indianapolis Band and the Indianapolis Opera House Orchestra. He returned to play concerts with Lathrope's Cornet Band in the summers of 1883 and 1884. Rogers went on to solo with the famous John Philip Sousa band for several years. Later he was the musical director of the Victor Phonograph Company during the era of recording Enrico Caruso. His signature appears on the stage wall of Delphi's opera house. (Courtesy Doris Shepard.)

Some recordings of Rogers would have been sold in the Gregg Music Store on South Washington Street. Here young Paul Gregg sits in front of a wide assortment of recordings and players. Later Joseph E. Ruffing and son, Edwin, had a music store on the east side of the square. (Courtesy Gail Baker Seest.)

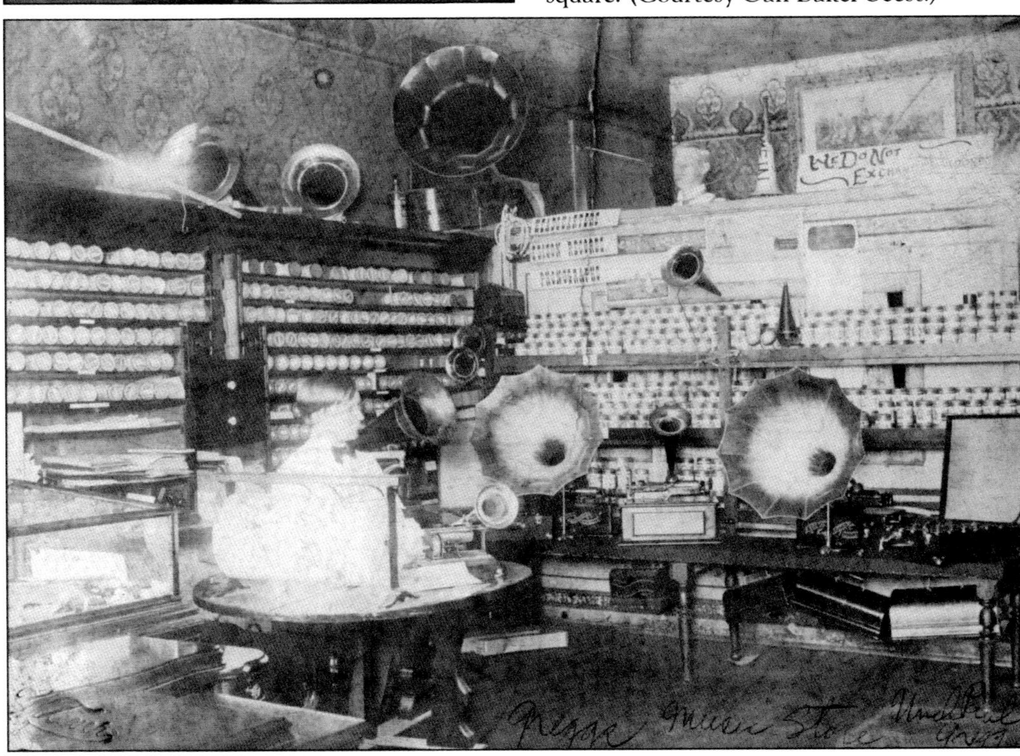

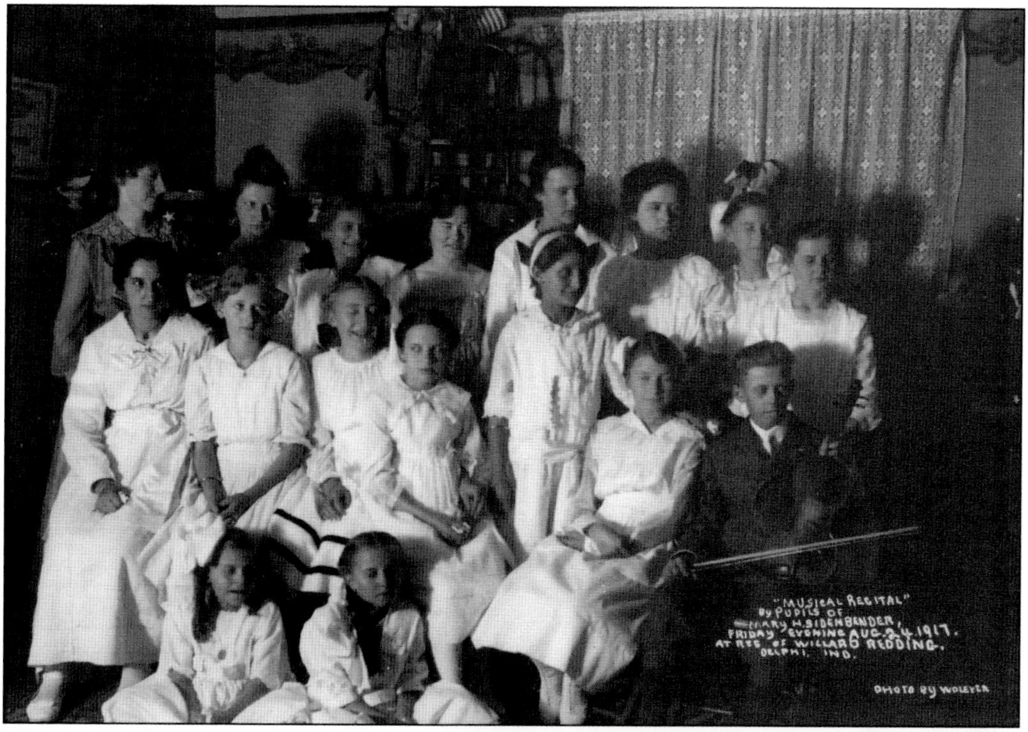

This group of young people, students of Mary Sidenbender, is shown at their recital in the home of William Redding in 1917. Note the stringed instrument in the hands of the only boy pupil.

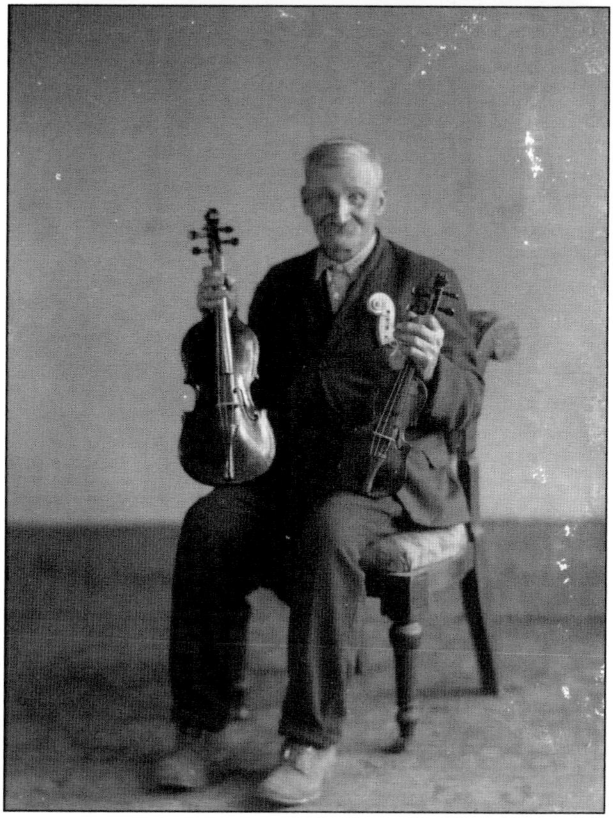

A skilled craftsman, James Calvin Kerlin (1836–1913) fashioned the cases of his violins from various fruitwoods, some of which were brought as starts from trees in his birthplace of Juniata County, Pennsylvania. While he could not play the violin, he could detect even subtle changes in the tonal values produced from different woods. On weekends, he would bring violins, produce, and fruit to Delphi from his home and workshop nearby on the Carrollton Road.

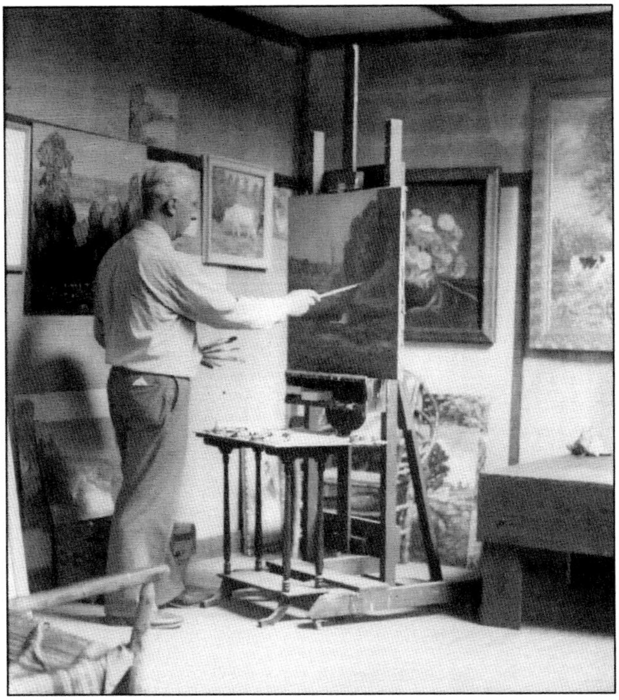

A telegraph operator for the Monon Railroad in Delphi, Leroy "Roy" Trobaugh (1878–1959) was a self-taught artist. He painted landscapes and still lifes in a style known as Brown County American Impressionism. With his free railroad pass, Trobaugh traveled extensively throughout the states and painted about 500 canvasses, many of which were given away locally. Another important local artist was Harry Milroy (1867–1935), noted for his sketches and sculptures.

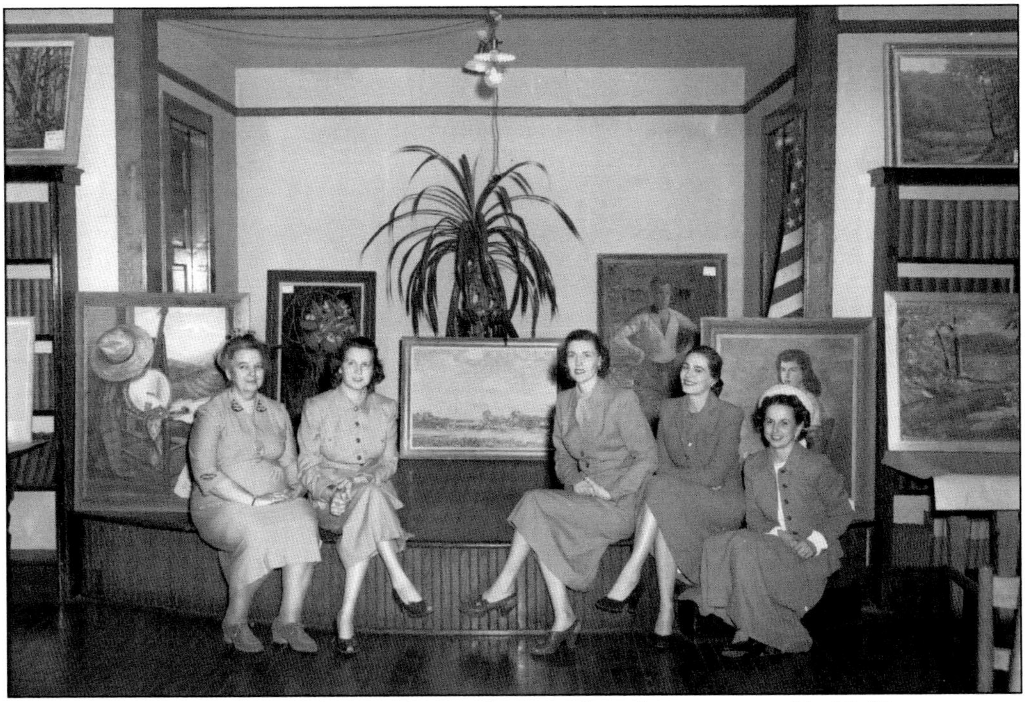

The importance of art in Delphi is evident in the annual art shows sponsored by Tri Kappa sorority and the school for many years. Psi Iota Xi is also a vigorous local arts supporter. The Delphi Art Club has been active since the 1950s and sponsors an annual show in the courthouse rotunda during the Old Settlers celebration. The community has been fortunate to have a number of outstanding art teachers.

Folsom Prison is playing at the Roxy Theater in this detail view. The Roxy was located on the north side of the square from about 1941 to the mid-1970s, when the theater building was torn down. It was Delphi's last movie theater. In the early 1900s, the Star Theater was located in this same quarter block in the Bradshaw building. Earlier movie houses included the Arc on the south side of the square. The Lyric Theater was in the Swegman building on Washington Street south of Main Street from about 1909 to at least 1912. (Courtesy Carroll County REMC.)

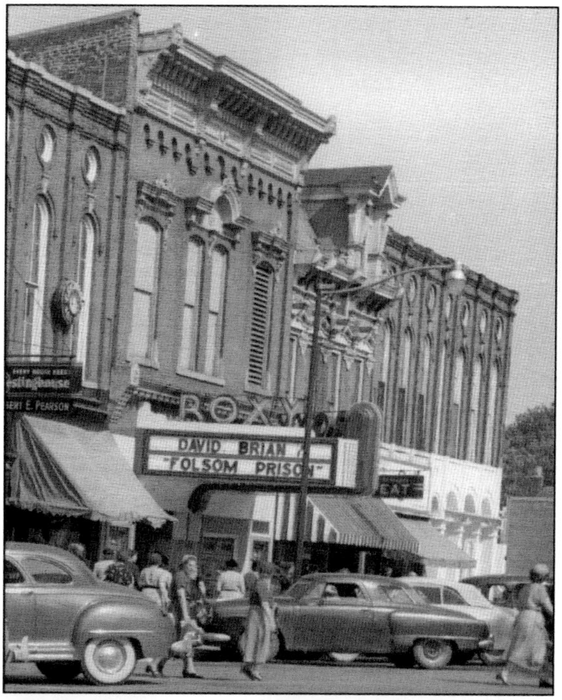

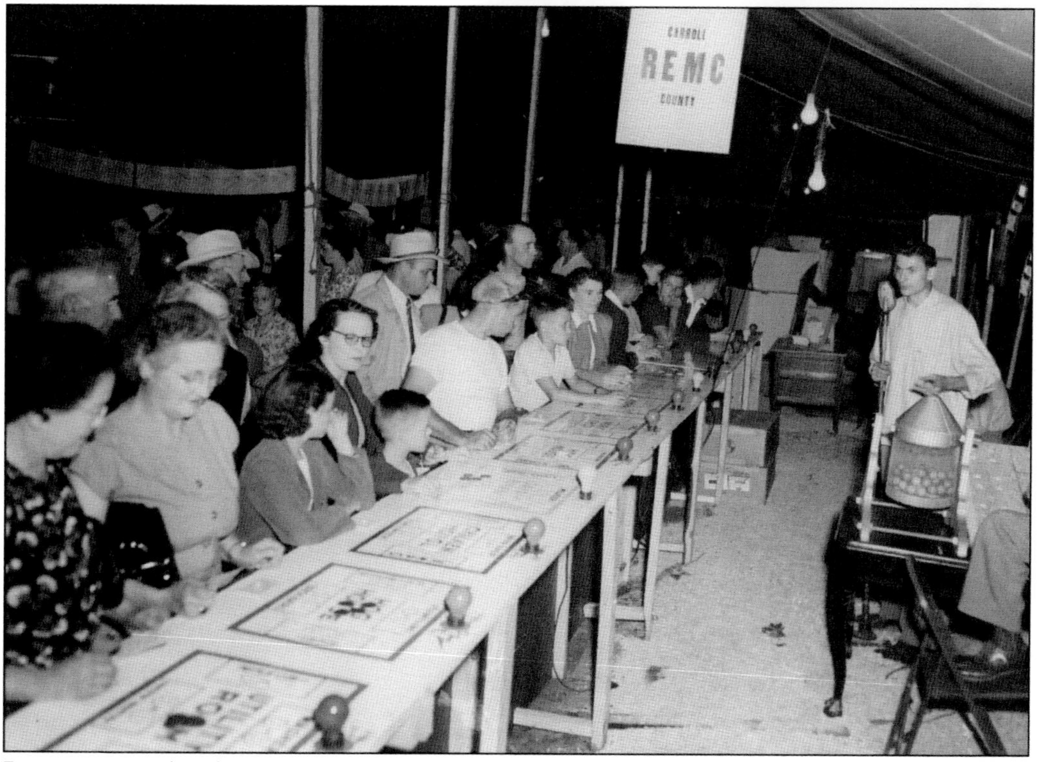

Bingo was another favorite entertainment. Here Ed Wingerd calls numbers at a Carroll County REMC event in the 1950s. Bingo was always offered in a tent on the square during Old Settlers. (Courtesy Carroll County REMC.)

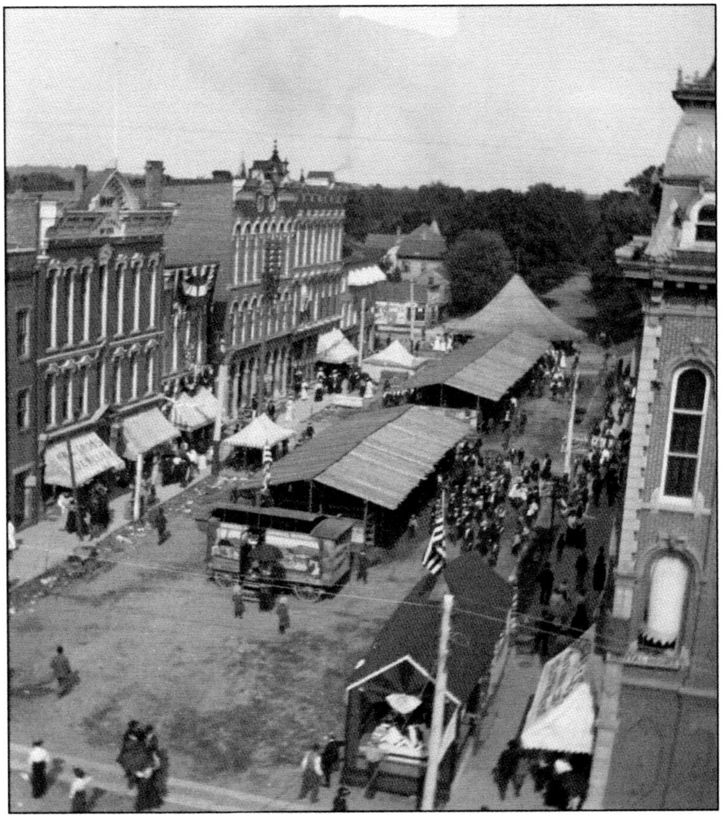

Free street fairs became annual events in the late 1800s. Merchants sold their wares, often in front of their own stores. Carnival vendors hawked goods from wagons or presented sideshows in colorful tents. Hot air balloon ascensions and daredevil acts were part of the fun. Over time, the homecoming gathering held in conjunction with the annual meeting of the Carroll County Old Settlers Association developed into a street fair. Having met continuously since 1855, Old Settlers is the oldest organization of its kind in Indiana. The celebration begins the first Wednesday in August and runs through that Saturday night.

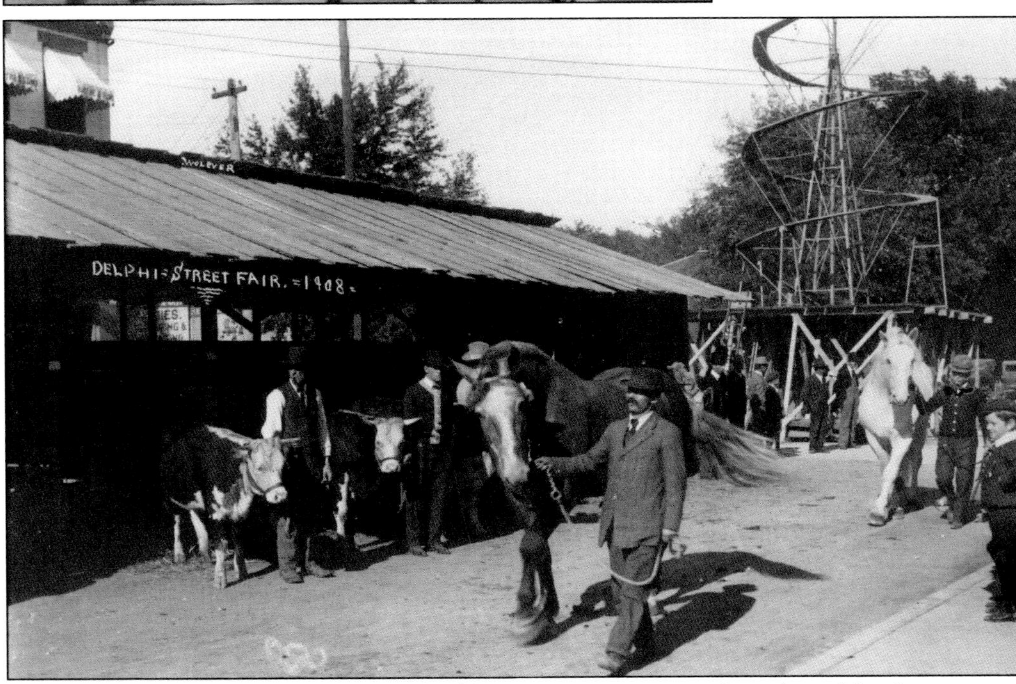

Livestock were displayed, reviewed, and sold, sometimes in covered pavilions like those seen in this 1908 county fair photograph. A track for a daredevil act is shown in the street behind.

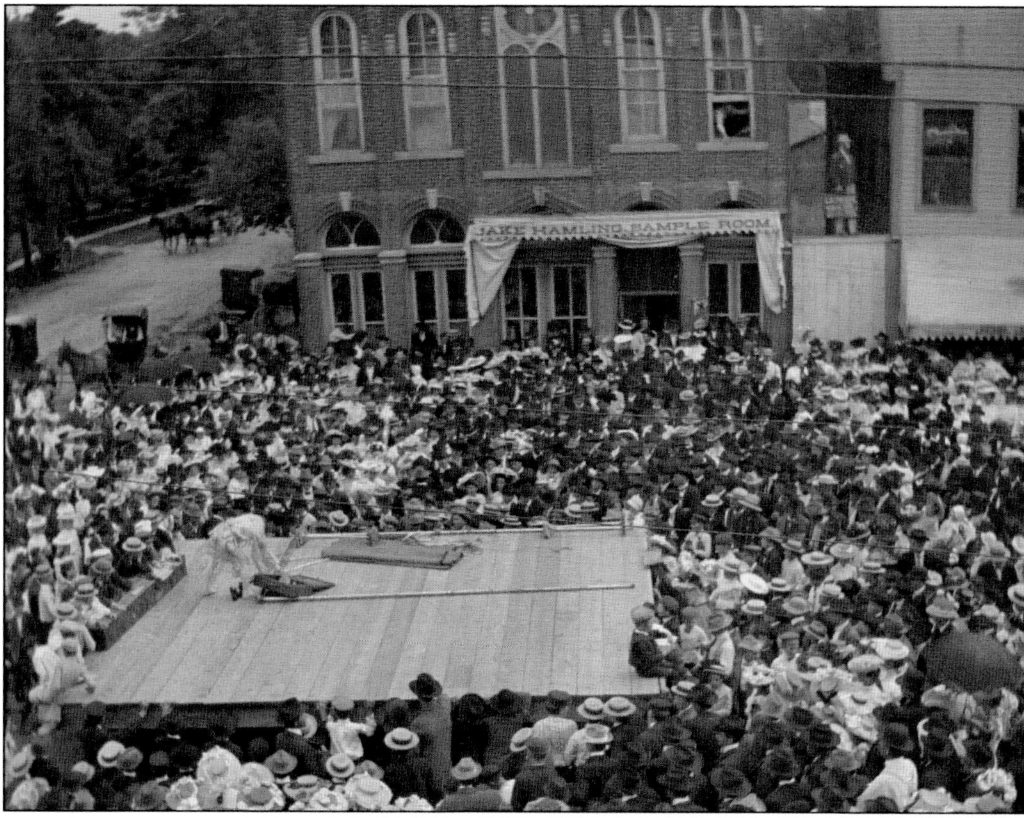

A trapeze artist is setting up on the stage in front of Jake Hamling's Tavern and Sample Room at the corner of Union and East Main Streets. A large crowd has already gathered in order to get a good viewing spot for the performance.

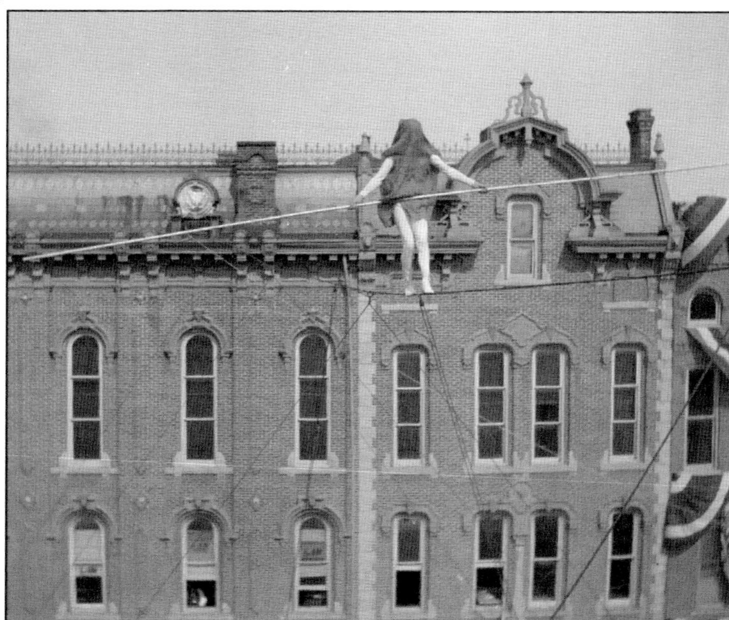

In this amazing photograph, a hooded tightrope walker is caught mid-trip on his way from the Washington Street side of the Odd Fellows building to the Moore block across the street. This surely qualifies as a daredevil stunt!

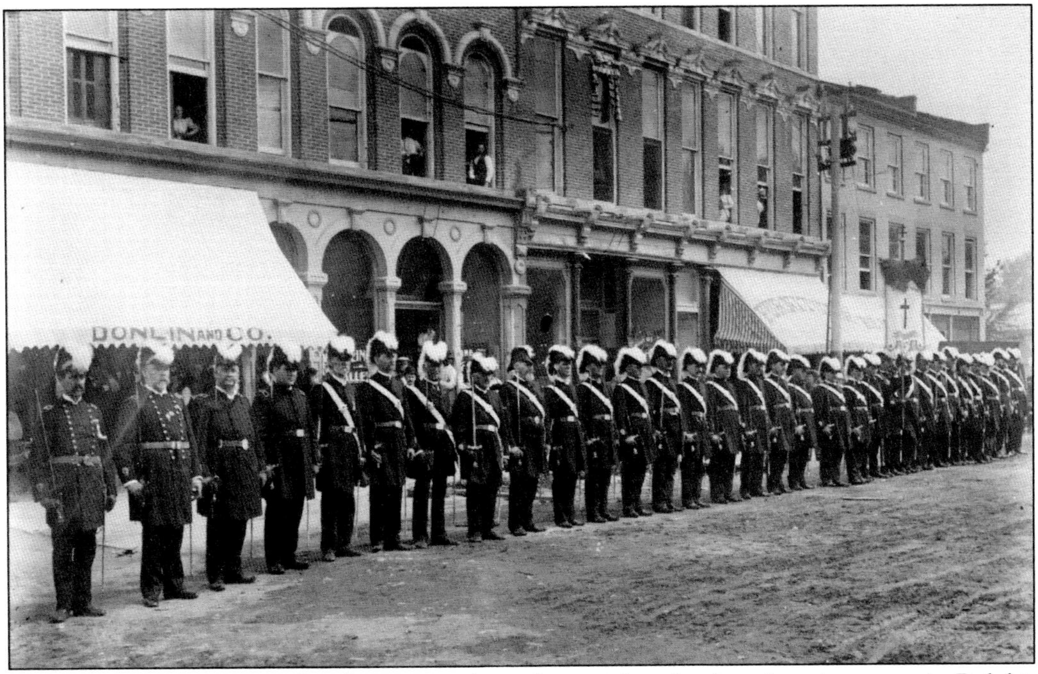

Benevolent organizations played a major role in the social and cultural environment in Delphi. Above, the Knights Templar are lined up for review in full uniform in the late 1800s. The north side of East Main Street in the background shows Donlin Grocery. Blythe Furniture store is farther down the street, located there 79 years until 1971. Previously, it was across Union Street at Main for nearly three decades. It began in 1860 by James Blythe after his emigration from Scotland and was maintained by three generations.

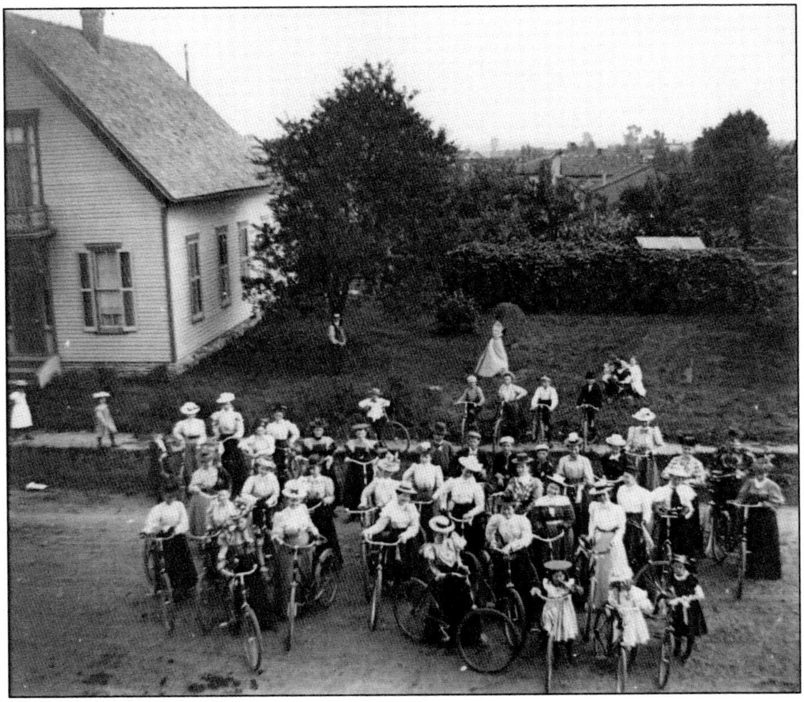

Delphi women formed a bicycle club in 1890. The bicycle was an important liberating force for women, providing an independent means of travel. The bicycle also led to changes in women's fashion to allow greater freedom of movement.

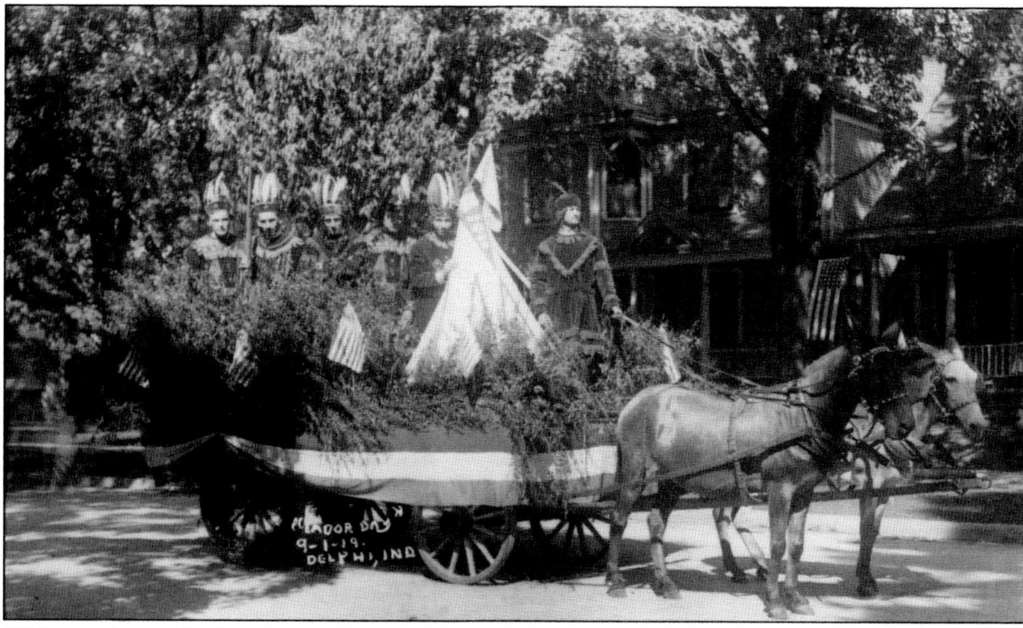

Welcome home! Labor Day on September 1, 1919, was an elaborate homecoming celebration to honor the troops who had served in the First World War. Buildings, vehicles, floats, and houses were decorated for the occasion. Crowds at the homecoming were estimated between 10,000 and 15,000. Neighborhood streets were clogged with parked cars and trucks of those streaming into town for the ceremonies. Each township created a float representing a different period of American history. The Order of the Red Men, an early patriotic and benevolent organization, rode on Clay Township's float illustrating the "Coming of the Indians." Religious, fraternal, and social organizations as well as businesses paraded their floats while community bands from Deer Creek, Flora, and Delphi provided music.

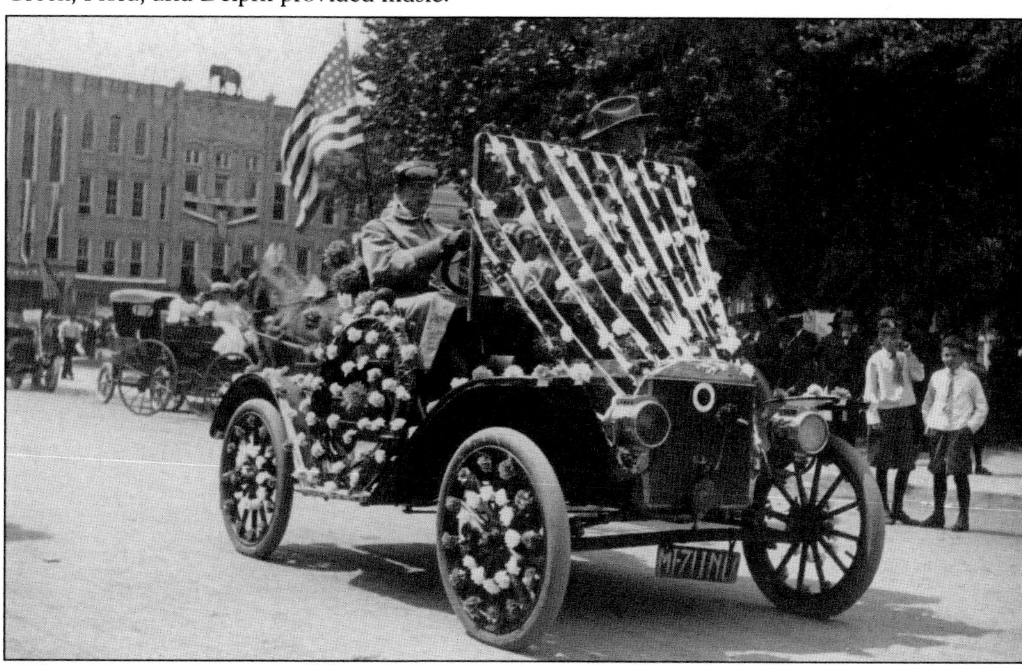

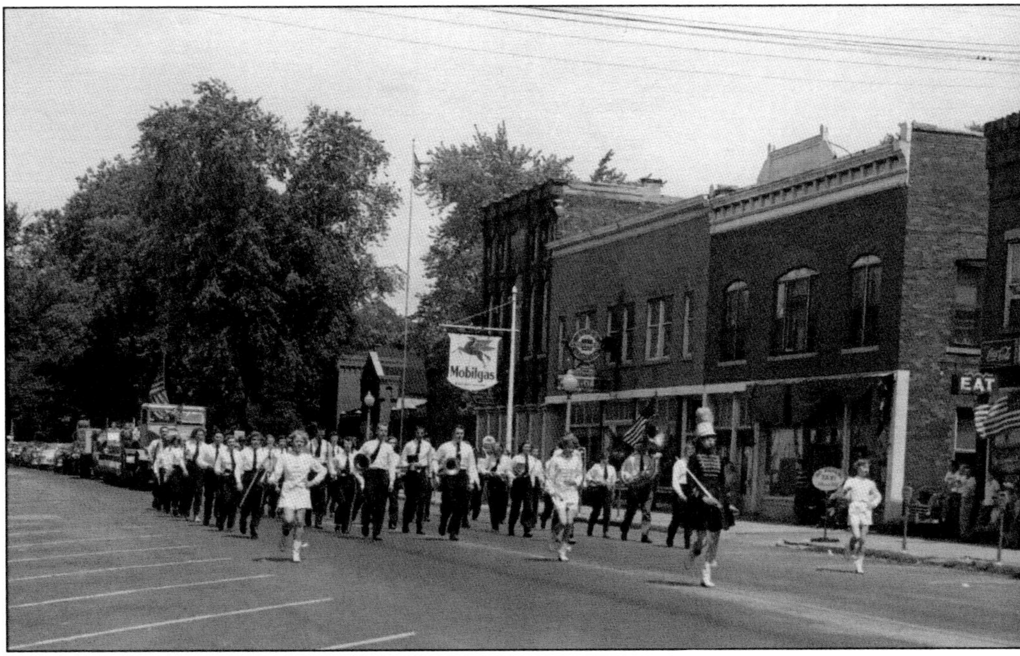

Fourth of July and Christmas parades are still important events in Delphi, kept alive by service organizations such as the Delphi Lions Club and enthusiastic community participation. There is always a reviewing stand on the courthouse square, commentary, prizes, and music. Leading the Fourth of July parade in 1950 was the Delphi High School marching band. Below, a float sponsored by the Carroll County REMC promotes modern electric appliances.

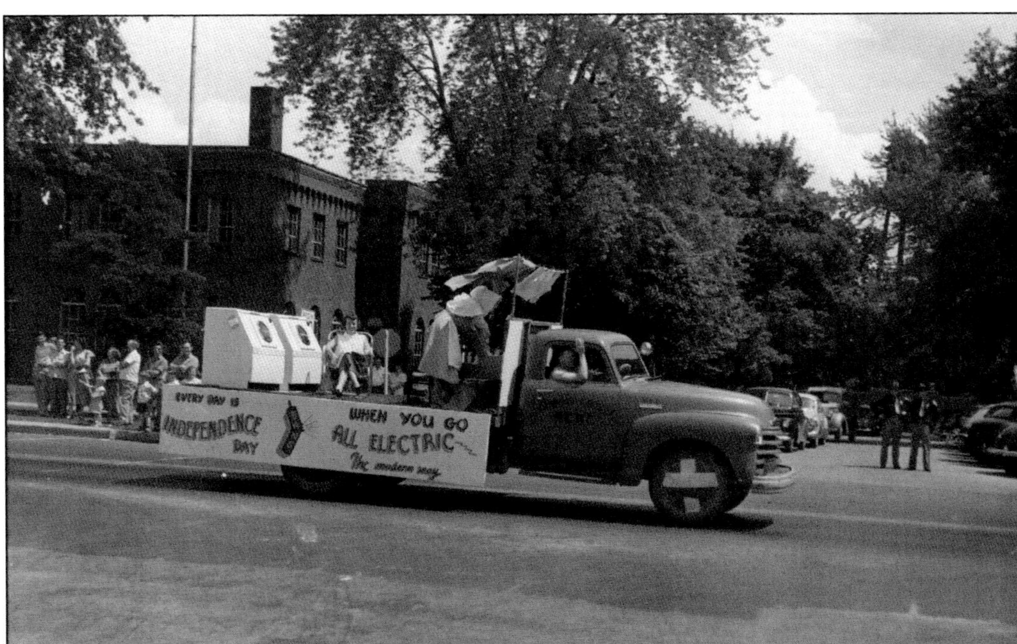

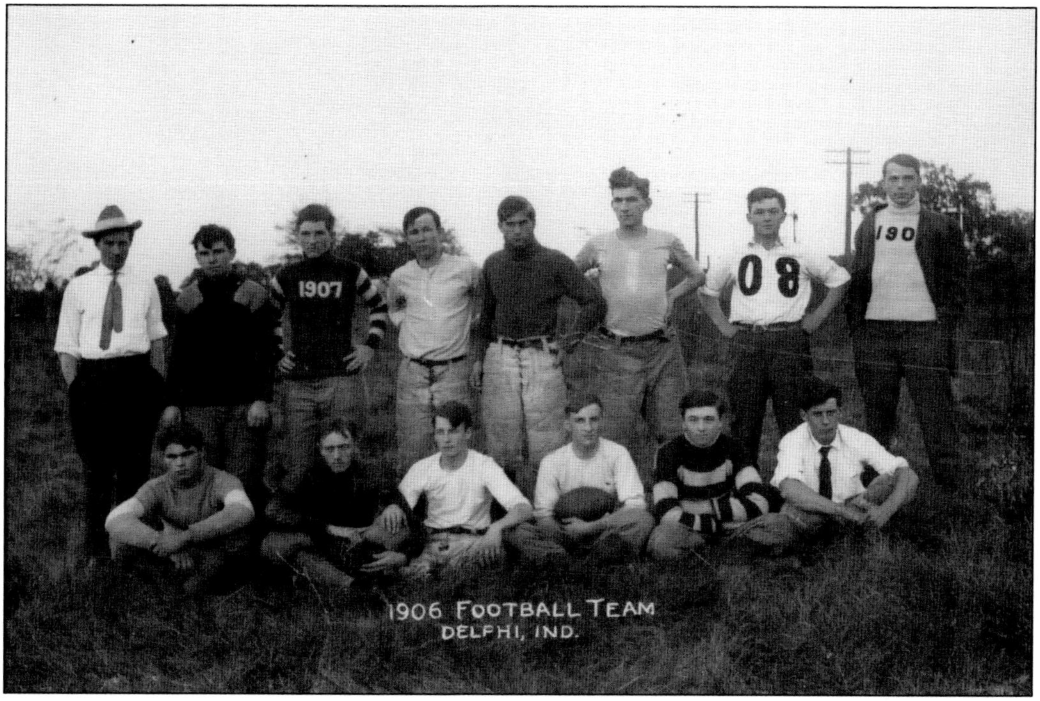

School athletics have long been an important source of entertainment and community pride in Delphi. As the film *Hoosiers* demonstrated so well, small-town teams can triumph against the odds. Such was the case when the Oracles sent basketball teams to the state finals several times in the 1920s and 1930s.

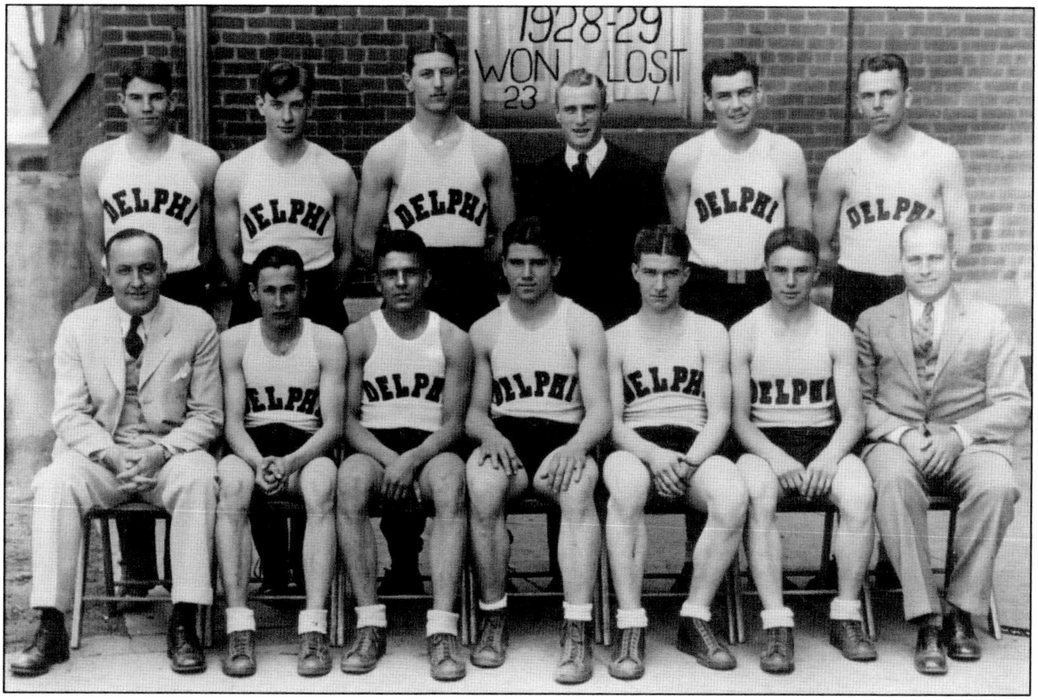

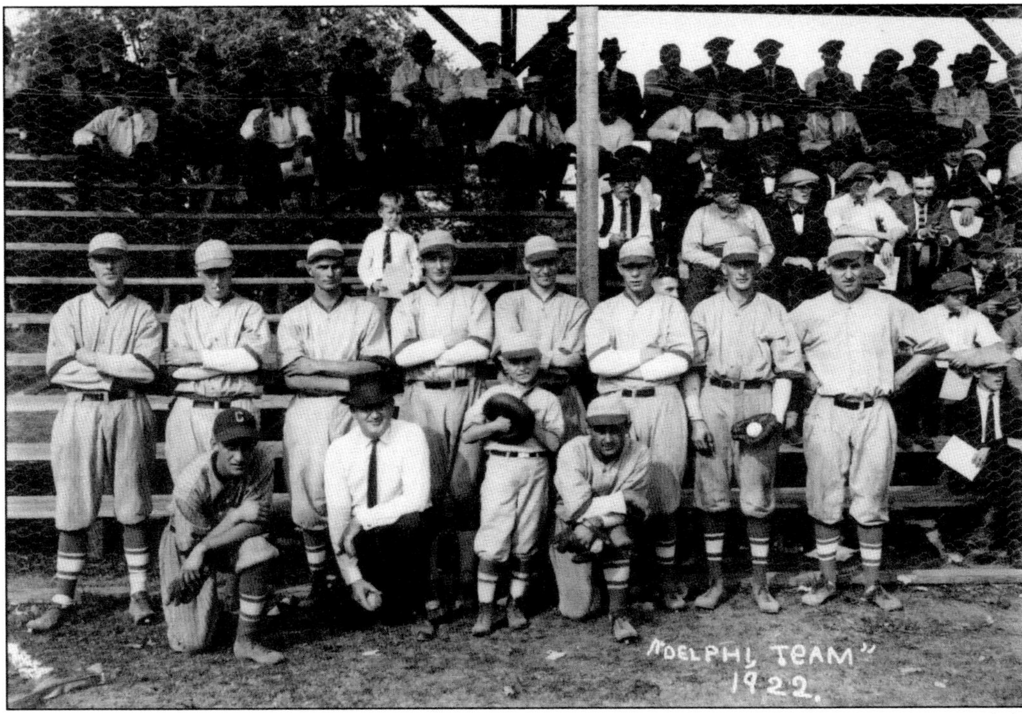

The nation's pastime was popular in Delphi as these two photographs show. The 1922 Delphi baseball team undoubtedly inspired the "Little Giants" posing on the courthouse square in 1924. Every tiny town had a team, and the competition was fierce from the 1890s on.

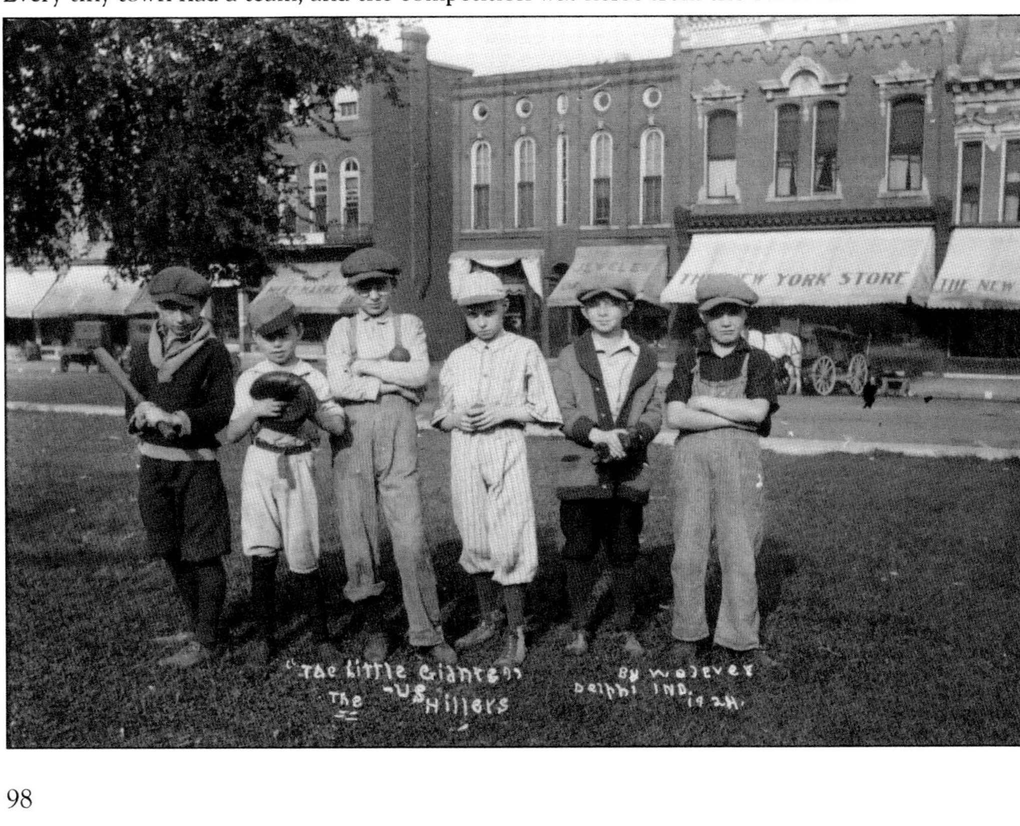

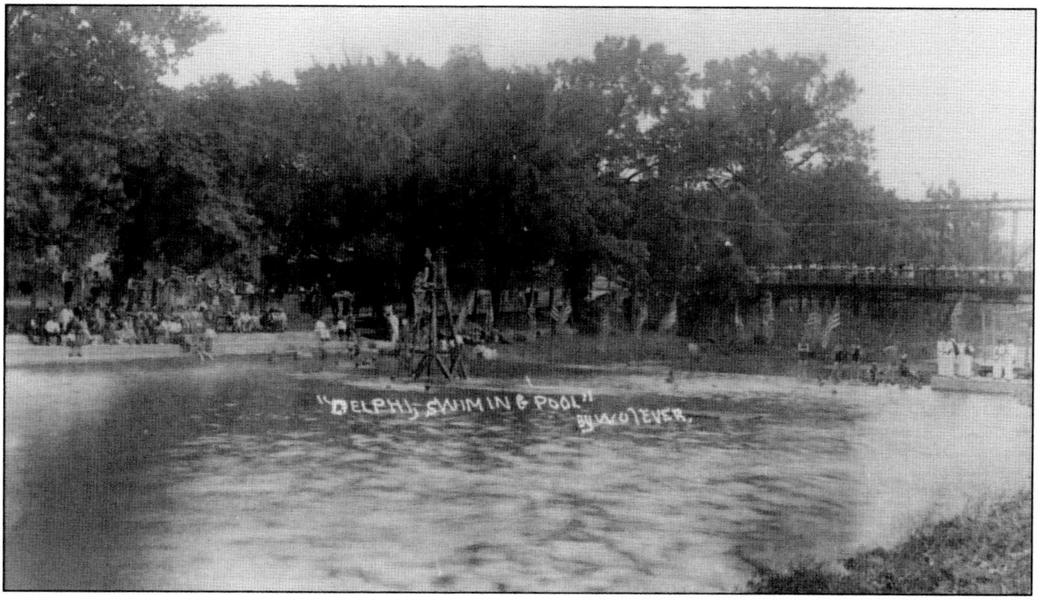

A dam was built across Deer Creek in 1925 to create a swimming pool near the Washington Street Bridge. More than 500 people attended the opening. Unfortunately, the dam washed out the next year. In 1930, it was rebuilt by Sutton Van Pelt, contractor for the Oakdale Dam on the Tippecanoe River. Steps and a new bathhouse were constructed, and the Riley Memorial Swimming Pool reopened and became very popular, attracting visitors from a large area. The year 1930 also marked the beginnings of what would become Riley Park with formal gardens, a skating rink, and athletic facilities. The park was used heavily for reunions and other events, as it is today. Of course, Deer Creek and its banks have remained great venues for fishing, boating, strolling, and picnics.

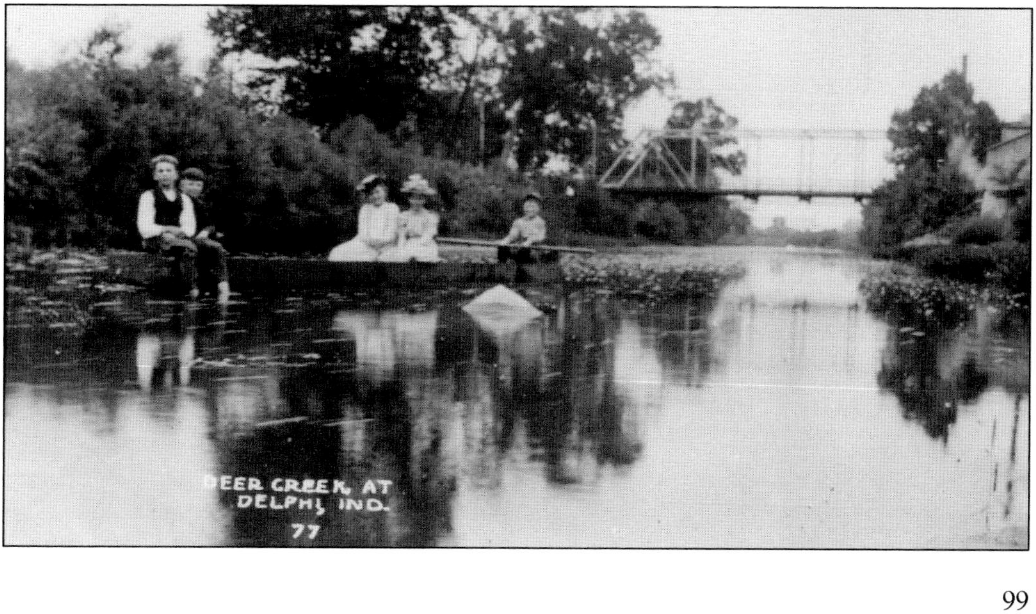

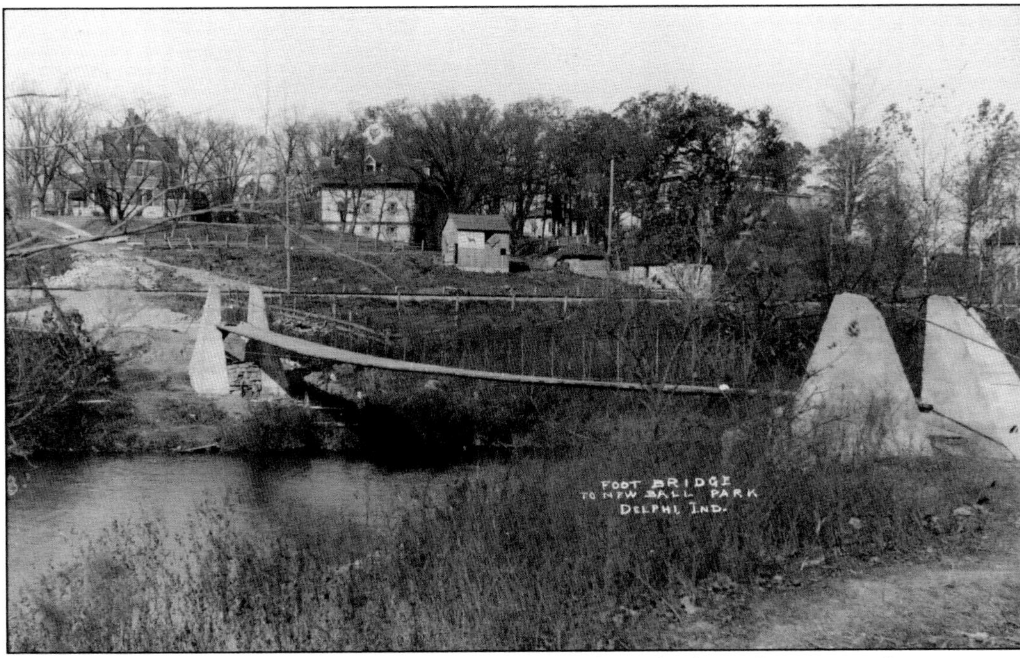

The first suspension pedestrian bridge across Deer Creek was built in 1911 to provide convenient access for students to the area developed later as Riley Park. The schools used the park for football, baseball, and track for many years. The bridge has fallen victim to flooding and has been rebuilt several times. It and the boardwalk along Deer Creek are included in the 10.5 miles of trails in the Delphi Historic Trails system.

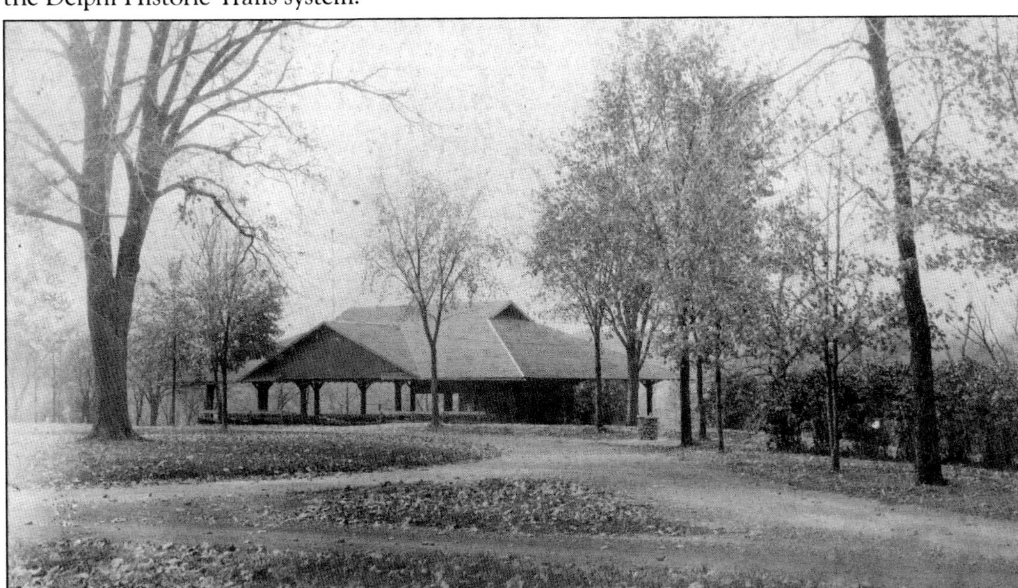

The shelter house at City Park was constructed in 1919 and stands relatively unchanged today. Franklin D. Roosevelt spoke here in his 1920 campaign stop. The park was first an Indian burial ground and the early cemetery for Delphi. After cemetery relocation, the area was developed as the school gardens in 1907. The Old Settlers annual meeting was held here for many years. The park is still heavily used.

Eight

Industry in the Rearview Mirror

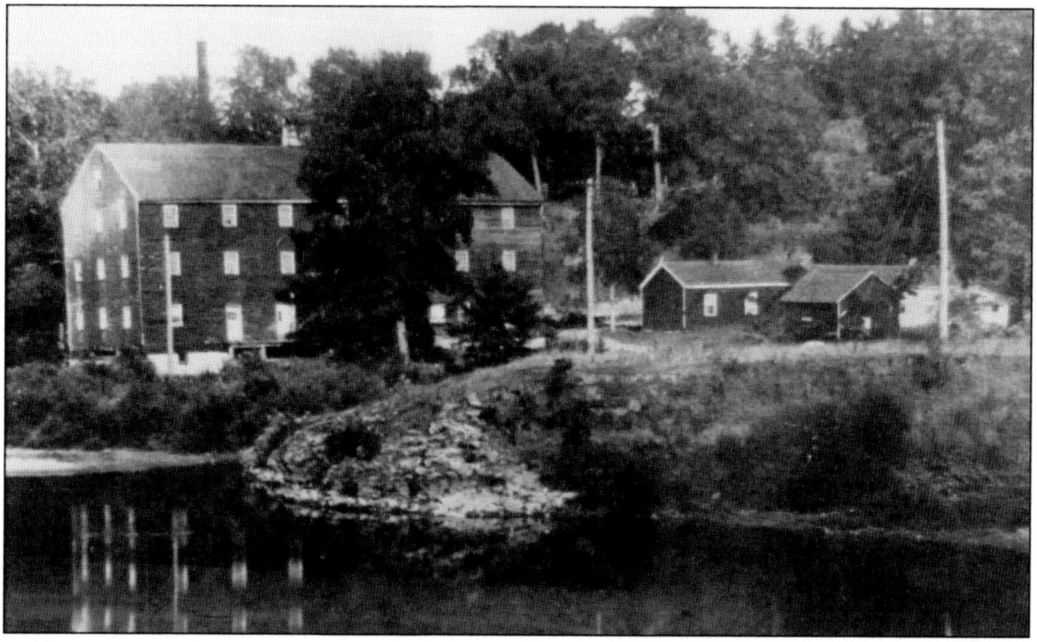

Mills were the earliest industries in Delphi, begun by first settler Henry Robinson. His son, Abner Robinson, designed their second mill (above) and headed construction until its opening in 1837. The Red Mill stood on the south bank of Deer Creek in what is now Riley Park. It was powered by water from a long race fed from a dam across Deer Creek. Wheat and corn were ground and exported in barrels made at the cooper shop. An attached sawmill generated lumber, and woodwork was made at the turning shop. Raw products were hauled down the steep Ox Hill road to the mill. The landmark structure was destroyed by fire in 1911.

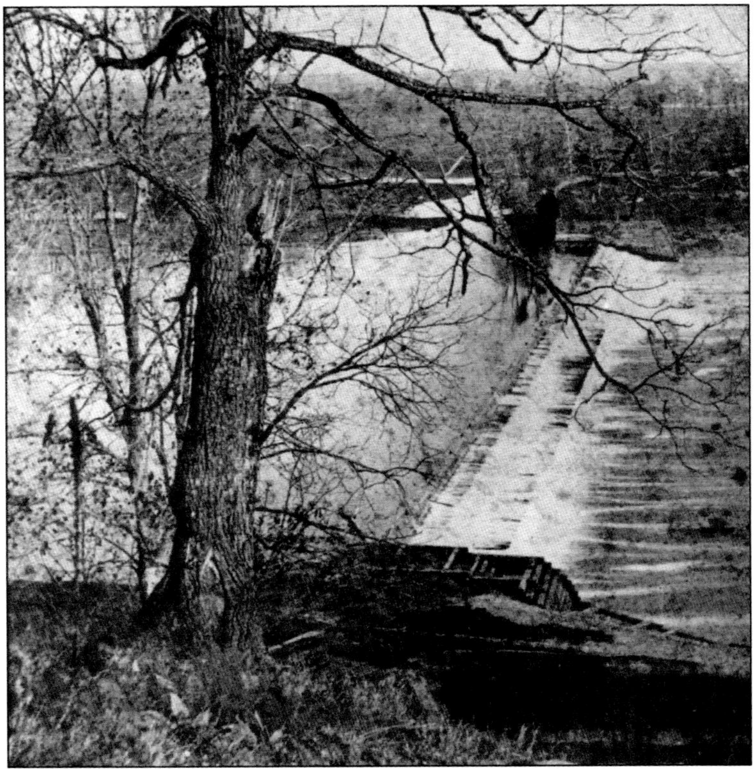

This 12-foot-high rock crib dam, completed in 1839 at Pittsburg northwest of Delphi, raised the water of the Wabash River to form a 6-mile-long lake. Its purpose was to divert water into the canal and to power local mills at Pittsburg and Delphi. At the bottom of the picture was the millrace with guard lock. To the top of the dam was the huge steamship lock built at the insistence of Logansport to gain riverboat access. It was used only once because rock outcroppings upstream made steamship travel impossible.

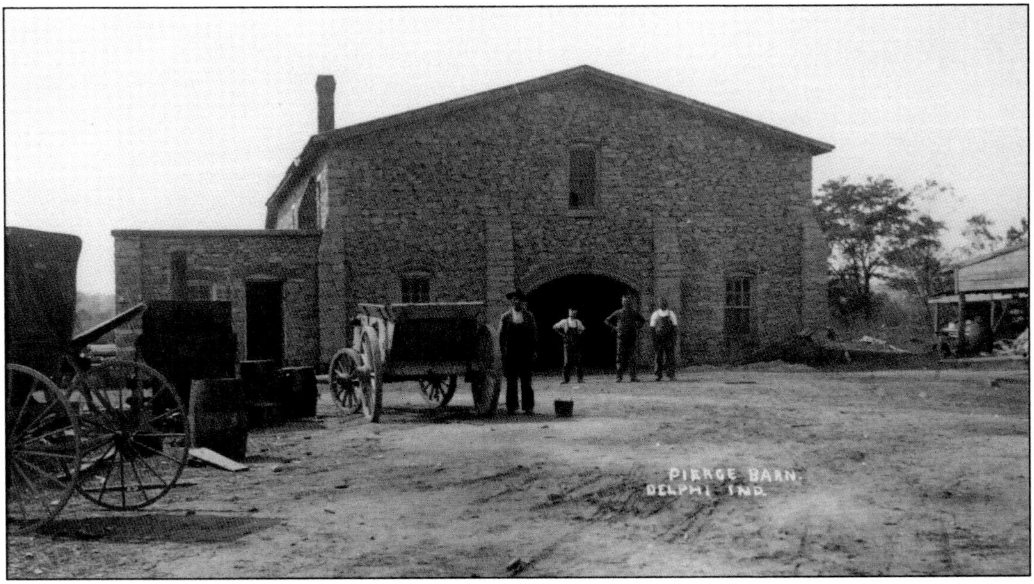

James M. Peirce built this stone barn in 1904 to house his road and bridge construction equipment. It later served Gustavel Furniture and Miami Produce and is now owned by the city and used as a senior center and parks office as well as home to the Delphi Lions Club.

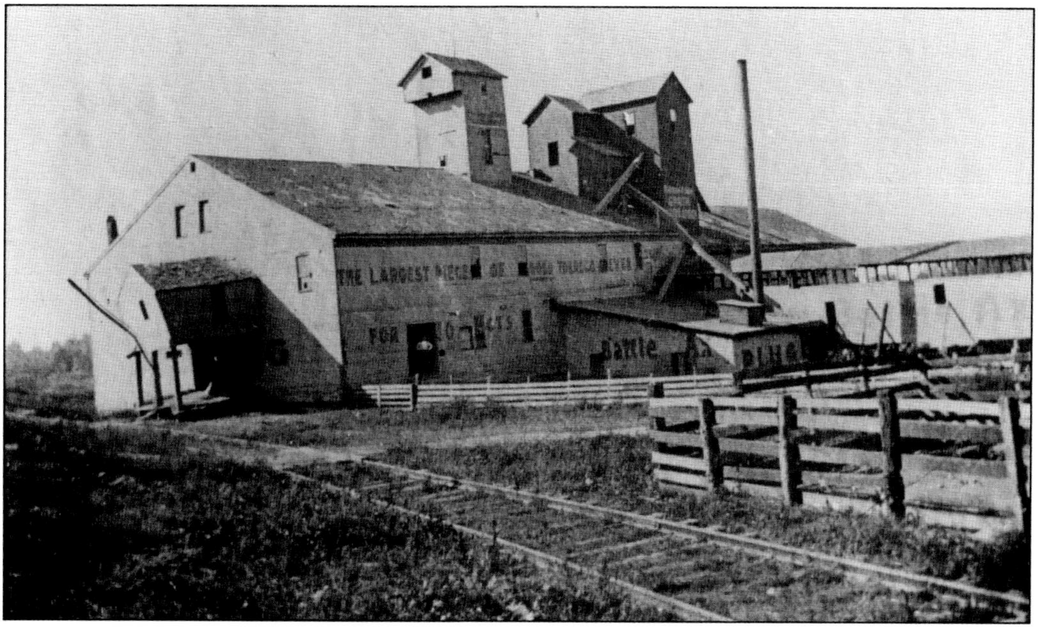

Kerlin and Son, established by Hiram Kerlin in 1880, operated one of several grain elevators in Delphi in the early 1900s. Another was Montman City Mills and its elevator, which was succeeded by Roach and Rathenbarger and then by Whiteman Brothers. Delphi's first elevator was built by Spears, Case and Company in 1845 on the canal side cut at West Main Street, and 100,000 to 300,000 bushels of grain per year were loaded onto canal boats at the warehouse. Later, grain was also loaded onto rail cars on the other side of the elevator. Kerlin's and Whiteman's elevators continued many years. Whiteman Brothers was the last to close in 2004 after 85 years in business.

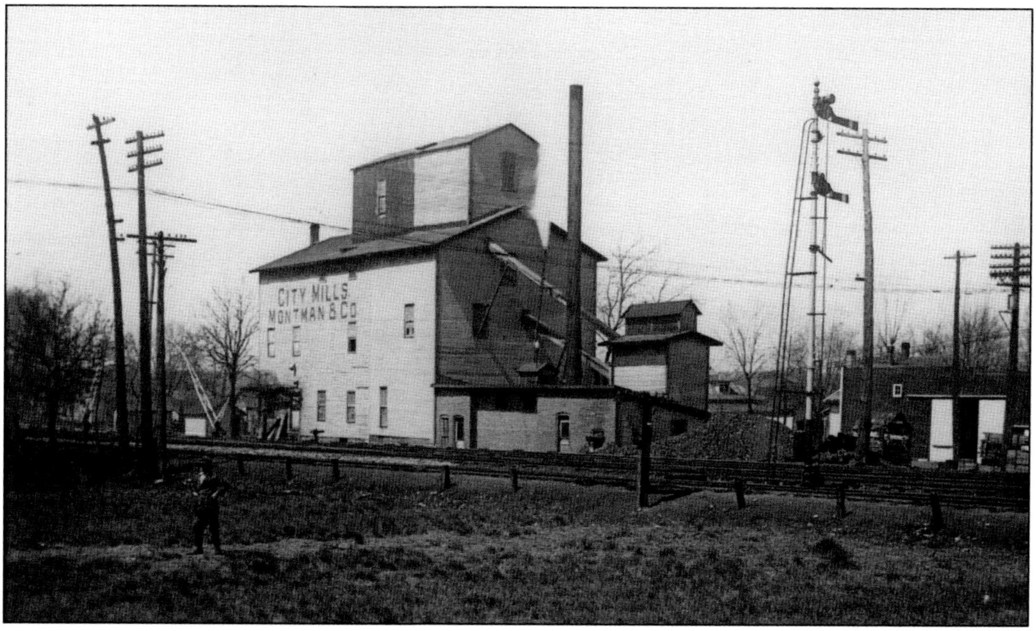

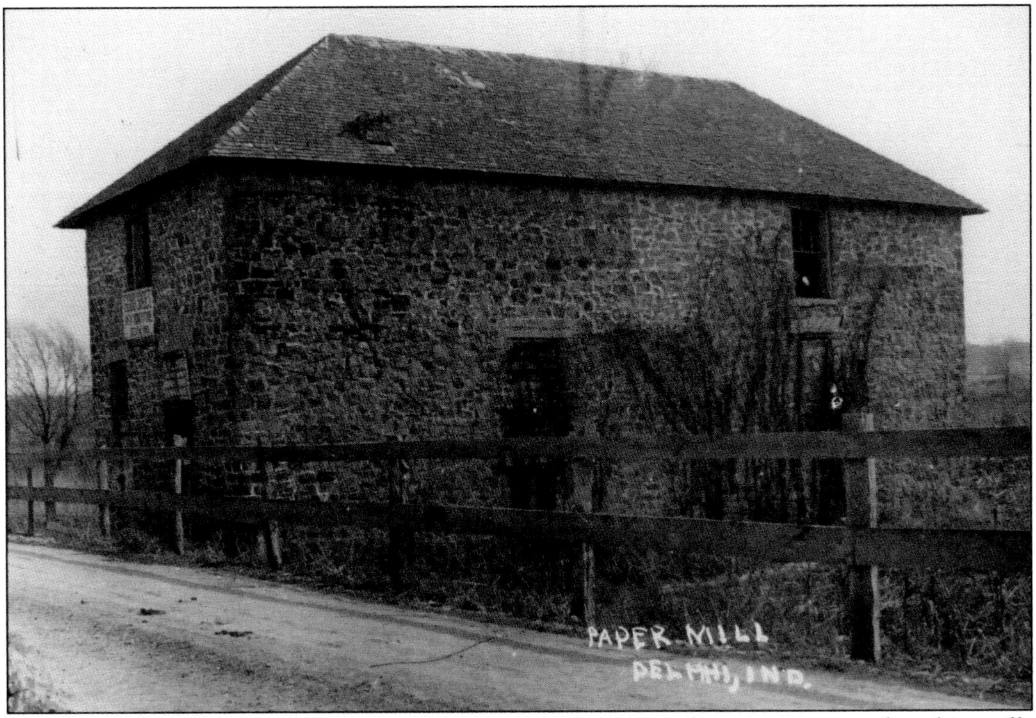

In the mid- to late 1800s Delphi was widely known for the quality rag paper produced in mills along the canal. This 1851 building owned by Enoch Rinehart and Charles Wood stood on the west side of the canal on the site of the George Robertson Paper Mill that had burned in 1849. Wood later sold his interest to A. H. Bowen. The mill could produce up to 2 tons of paper per day from discarded rags. The paper was prized for newspapers and general printing and survives in pristine condition today. Wagon-loads of paper were taken to Chicago, Cincinnati, and other cities, returning with loads of rag. Dependent on water from the canal, the mills ceased to operate in 1881, when the Pittsburg dam was destroyed.

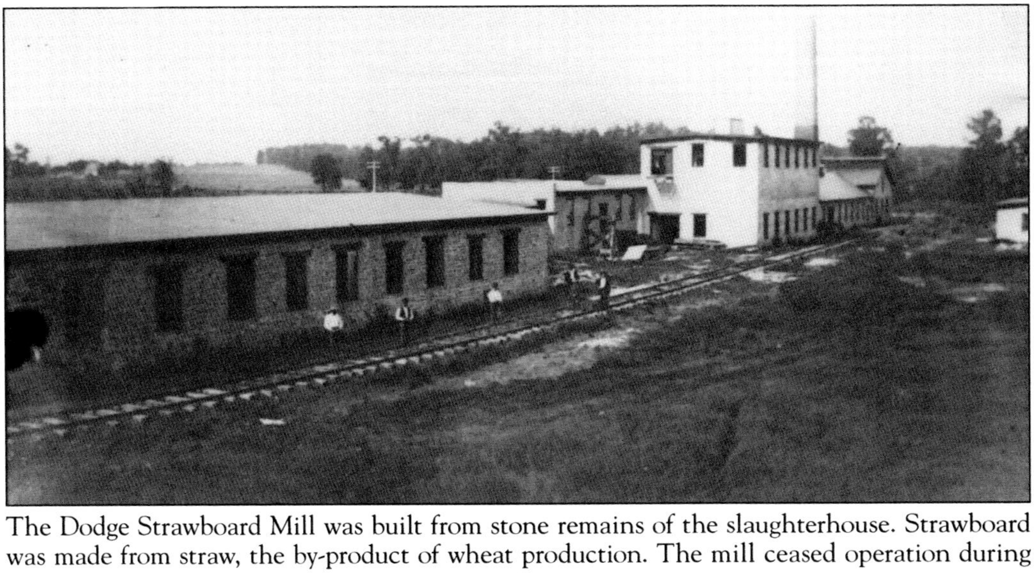

The Dodge Strawboard Mill was built from stone remains of the slaughterhouse. Strawboard was made from straw, the by-product of wheat production. The mill ceased operation during the Depression.

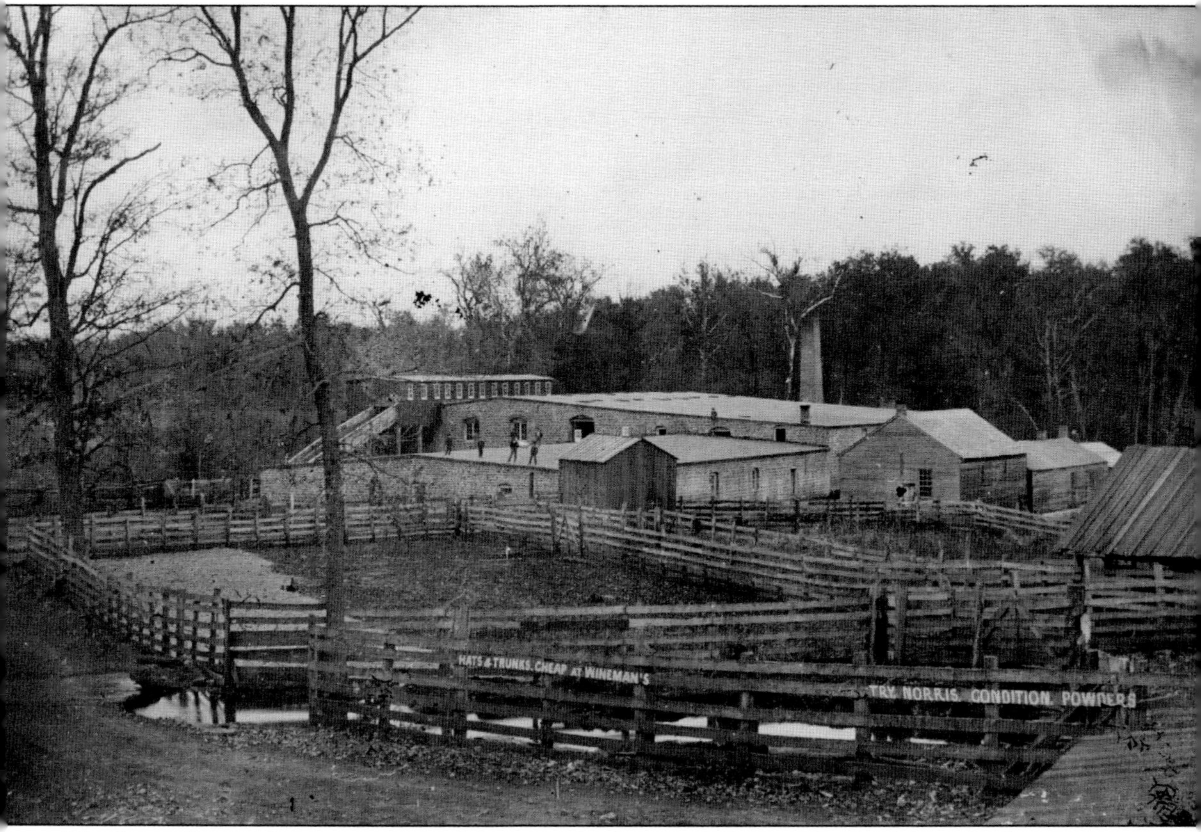

The Spears Dugan Company pictured above was built in 1863. During the Civil War, the firm was said to be the largest packinghouse in Indiana, slaughtering 1,000 hogs per day during packing season. The plant was located in east Delphi on Robinson's Run, which became known as "Gut Creek." Barrels of lard and pork were shipped by canal and rail until 1871. Packing plants had been located near the canal in the 1840s but were forced to move farther from downtown. Today Delphi is home to a modern pork-packing facility with Indiana Packers Corporation (IPC) south of town, employing over 1,600 people and processing 16,000 hogs daily. IPC is active in community affairs and is a generous supporter of many activities in this rural area.

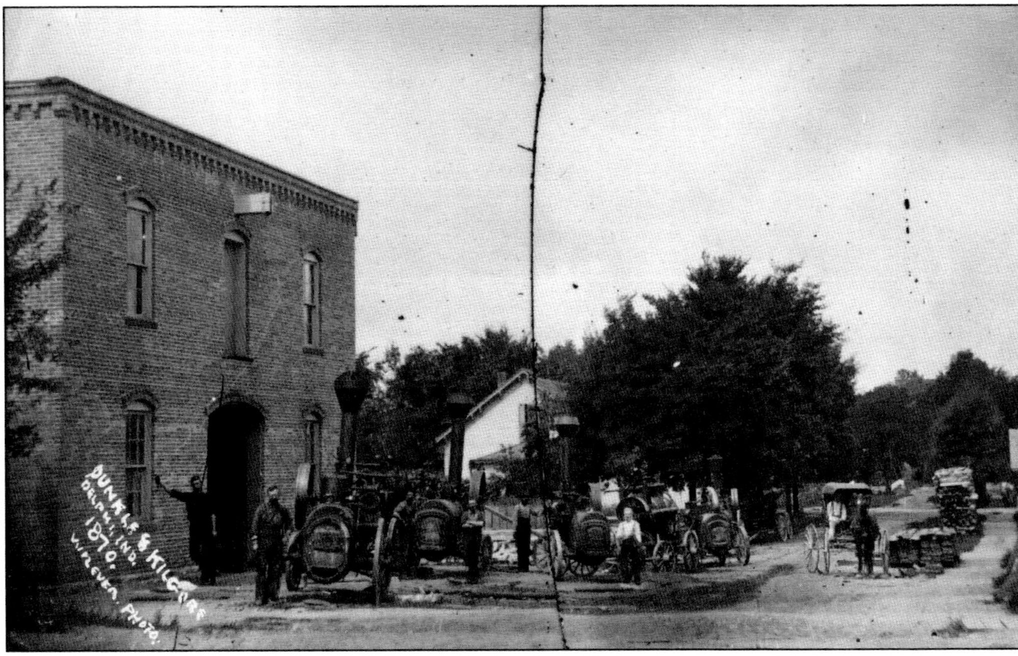

William Dunkle and James Kilgore began manufacturing the first plows and two-horse wagons made in this part of Indiana at Wilson and Franklin Streets in 1848. In the mid-1850s, they also opened a store to sell agricultural implements downtown. In 1872, a new brick building at the original site allowed them to build boilers and steam engines, including the steam-powered threshing machine shown above. The Little Corporal upright engine used in printing offices and other venues was another successful product. In 1879, Jacob Fisher and Lambert Hare bought the wagon business, making Fisher Wagons until 1888, when William Bradshaw bought out first Hare and later Fisher. Delphi Wagon Works produced the Delphi Wagon at the former Lew Moore Planing Mill south of downtown. It was already outfitted with much of the machinery necessary for wagon manufacture.

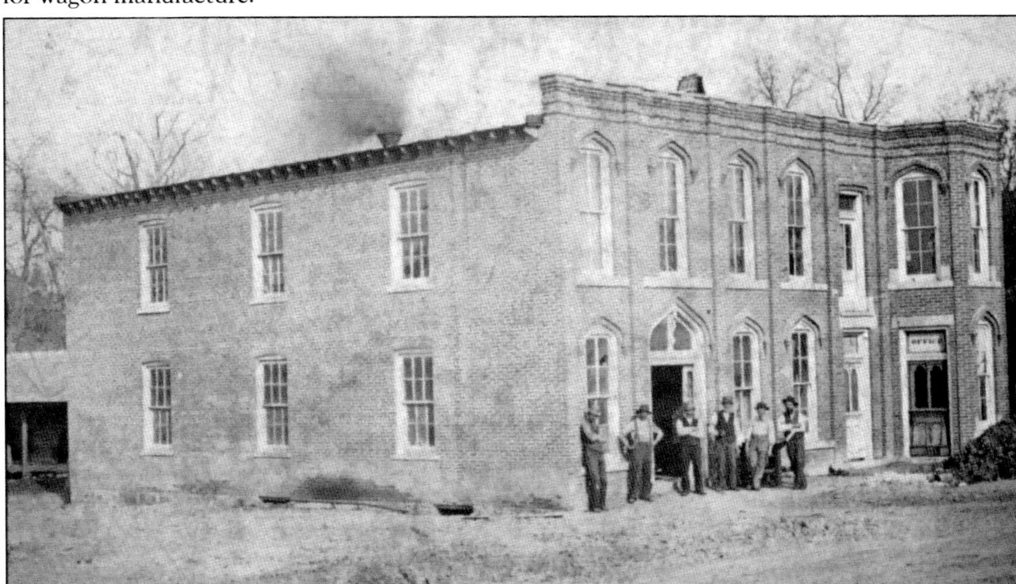

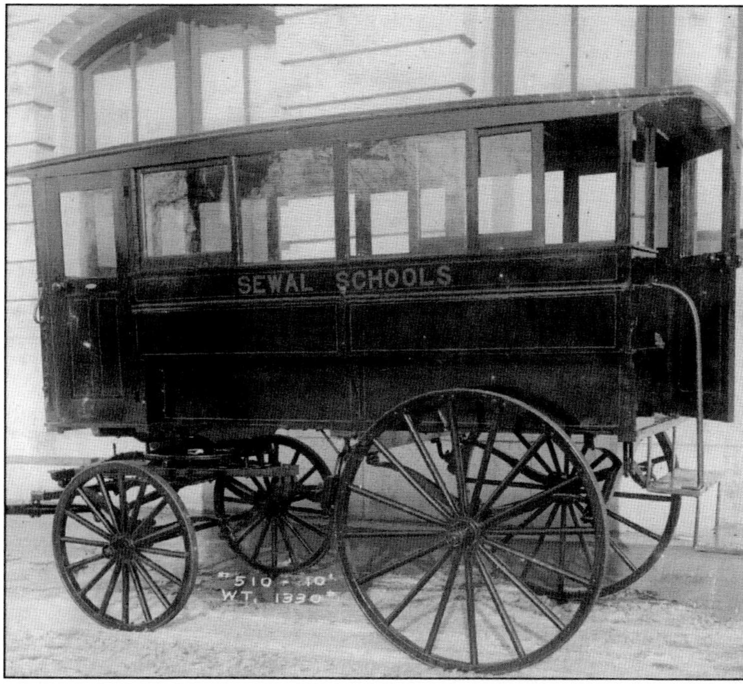

William Bradshaw's son, W. H., entered the business in 1895. In the late 1890s, Delphi Wagon Works manufactured lightweight wagons for mail delivery following the passage of the Rural Free Delivery Act. In 1899, they built a closed-body school wagon—the first such conveyance in the United States. School bus bodies for trucks became a major part of the business, and the company's name was changed to Delphi Body Works in 1929. (Photograph courtesy Delphi Body Works.)

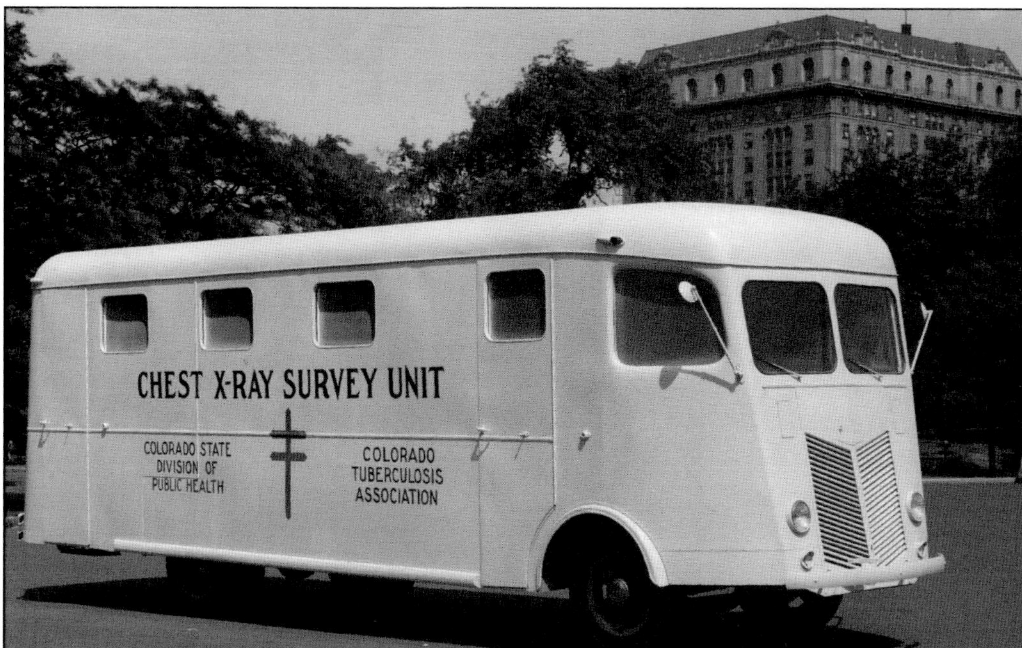

W. H. Bradshaw's son, Charles, became a partner, and in the 1930s, they began production of utility company service vehicle bodies, shifting construction from wood to steel. During World War II, the firm machined aircraft parts for the war effort and manufactured mobile X-ray units. In its 163rd year of operation, Charles's son, Richard, and grandson, Matthew, oversee production of utility truck bodies and lifts. It is the only Indiana company with such a long history. (Photograph courtesy Delphi Body Works.)

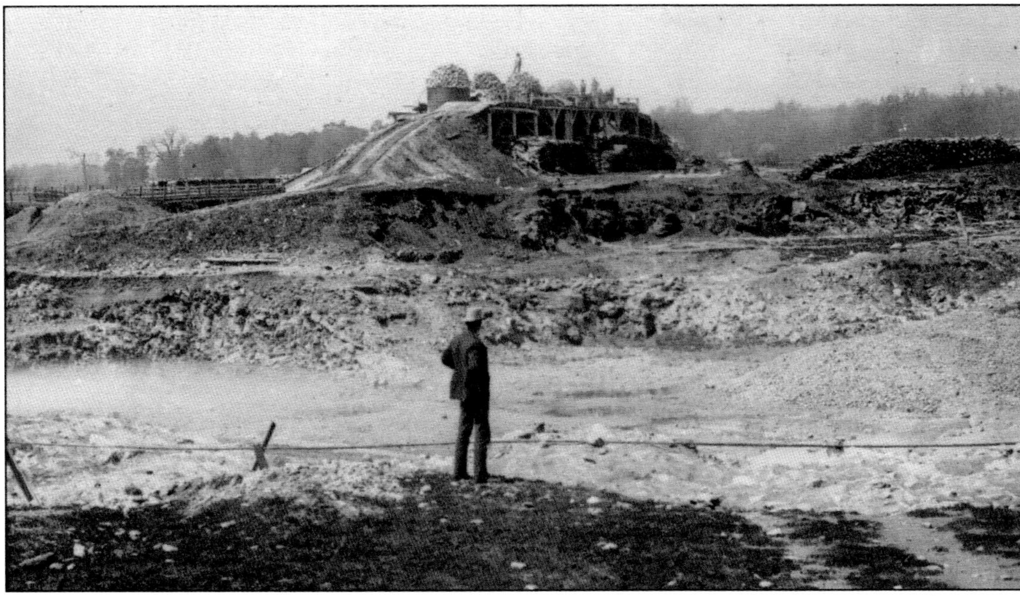

Delphi lime, prized for use in decorative plaster, was a major industry beginning in the 1850s. Huge stone kilns burned the lime down to the fine-sifted powder that was delivered to New York and Chicago by canal and rail. Dirt ramps and a platform allowed stone to be hauled to the top and packed into the kilns. Vast numbers of logs were needed to fire the Harley and Hubbard kilns. Land purchased south of Delphi kept 25 men employed year-round cutting logs. The Monon Railroad brought fuel from Harley Siding via a Belt Railway loop, which provided access to north Delphi industries.

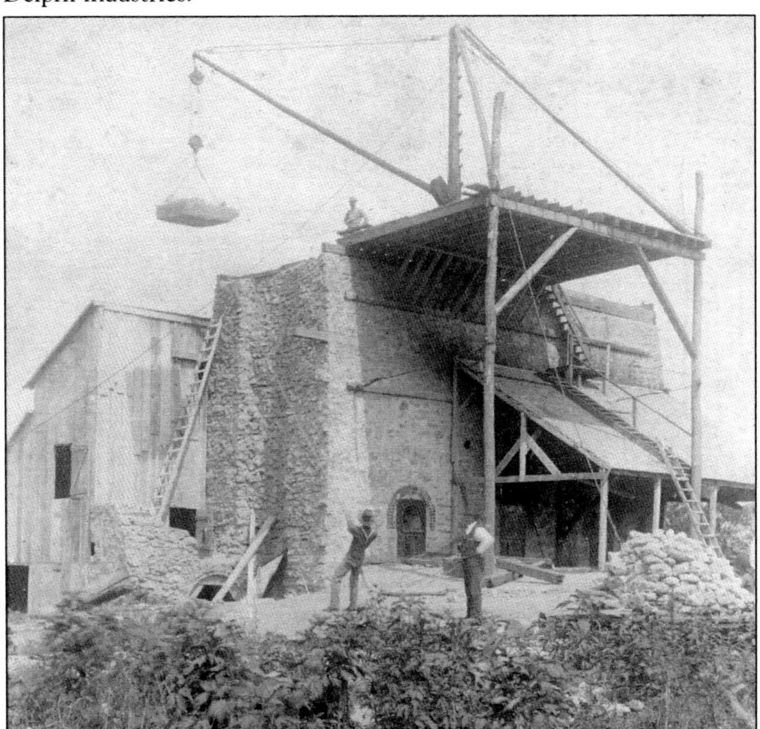

This kiln operation utilized a gin pole to hoist and dump stone. A replica kiln at the Wabash and Erie Canal Park Annex illustrates the importance of this industry. Local McCains descend from the Harley and McCain kiln owners.

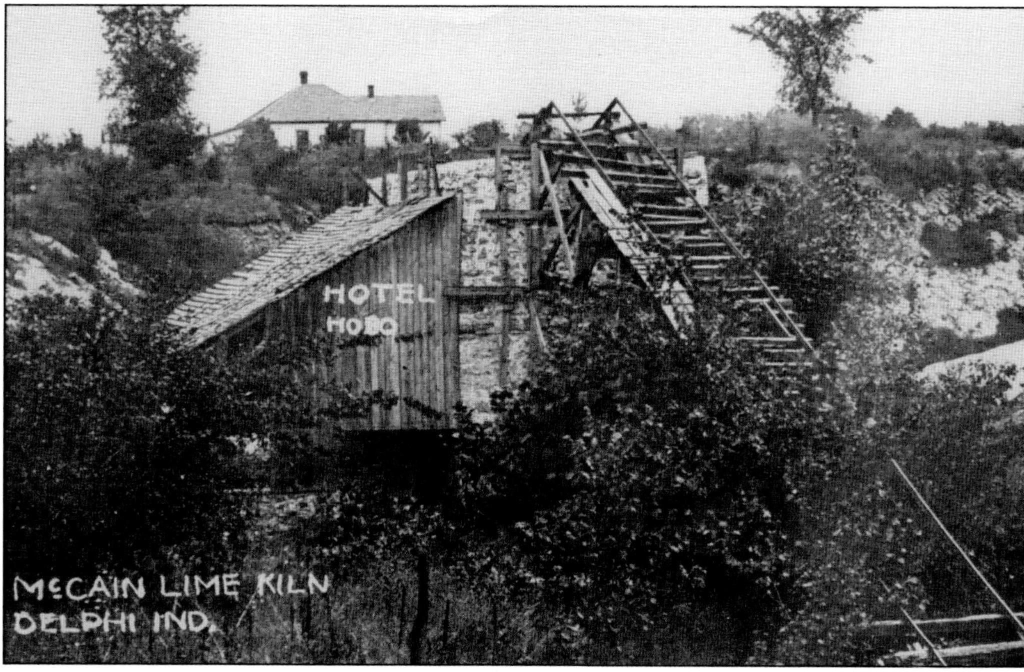

By 1917, the burning of lime for plaster was no longer a local industry, and the kilns fell into ruins. Other uses were found for Delphi's mineral resource, including the production of crushed stone and agricultural lime as shown in the photograph below. A crusher is used to break down the stone and to screen it to the particle size required for spreading. Crushed stone is also graded in sizes required for many uses, including road production, railroad beds, foundation fill, and erosion control. In 1944, Edgar Stuntz and Dale Yeoman began a quarry west of Delphi. In the 1950s, Stuntz became the sole owner, changing the name to Delphi Limestone Company. The quarry operation is owned today by U.S. Aggregates and continues as a major industry and valued corporate citizen.

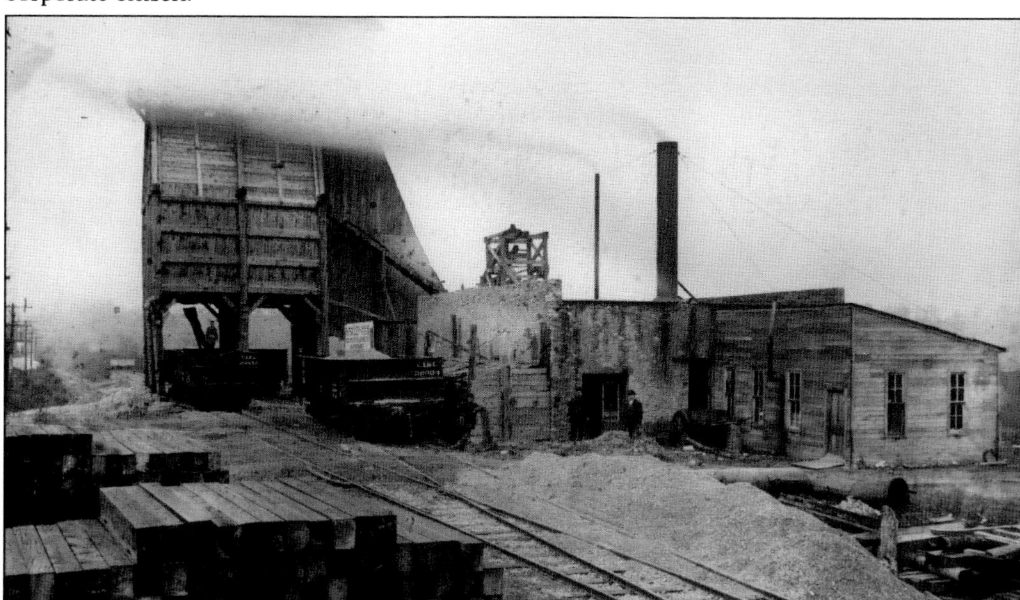

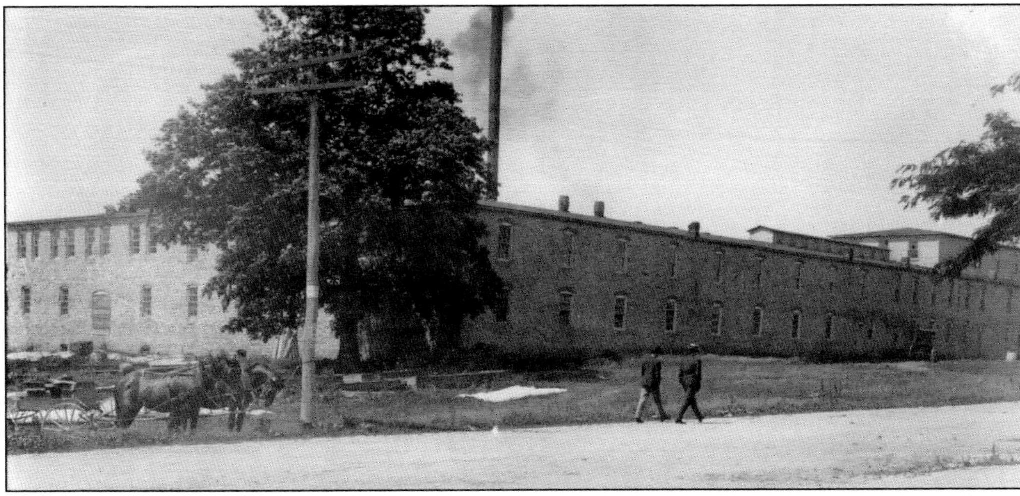

The Great Western Canning Factory operated seasonally in Delphi from 1903 to 1946, employing as many as 75 workers. Local produce was packed and shipped by rail to distribution centers. Fire destroyed the plant in 1914 and the warehouse in 1928, but the locally owned business was rebuilt each time.

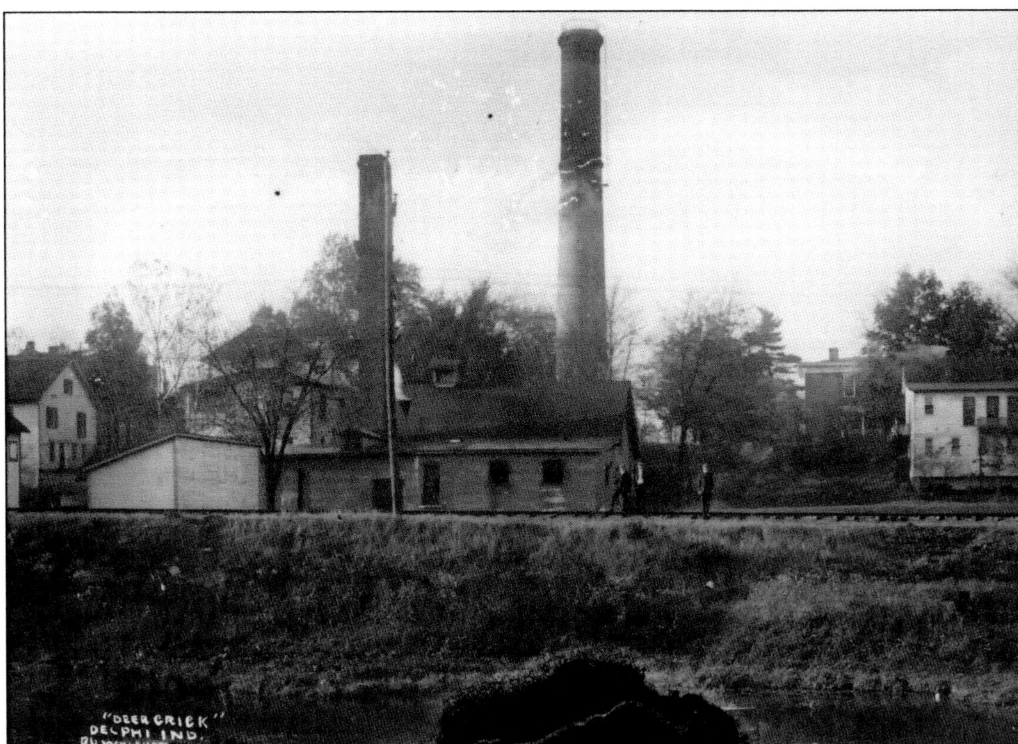

The water works facility and tower were erected in Delphi in 1891 at a total cost of $40,000. A. W. Wolever was mayor at the time the system was planned. The tower was 111 feet tall and 25 feet in diameter at the base, with the brick portion measuring 75 feet high. The water tank was 36 feet in height with a capacity of 15,000 gallons. A second tank inside the brick tower at the bottom was filled by gravity flow from Snyder Springs. The pumping station took water to the upper tank. The water tower was torn down in 1922 after the installation of a metal water tower.

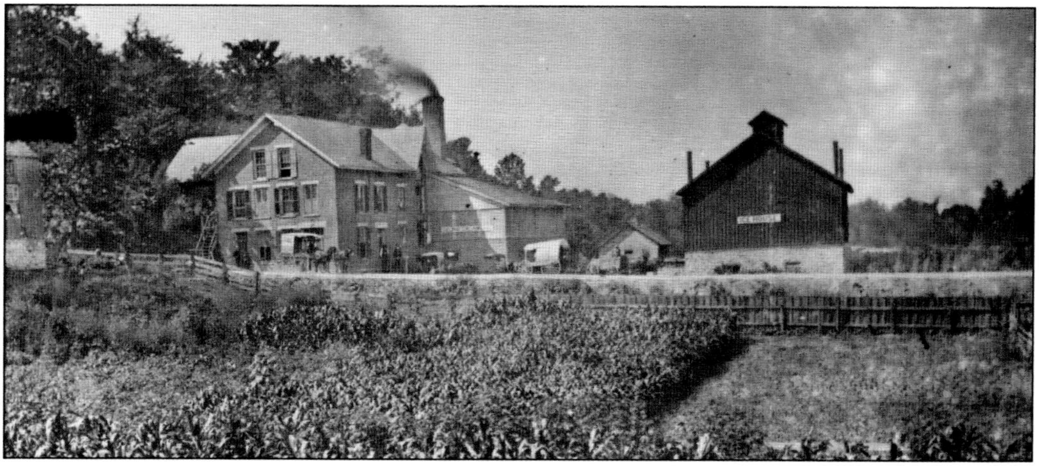

Formerly the "new brewery," making and selling beer, the three-story brick building became the Delphi Creamery in 1882. To the right is the icehouse. The "old brewery" can just be seen at the left in this photograph. The field in the foreground is now part of Riley Park.

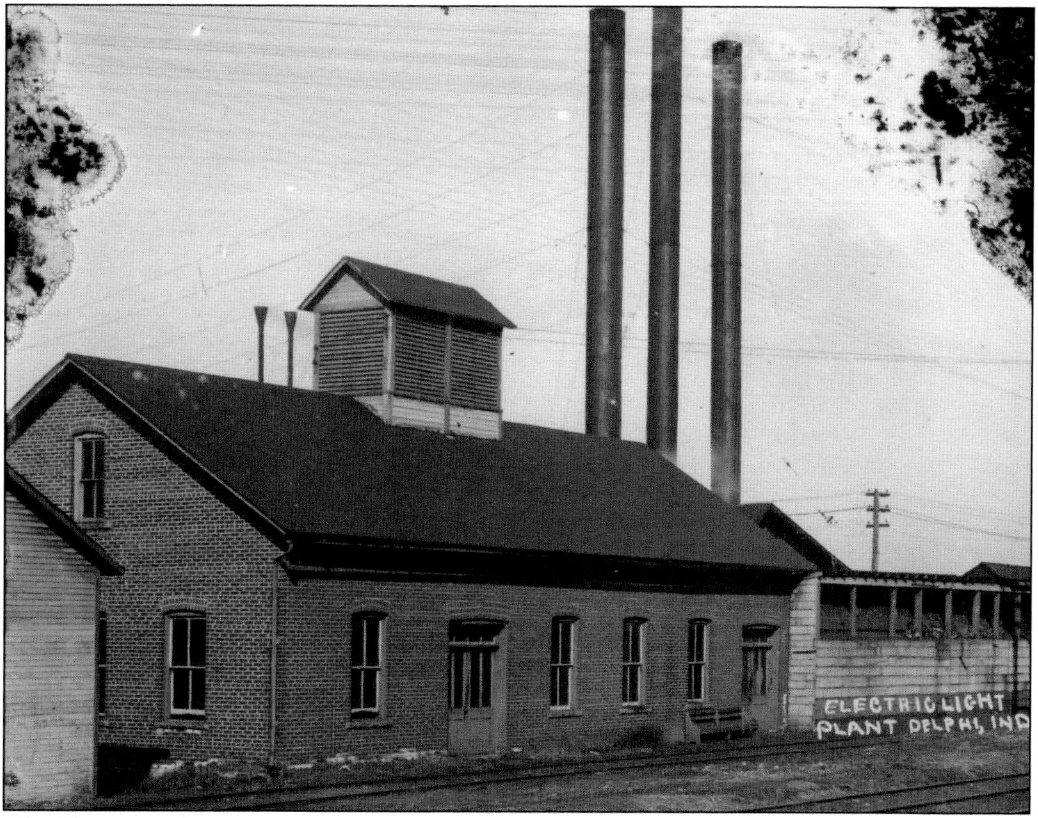

The Electric Light Company was organized in early 1888. On Saturday night, April 21, 1888, twenty arc lamps were turned on to light Delphi streets. Electricity was supplied first to Delphi businesses and then to residences to replace oil and gas lamps. By 1896, the lines had been extended to South Delphi. The electric light plant was built in the summer of 1898 on the south side of Monroe Street west of the Wabash Railroad with initial power provided by two 250 horsepower steam engines. The light plant was sold to the interurban company in 1910.

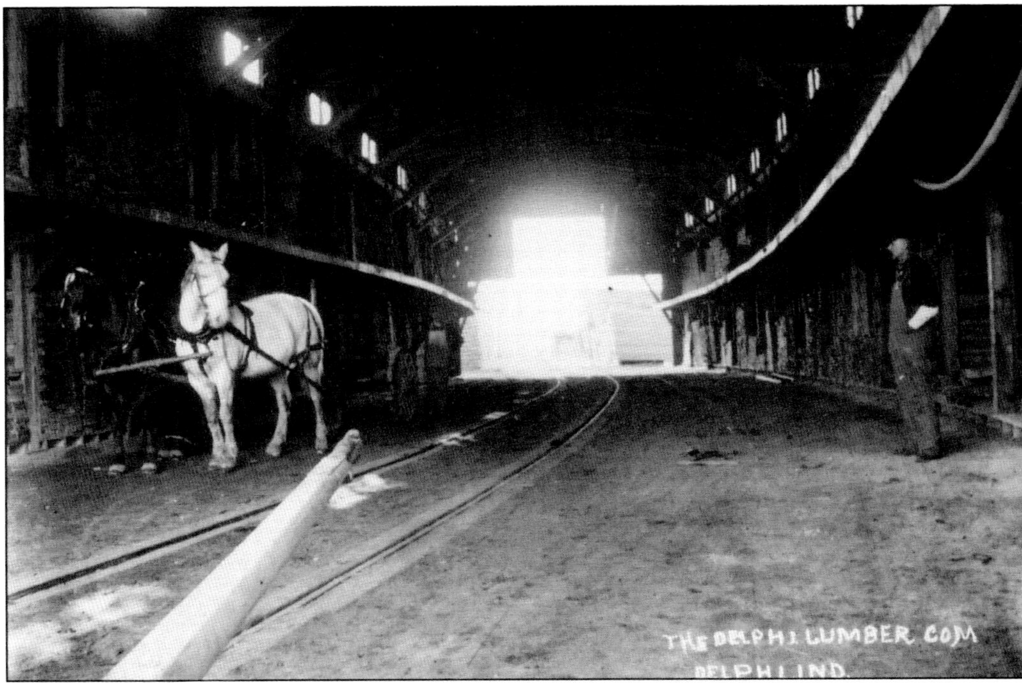

Tracks ran through the Delphi Lumber Company warehouse, connecting to the Beltline spur, which was built by the Monon Railroad to reach the lime kilns in North Delphi. Railcars could be loaded with moldings and lumber produced in the mills.

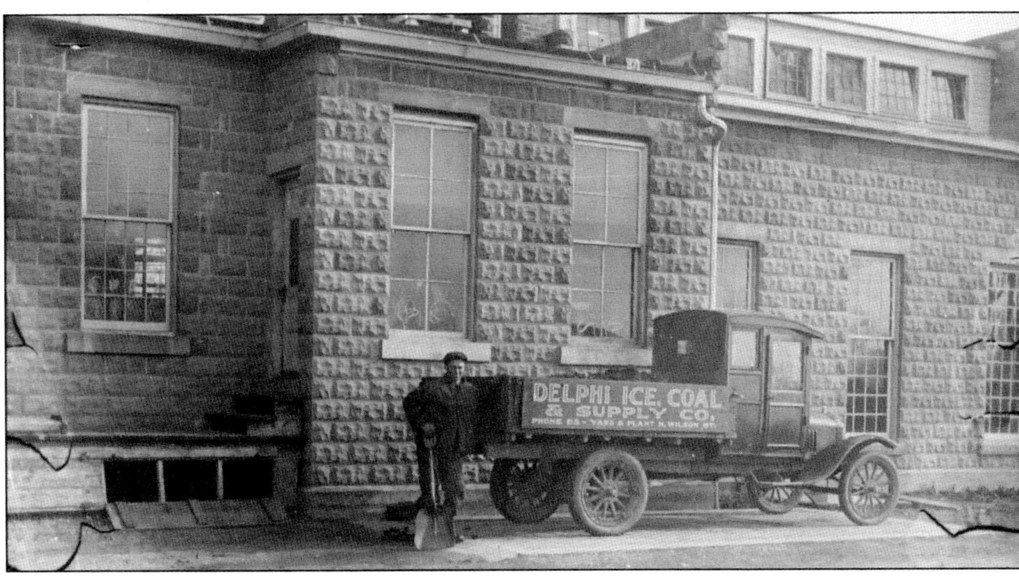

Formed in 1920, the Delphi Ice, Coal and Supply Company's plant was built on North Wilson Street next to the Beltline Railroad spur to enable railroad cars to deliver coal. Refrigeration to make the ice was likely produced by coal-fired boilers. Springwater was used for the ice, which was known for its clarity.

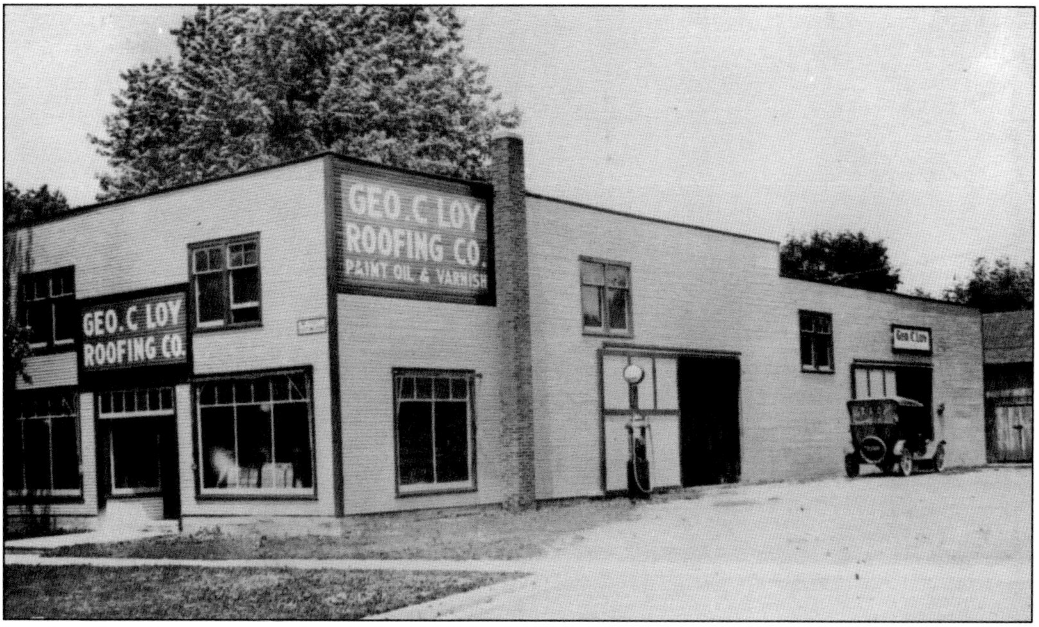

Loy Roofing Company was founded in 1910 by George C. Loy who had previously made his living teaching school. From 1918 until it was destroyed by fire in 1976, the business operated from this site on North Washington Street. It has been operated by members of the Loy family or their Quinn in-laws throughout its history and is now headquartered in Lafayette.

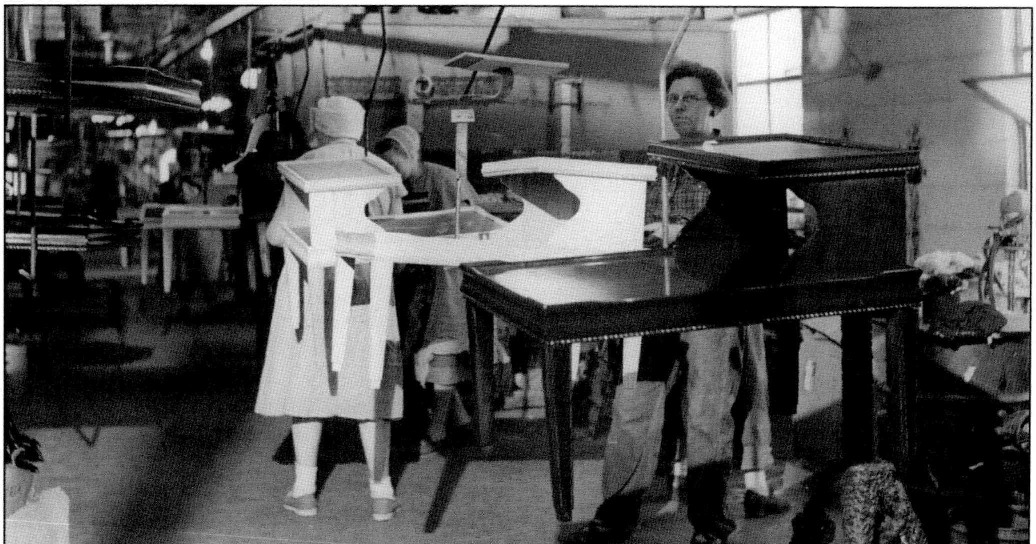

In 1946, T. L. Peters founded the Peters Manufacturing Company in Delphi for the production of novelty wall racks. A year later, George Revington joined the firm, and in 1958, the company's name was changed to Peters-Revington. Located on the former site of the Great Western Canning Company, Peters-Revington was a major employer until 2008, manufacturing fine furniture including the end tables seen here. Today, with the manufacturing done overseas, only a warehouse remains in Delphi.

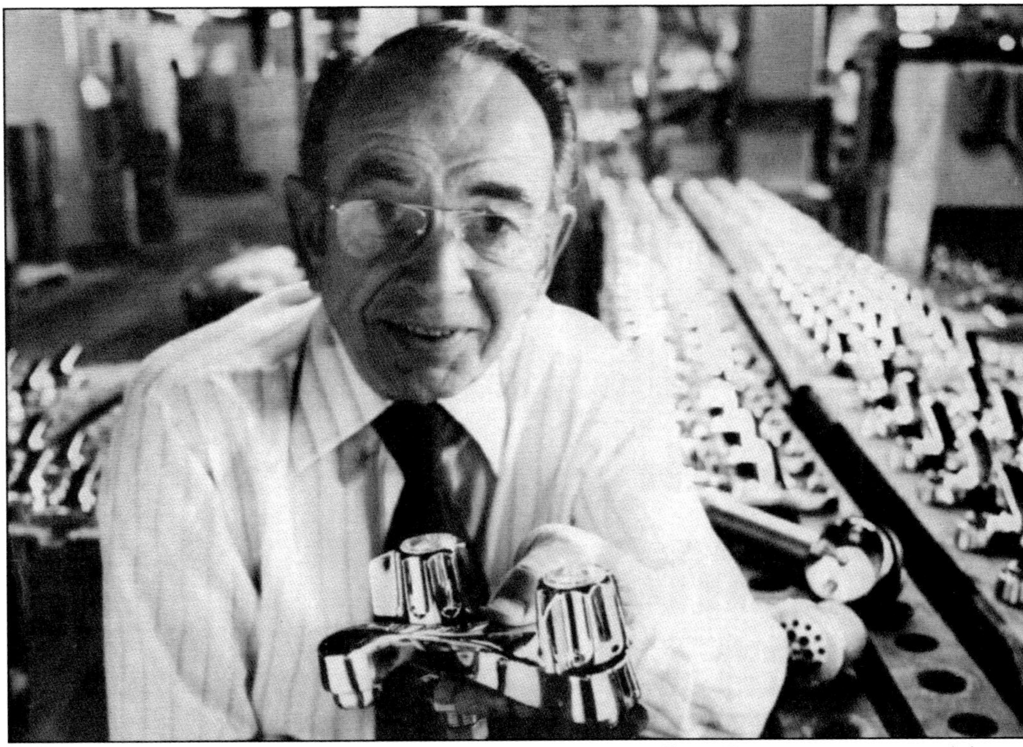

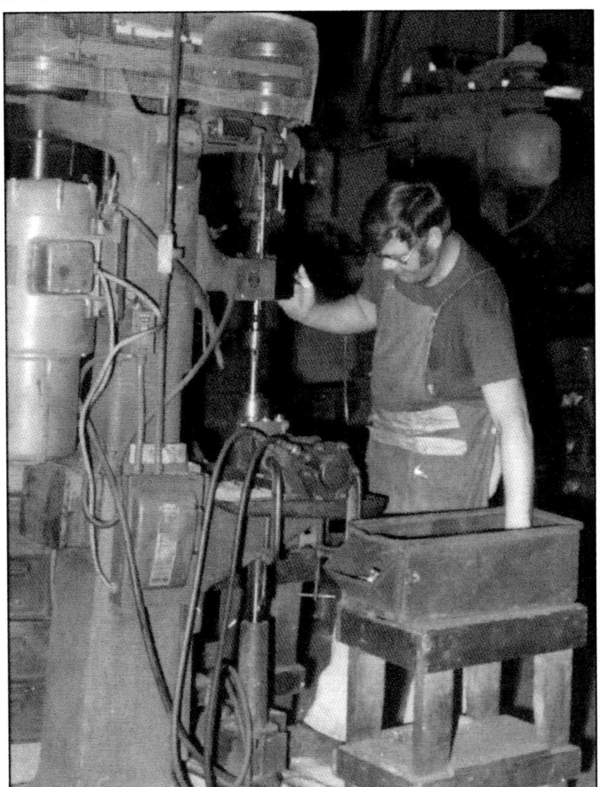

William Freeman, manager of the Globe Valve and Gerber plant in Delphi from 1947 until his retirement in 1981, is pictured above with the faucets manufactured in the brass-works operation. Employing more than 300 people at one time, the closing of the operation in 2003 was a tremendous blow to the community. (Courtesy Thomas and William Freeman Jr.)

Max Gerber of Chicago located Globe Valve in Delphi in 1939, beginning production with 25 employees. Gerber Industries, which manufactured shower stalls, was part of the operation from 1947 through 1983. Globe modernized its foundry with new technology and was considered a major community contributor, not only with jobs but sponsorship of ball teams, annual Christmas parties, and funding the Gerber Globe Valve room in the expanded Delphi Public Library. (Courtesy Thomas and William Freeman Jr.)

Nine

A Heritage of Transportation

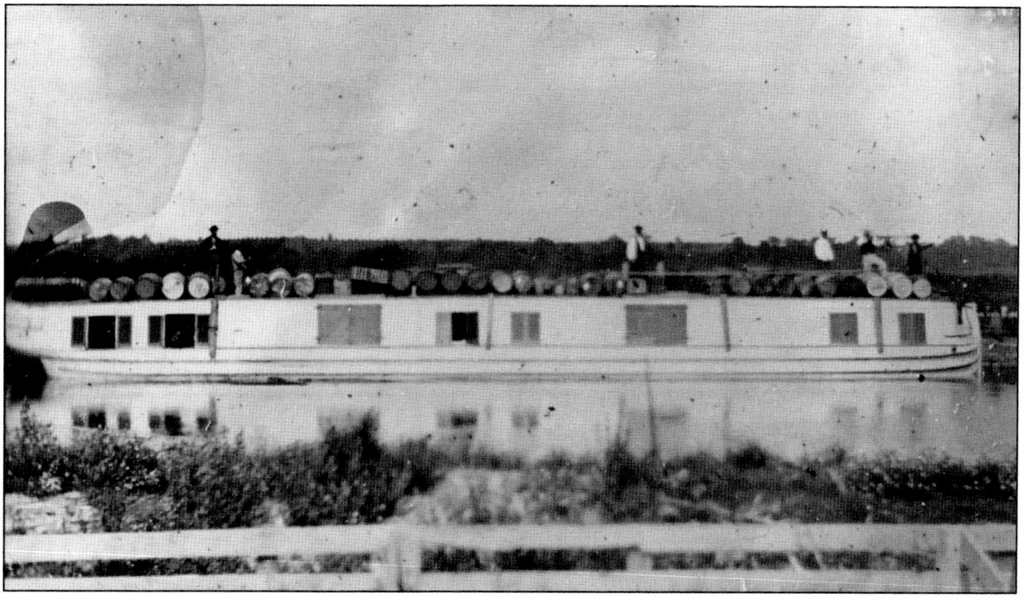

Delphi's location made it a hub for early travel by waterways and primitive roads. The Wabash and Erie Canal was immensely important to the development of Delphi and the surrounding area. The canal first opened from Fort Wayne to Delphi in 1840. By 1843, one could reach Lake Erie at Toledo making two-way commerce possible with trading centers in the east. The photograph is an 1860s image of a Speece Brothers' canal boat near Delphi. (Courtesy Indiana Historical Society.)

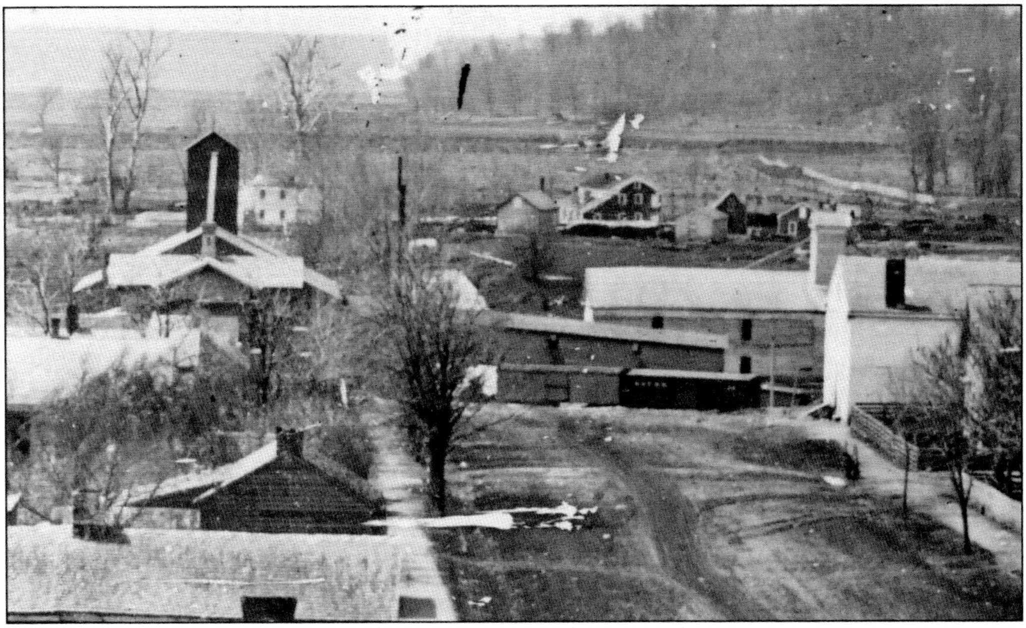

This detail from a mid-1860s photograph of West Main Street illustrates the forces at work in the rise and fall of the Wabash and Erie Canal. A side-slip and turning basin connect the canal with the elevator (left) to load boats with grain. Boats bringing merchandise were unloaded at the warehouse, reloaded with goods for shipment, and returned to the canal. Since the railroad at the front of the warehouse provided faster, year-round transport, canal shipping prices were lowered, eliminating all profit. The canal had ceased all but local operation by the 1870s.

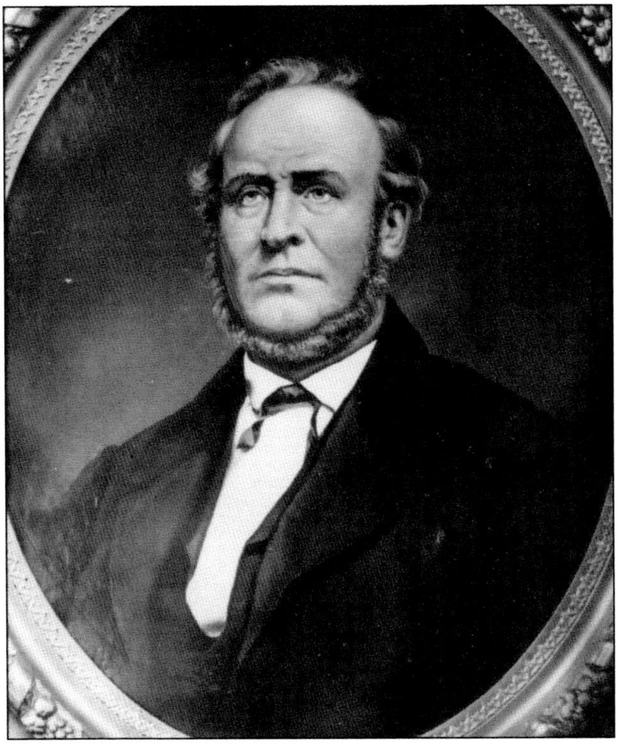

Reed Case (1808–1871) was a contractor in the construction of the canal. With James Spears in 1839, he built the steamboat canal and locks on the Wabash River at Pittsburg. In 1842, they constructed the millrace to the paper mills and canal side-cut. He was also central to the packinghouse, grain warehouse, and banking industries in early Delphi.

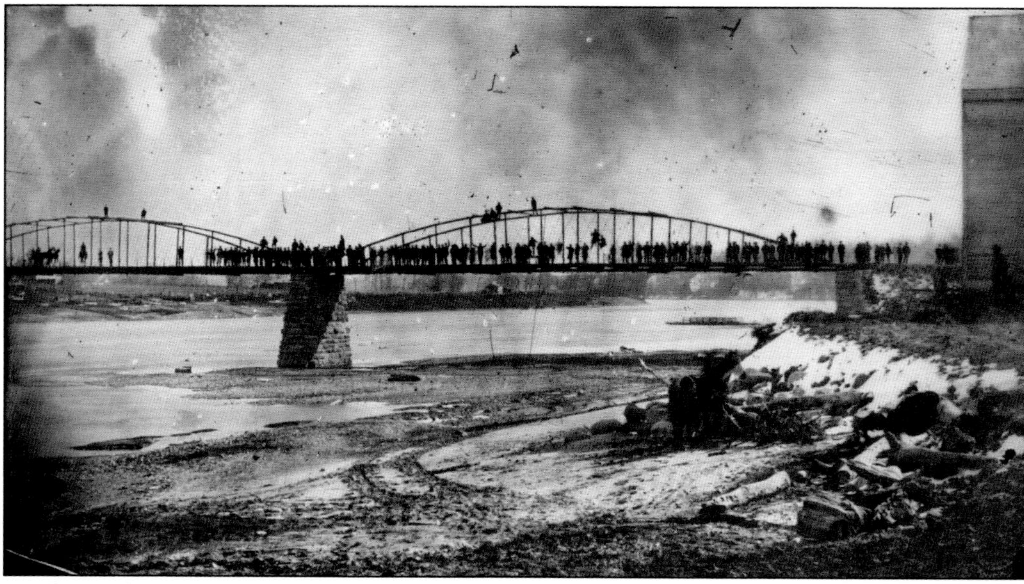

Pittsburg, platted in 1836, is northwest of Delphi on the Wabash River. Numerous mills operated here after the State Dam was constructed, and Pittsburg thrived because of easy access to barge transportation. The 600-foot iron bridge was built in 1868 between Delphi and Pittsburg. The flat-bottom ferry beneath the bridge had previously been the main means of transportation between the towns. William Bolles and Spears and Case had enterprises in both towns, and Bolles also had a warehouse in Toledo.

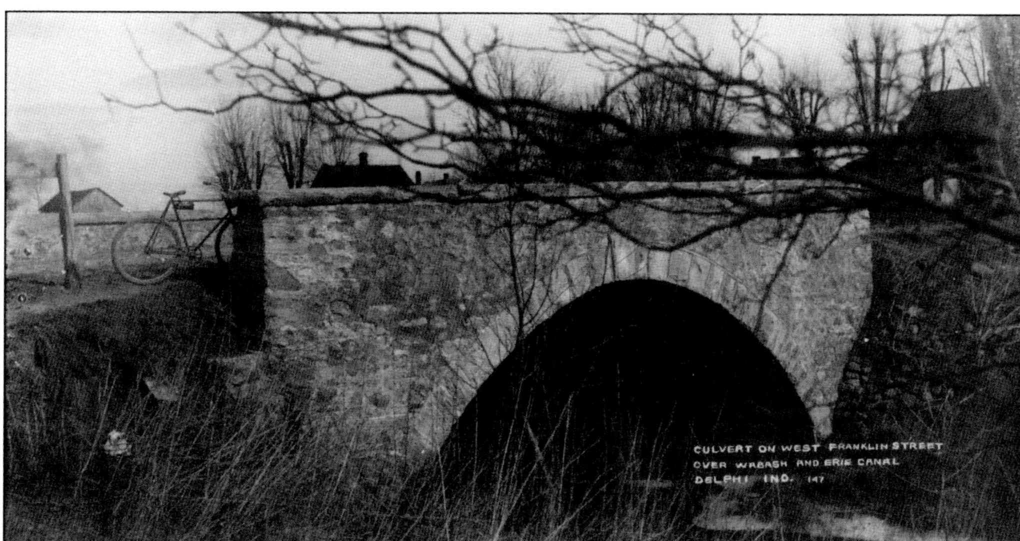

This stone-arch bridge at West Franklin Street was built over the Wabash and Erie Canal in 1905, long after canal operations had ceased. A "pivot bridge" was used at this location when the canal was in use. Another stone-arch bridge is over the canal at North Washington Street, once called Pittsburg Road. During the canal era, an arched wooden bridge was there, collapsing just as the canal chapter closed.

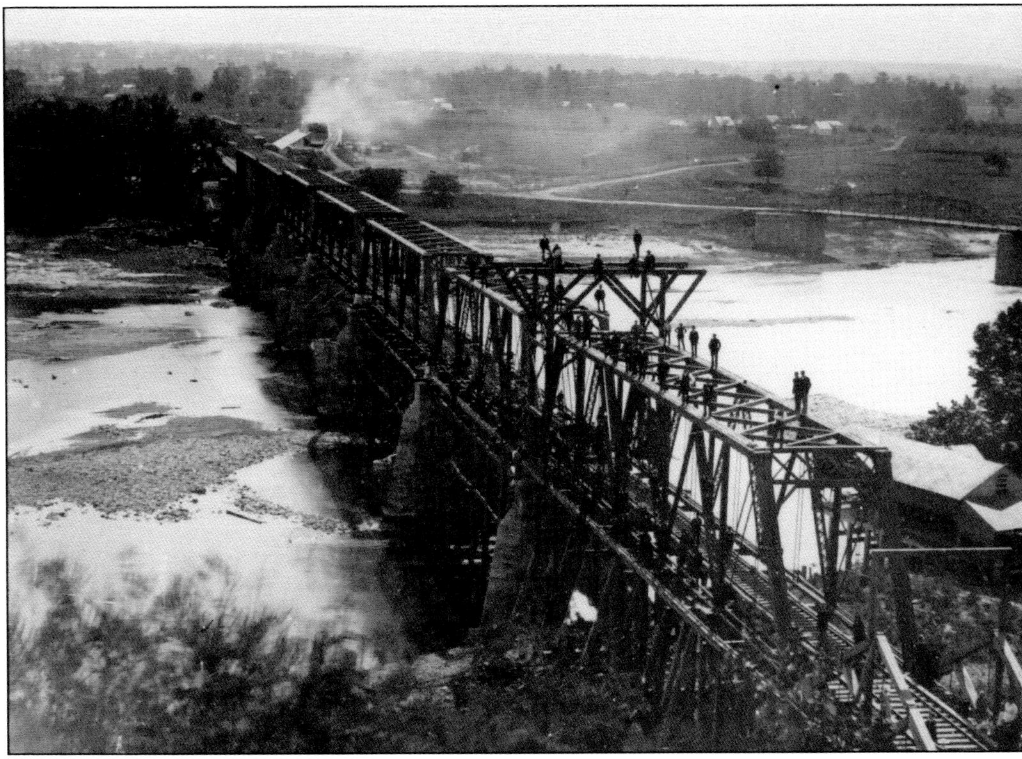

This Monon Railroad bridge over the Wabash River at 1,200 feet was the longest bridge on the Monon system. To its right is the iron bridge connecting Delphi to Pittsburg via the road veering right. Built initially as a toll plank road, it was completed in 1852. A free ferry across the river completed the connection. In 1880, the road became a free gravel road. The smoke in the background rises from a lime kiln.

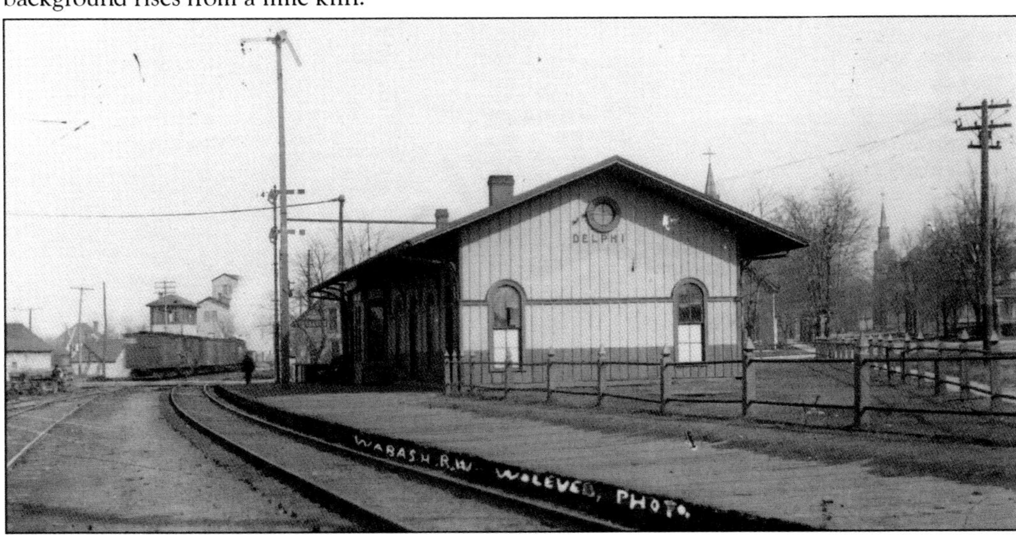

In June 1856, the Lake Erie, Wabash, and St. Louis Railroad Company completed a line from Toledo to Lafayette through the Wabash River Valley. This brought the first train to Delphi, connecting it to all parts east and south to the Gulf. The Wabash Railway Depot welcomed passengers to Delphi.

Servicing the electric lines of the interurban required special equipment and skills. Wire workers ride along the track on a scaffolding cart to check and repair the lines.

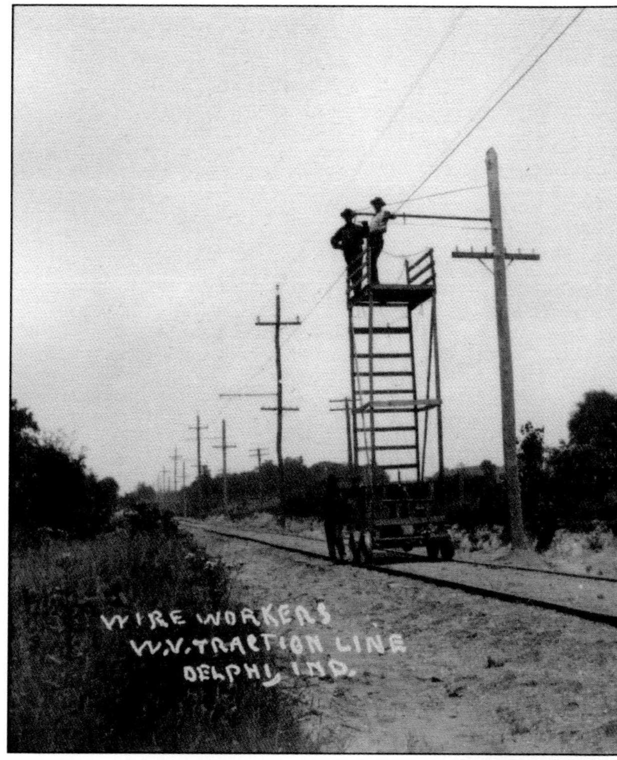

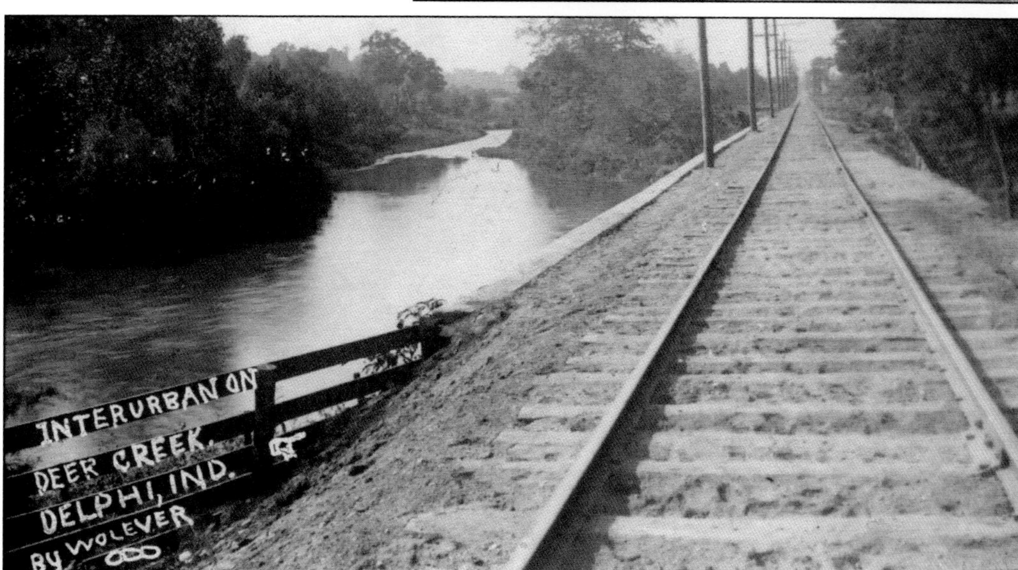

As automobiles gained in numbers and the roads improved, the interurban lost most of its passenger base and was discontinued. Remnants of the rail bed can still be seen around Delphi, and it forms one of the historic walking trails. A trolley bus fashioned as an interurban car currently operates for special events, especially during the Heritage Transportation Festival held every Father's Day weekend. The festival celebrates all modes of local transportation—both historic and current—through demonstrations and exhibits. Rides are available by horse and carriage, trolley bus, or on *The Delphi* replica boat on the 3-mile watered section of the Wabash and Erie Canal.

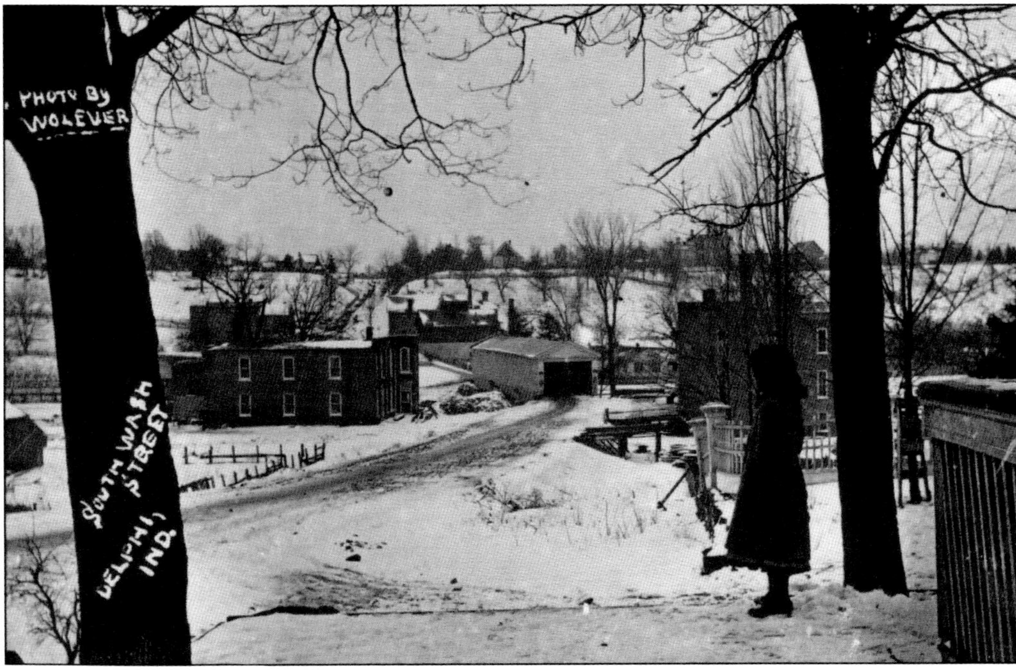

The covered bridge over Deer Creek was built in 1848. It replaced an earlier plank bridge on wooden trestles that was constructed during the early settlement years. The covered bridge was demolished in 1893 when James W. Peirce and Craven Smith constructed the iron bridge seen below. That has since been twice replaced by concrete bridges.

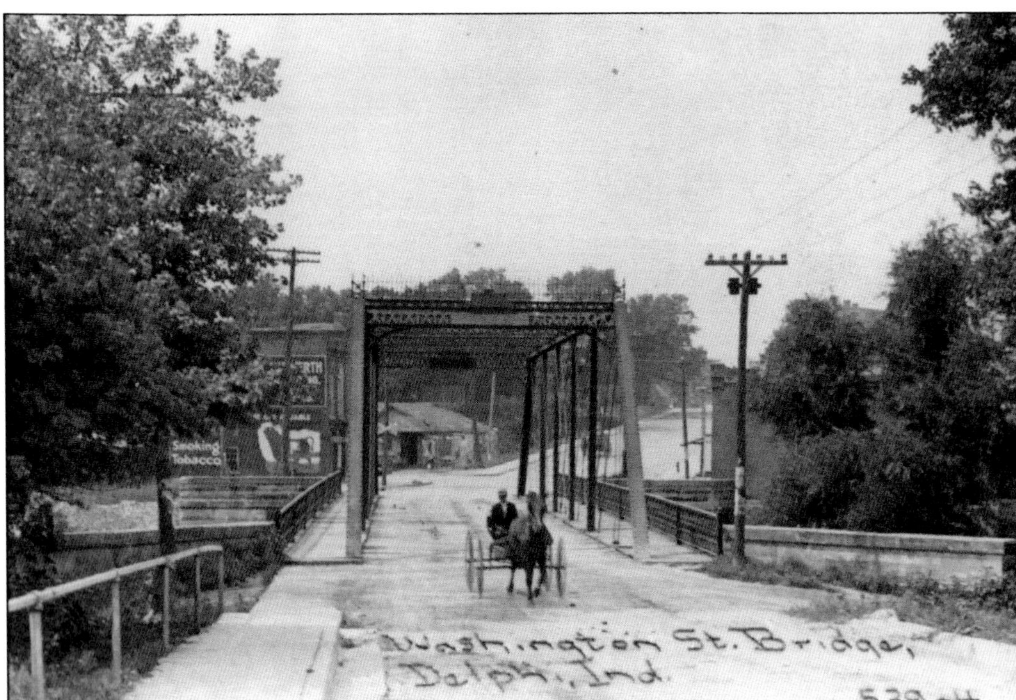

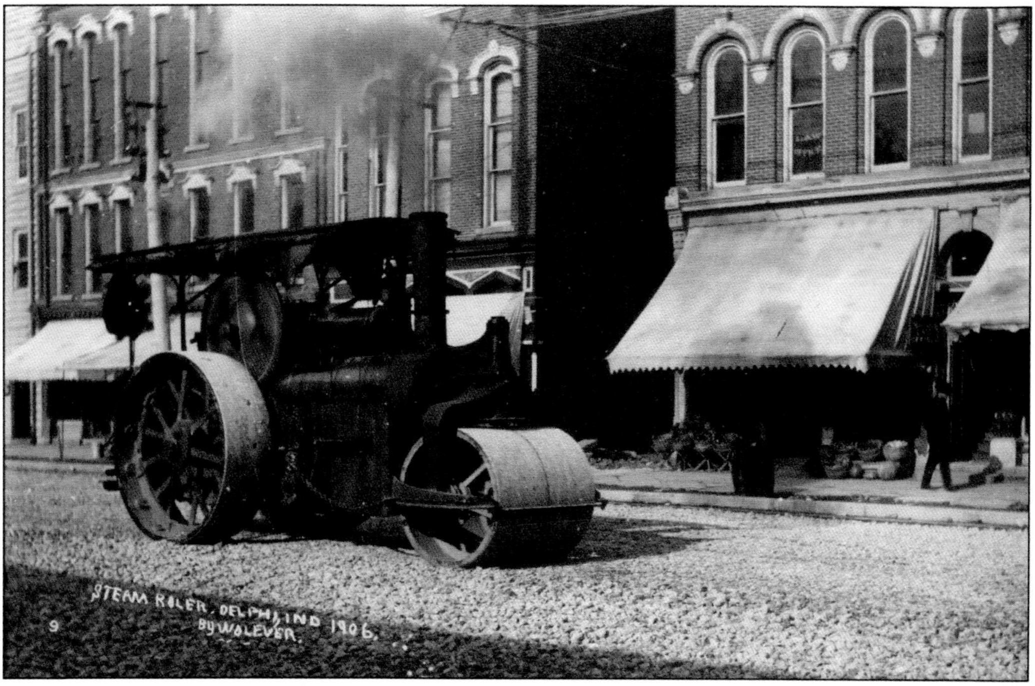

Louis Niewerth purchased the first local automobile in 1903—a Stanley Steamer. As the number of cars increased, the need for improved streets became a high priority. Gravel is being compacted on East Main Street in preparation for laying pavement in this 1906 photograph. Below, workers use a steam-driven mixer to prepare concrete for sidewalks and curbing on Main Street in the early 1900s.

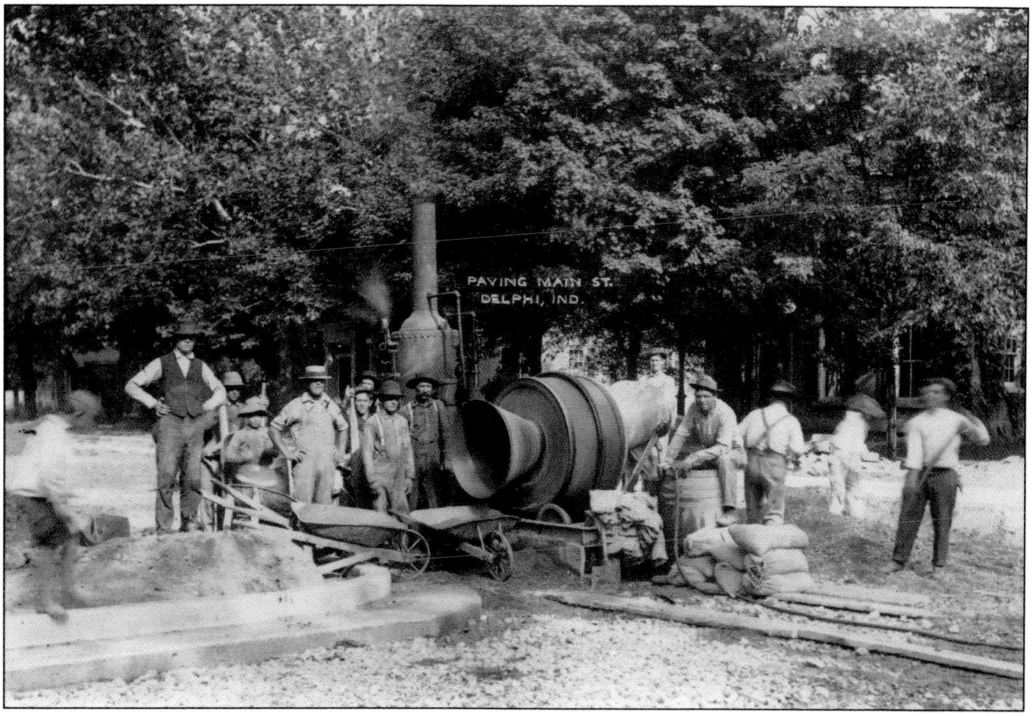

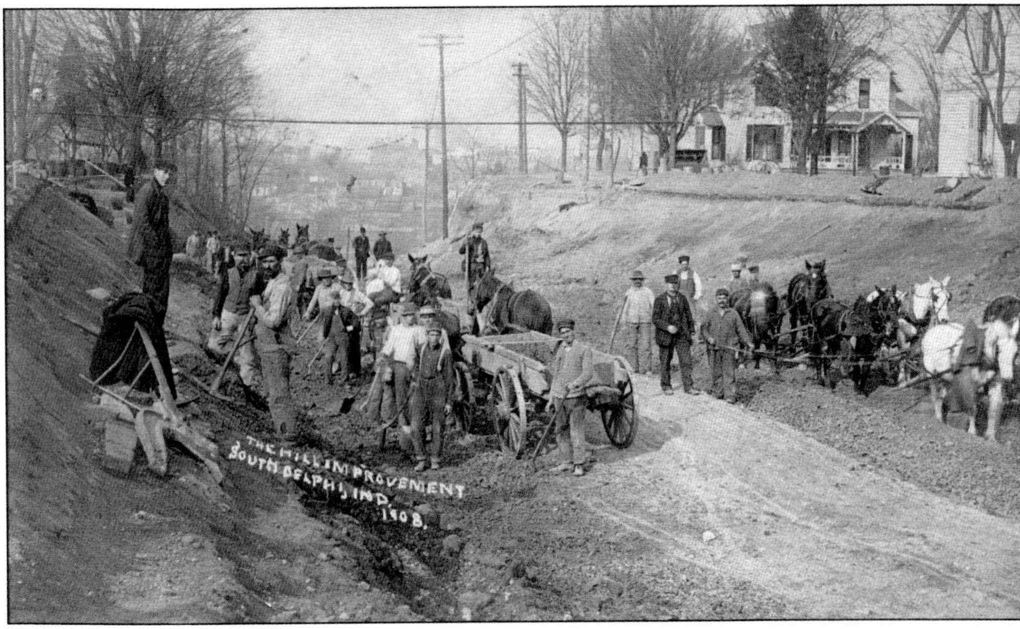

The early road from Delphi south was a plank road to Prince William in southern Carroll County and then on to Frankfort. It avoided this steep hill directly south of town by veering eastward at the base of the "South Hill" on the Prince William Road. The 1908 improvements underway in these photographs would provide a more direct route into Delphi's downtown from points south, including the town of South Delphi, which had been incorporated into the city in 1903.

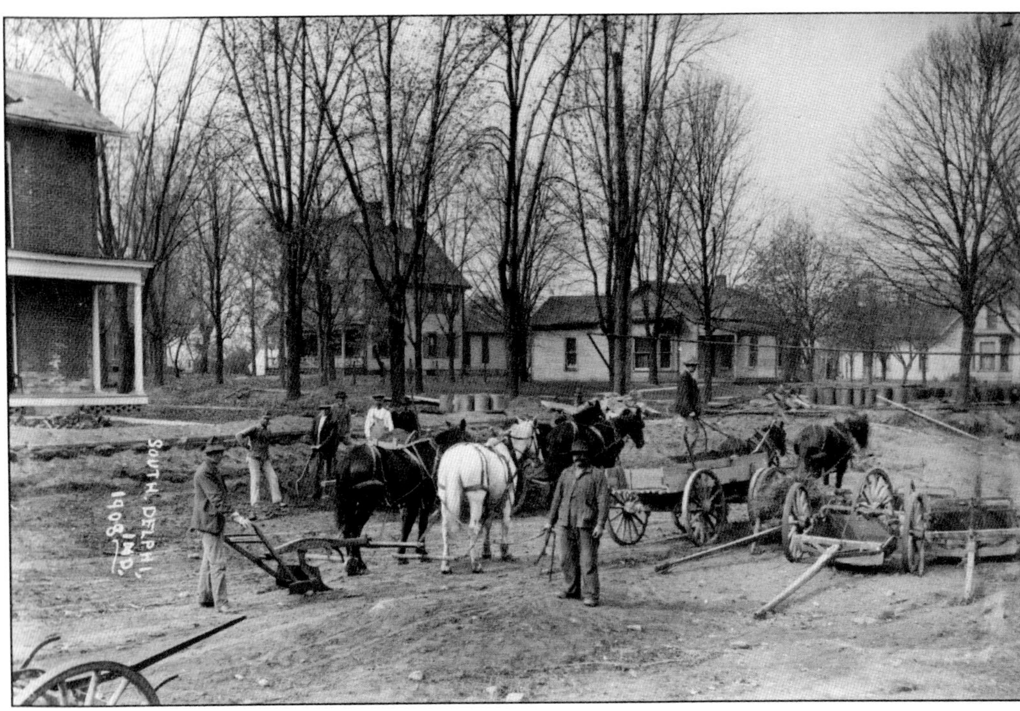

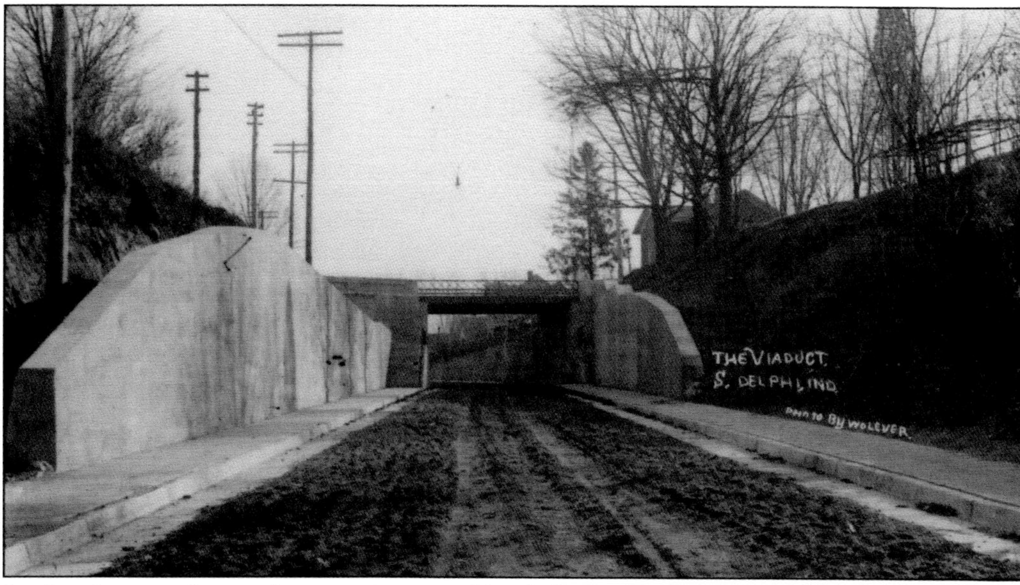

In the photographs on the opposite page, North Street has been severed by the huge trench required for the grade extending Washington Street to the Prince William Road farther to the south. The top photograph to the left is the view from Washington Street; the bottom is the view from North Street. Part of the hill improvement project was the creation of a viaduct to carry North Street (the northernmost street of South Delphi) over Washington Street. The completed viaduct is seen above with North Street reconnected.

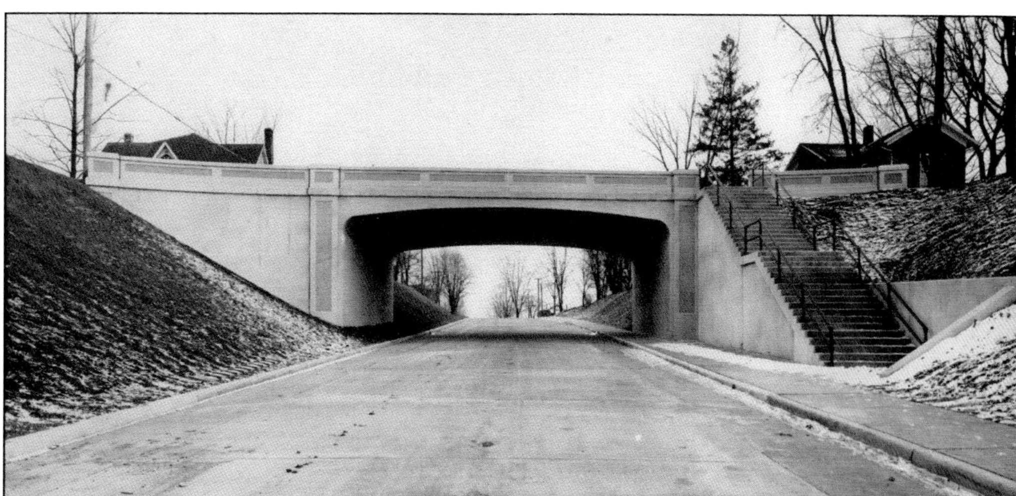

Washington Street was widened and the viaduct rebuilt in 1936 along with the steps to North Street. This is now the route of U.S. Highway 421 and State Roads 39 and 18 through Delphi. Also in the mid-1930s, the iron bridge over Deer Creek was removed and replaced with a double-arch concrete span, which in turn, was replaced recently. (Courtesy Carolyn Orr.)

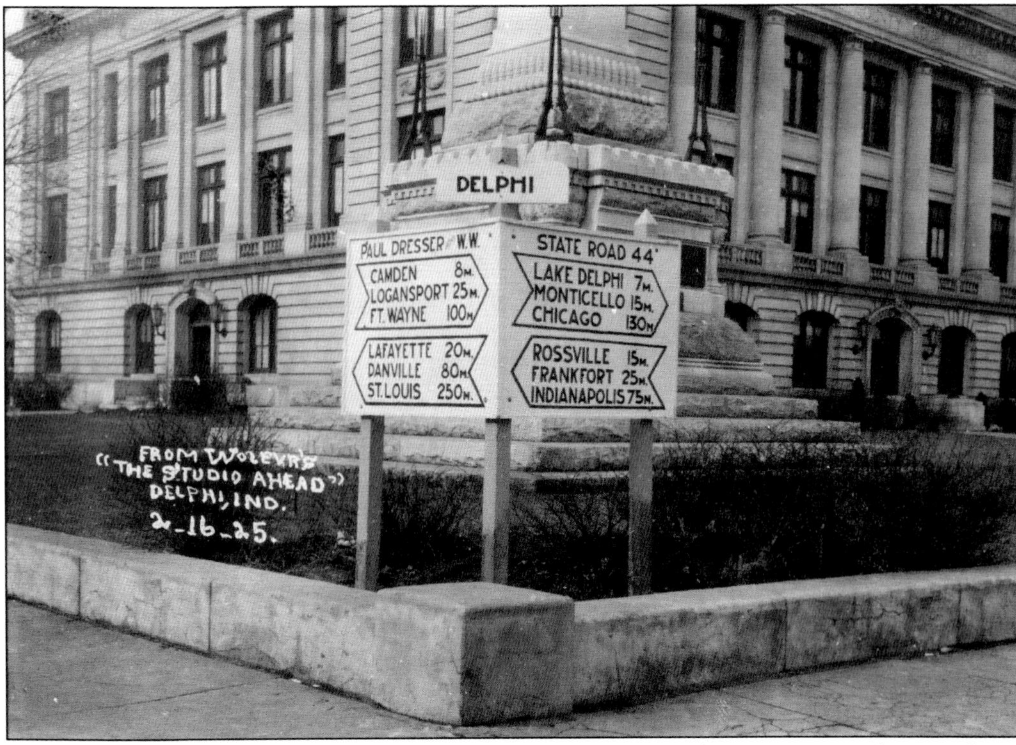

As the signpost in this 1925 photograph indicates, the highways that converge at the courthouse square locate Delphi centrally to cities such as Lafayette, Logansport, and Frankfort and within comfortable distances to Indianapolis, Fort Wayne, and Chicago. We invite you to come share Delphi's rich architectural and cultural heritage.

DELPHI *preservation* SOCIETY

The Delphi Preservation Society, Inc. was founded in 1994. It is a not-for-profit corporation dedicated to the preservation and restoration of historic structures in the greater Delphi community. For information about our organization, projects, and activities, visit our Web site at www.delphipreservationsociety.org.

Bibliography

A Map of Carroll County, Indiana. Delphi, IN: Skinner & Bennett, 1863.

Carroll County Interim Report: Indiana Historic Sites & Structures Inventory. Indianapolis, IN: Division of Historic Preservation, 1980.

Castaldi, Tom E. *Wabash & Erie Canal Journey, 1832–1876*. Delphi, IN: Carroll County Wabash & Erie Canal, Inc., 2004.

Durant, Samuel W. and Pliny A. Durant. *An Illustrated Historical Atlas of Carroll County, Indiana*. Chicago, IL: O. L. Baskin & Co., 1874.

Gerard, Charles E. *Delphi—A Mirror of Remembrance, July of 1985*. Delphi, IN: Indiana Graphic Arts Co., 1985.

Gerard, Charles E. *The Mystique of Deer Creek*. Delphi, IN: Delphi Preservation Society, 2009 revision.

Gerard, Charles E. *First Research on the Lathrope and Ruffing Opera House*. Delphi, IN: Delphi Preservation Society, Inc., 2010 revision.

Gerard, Charles E. and Michael G. Griffey. *The Carroll County Sesquicentennial Publication, 1824–1928—1874–1978: A Photographic Portrayal of Old Life in a Hoosier Community: The Pictorial History of Carroll County*. Lafayette, IN: Haywood Printing Co., 1977.

Helm, Thomas B. *History of Carroll County, Indiana: with Illustrations and Biographical Sketches of Some of its Prominent Men and Pioneers*. Chicago, IL: Kingman Brothers, 1882.

Maxwell, Bonnie J. and Anita L. Werling. *Carroll County, Indiana, Legacy, 1824–2005*. Delphi, IN: Carroll County Historical Museum, 2005.

Mayhill, Dora Thomas. *Carroll County, Indiana: Postal History, Rural Settlements, Towns, Development of Modes of Travel*. Knightstown, IN: Banner Publishing Co., 1954.

Mayhill, Dora Thomas. *Old Wabash and Erie Canal in Carroll County and Pre-Canal History of the Wabash River*. Knightstown, IN: Banner Publishing Co., 1953.

Odell, John C. *History of Carroll County, Indiana: Its People, Industries and Institutions*. Indianapolis, IN: B. F. Bowen & Co., 1916.

Peterson, John C. and Doris M. Peterson. *Carroll County, Indiana, Rural Organizations, 1828–1979*. Delphi, IN: Petersons, 1980.

Stewart, James Hervey. *Recollections of the Early Settlement of Carroll County, Indiana*. Cincinnati, OH: Hitchcock and Walden, 1872.

Yoder, Susan. *Faces Behind the Façades*. Delphi, IN: Carroll County Wabash & Erie Canal, Inc., 2004.